MW00461667

PAPER SOLDIERS

PAPER SOLDIERS

How the Weaponization
of the Dollar Changed
the World Order

SALEHA MOHSIN

Portfolio | Penguin

Portfolio / Penguin
An imprint of Penguin Random House LLC
penguinrandomhouse.com

Copyright © 2024 by Saleha Mohsin
Penguin Random House supports copyright. Copyright fuels creativity,
encourages diverse voices, promotes free speech, and creates a vibrant culture.
Thank you for buying an authorized edition of this book and for complying with
copyright laws by not reproducing, scanning, or distributing any part of it in
any form without permission. You are supporting writers and allowing
Penguin Random House to continue to publish books for every reader.

Most Portfolio books are available at a discount when purchased in quantity for
sales promotions or corporate use. Special editions, which include personalized covers,
excerpts, and corporate imprints, can be created when purchased in large quantities.
For more information, please call (212) 572-2232 or email specialmarkets
@penguinrandomhouse.com. Your local bookstore can also assist with
discounted bulk purchases using the Penguin Random House
corporate Business-to-Business program. For assistance in locating a
participating retailer, email B2B@penguinrandomhouse.com.

Portions of this book first appeared in different form in
Bloomberg News or *Bloomberg Businessweek*.

Library of Congress Cataloging-in-Publication Data

Names: Mohsin, Saleha, author.
Title: Paper soldiers : how the weaponization of the dollar
changed the world order / Saleha Mohsin.
Description: New York : Portfolio/Penguin, [2024] |
Includes bibliographical references and index.
Identifiers: LCCN 2023049472 (print) | LCCN 2023049473 (ebook) |
ISBN 9780593539118 (hardcover) | ISBN 9780593539125 (ebook)
Subjects: LCSH: United States. Department of the Treasury. | Economic
history. | United States—Economic conditions. | Dollar, American.
Classification: LCC HJ261 .M64 2024 (print) |
LCC HJ261 (ebook) | DDC 352.40973—d 23/eng/20231026
LC record available at https://lccn.loc.gov/2023049472
LC ebook record available at https://lccn.loc.gov/2023049473

Printed in the United States of America
1st Printing

BOOK DESIGN BY CHRIS WELCH

For Abba

CONTENTS

CAST OF CHARACTERS

Jim Baker. As Treasury chief serving the Reagan administration, during a secret meeting in New York City, he brokered a deal with the finance ministers of the most influential countries to collectively weaken the dollar.

Tim Geithner. Working as a civil servant in Bob Rubin's Treasury department, he helped create the strong dollar policy that ruled economic policymaking for two decades. He would become the seventy-fifth Treasury secretary.

Stuart Levey. The first official to run Treasury's expanded sanctions office, he helped the department attain formidable influence in the country's national security apparatus.

Jack Lew. Foreshadowed the evolution of economic sanctions into an often misused weapon that posed risks to the sanctity of the dollar's status as currency supreme.

Steven Mnuchin. Stood as the last line of defense against the president's attempts to aggressively control the value of the U.S. dollar.

Paul O'Neill. Served on the front lines of George W. Bush's war on terror after 9/11, overseeing the modern weaponization of the U.S. dollar to protect American security interests.

Hank Paulson. Established a closer relationship between the United States and China, which became key when he and his successors dealt with the fallout of the global financial crisis.

Robert "Bob" Rubin. Created the strong dollar policy to underpin the dawning of globalization, while at the same time bringing calm and order that had eluded U.S. currency policy for two decades.

John Snow. Oversaw the creation of a new economic sanctions unit at Treasury as the United States used access to the dollar as a cudgel to achieve foreign policy objectives.

Mark Sobel. An apolitical civil servant who worked on U.S. currency issues for four decades and carried the dollar policy across multiple administrations.

Janet Yellen. The first woman to ever run Treasury, she oversaw the dollar's use as a weapon to protect an eighty-year-old global order when the Russian president Vladimir Putin launched the biggest military assault in Europe since World War II.

INTRODUCTION

It is possible that 5:13 p.m. on Saturday, February 26, 2022, will one day be seen as the precise moment the ebb of the dollar empire began. While we won't know for decades if the almighty buck's global status as currency supreme is permanently lost, one thing is certain: all empires think they're special, and all empires fall. Right now the flourishing of American power—and that of its dollar—is dizzying, but are the nation's leaders accelerating its downfall just as the world enters a new age of great-power rivalry that is redrawing alliances? Or will the latest threat pass?

On that wintry February day in Washington, D.C., the world's most powerful finance minister was staring down historic challenges. In the preceding forty-eight hours, Russia had instigated the greatest military crisis since World War II. World leaders were faced with a disaster: global order that had lasted eighty years, built around democracy and economic integration, with the American dollar at the core as the world's reserve asset, was suddenly thrown into chaos. In this tradition, governments wouldn't dream of aiming missiles at each other because of the potential for self-inflicted wounds—the world had become too interconnected for one bruise not to hurt the rest.

But Putin had done the unthinkable. The U.S. president, however, had firmly ruled out military action, putting added emphasis on the potency of the next option: economic sanctions. And the strongest weapon sat with Secretary of the Treasury Janet Yellen.

At around 8:00 a.m., she joined President Joe Biden and senior members of the administration on a secure teleconference line to talk through how to deal with President Vladmir Putin's murderous invasion of Ukraine. Jake Sullivan, the national security adviser, recommended that Biden enact what many called the "nuclear option" in America's economic arsenal: cutting off a central bank from the U.S. dollar. By putting Putin's half-trillion-dollar war chest out of his reach, they would financially excommunicate most of Russia's banking sector from the rest of the world.

Biden signaled that he was ready for that extreme step, and then he looked to Yellen. As secretary of the Treasury and signatory of the U.S. dollar, she would be the one to tell financial markets to dramatically reduce Russia's access to the currency. One update to the website on Treasury.gov's sanctions designation list and the money managers carefully monitoring that page would know they had to stop trading and dealing with the Russian banks, companies, and individuals that were being financially ostracized.

Yellen wasn't immediately convinced that this step was necessary. Bound by an oath taken on her first day in office to serve as the steward of the world's reserve asset, she needed to be acutely focused on the impacts of such a move.

For one, she worried that it would turn the dollar into an unequivocal weapon of war. It wouldn't be the first time, but extreme measures against the central bank of a Group of Twenty nation would dent the dollar's standing as the world's bedrock currency if allied governments could no longer consider the United States a safe place to store assets. The other problem was that the potential economic sanctions package had the makings of a financial carpet-bombing: economic destruction that would ravage the livelihoods of innocent civilians in Russia, the world's eleventh-largest economy, and inflict certain harm on global financial markets. It would also strain everyday commodities, like food and energy, around the world. Was this a justified use of power, or an abuse of it?

It had taken more than two centuries for the United States to ascend to this position of power. Over that period, it went from an experiment in independence predicted to fail to a global superpower and bastion of democracy. The story of America's rise and endurance is also the story of the dollar. Nourished in almost ideal conditions—a stable and predictable democracy built on free and fair elections, rule of law, and independent courts—the U.S. currency came to rule the global financial system, magnifying American dominance in commerce and global security.

The United States Department of the Treasury is at the very core of this mission.

Despite its impressive granite colonnade and neoclassical Greek revival columns across two city blocks, visiting the U.S. Treasury department's headquarters at 1500 Pennsylvania Avenue is rarely on the bucket list of destinations for tourists who flock to Washington,

D.C. Gawkers prefer to gather outside its more prestigious neighbor, the White House. But the occupants of both buildings have arguably played an equally central role in creating the American dream—work hard and you'll get a better life.

Founded in 1789 during the tumultuous years following the Revolutionary War, Treasury took over management of the nation's finances, overseeing the launch of the dollar and stabilizing the country's credit. Its work lubricates the system of free markets and open trade. That system is inextricably linked to democracy: Make it more difficult for Americans to climb the economic ladder, and they start to lose faith in the political system. Undermine democracy, and companies could lose confidence in the United States as a place to do business.

It took the global convulsions of World Wars I and II for the dollar to take hold as the world's most important asset, but the consolidation of that power occurred over the past three decades. *Paper Soldiers* is about the dollar's astonishing rise, and how it came to be wielded as the United States' most consequential weapon. It also chronicles the unintended, and sometimes devastating, impact the strong dollar policy had both inside and outside our borders. This story is best understood through the actions of the dollar's stewards: the individuals who have served as Treasury secretary amid economic and political turmoil, whose most essential task is to protect and maintain the dollar as a source of influence. These figures include not only Janet Yellen, but Robert Rubin, Hank Paulson, Steven Mnuchin, and the thousands of unsung heroes and heroines at Treasury who spend their careers fortifying the nation's democracy by protecting the global financial system. As a reporter for Bloomberg News, I have conducted hundreds of interviews with the key figures involved: current and former Treasury secretaries; officials from the Federal Reserve,

White House, International Monetary Fund, World Bank, and private sector officials; along with current and former foreign diplomats. All of these interviews revealed how Treasury's dollar policy was shaped over the past thirty years.

Despite Yellen's hesitations during that urgent teleconference with the White House, the inescapable fact was that Vladimir Putin had launched an assault on global peace and stability—despite Russia's membership in the G20 nations, the International Monetary Fund, and other world coalitions created to prevent just this type of attack.

Images of bloodstained faces of women, children, and grandparents, piled into underground tunnels to escape the destruction of their homes above, spilled across the world's newspapers and televisions. Within a few hours, Yellen was on board with the White House's plan. After finalizing the next steps and coordinating with allies, that Saturday night the United States marshaled the power of an integrated global system that it anchored by bringing together thirty countries (representing more than half the world economy) to launch an economic war against Russia, with the dollar as the most severe weapon in the battle to protect the world. "Russia's war represents an assault on fundamental international rules and norms that have prevailed since the Second World War, which we are committed to defending," read the White House statement announcing the unprecedented measures. The administration vowed to isolate Russia from the international financial system.

The United States needed to "act in support . . . of our principles and in alignment with our commitment to a rule-based order that protects peace," Yellen later said about those first crucial decisions after Ukraine was invaded. The choice before her on February 26 reflected the very image printed on every one-dollar bill: a bald eagle holding both olive branches and arrows, signaling a preference for peace but a preparedness to defend.

Janet Yellen's concerns in early 2022 about weaponizing the dollar weren't unfounded. A year later, in April 2023, Brazil's President Luiz Inácio Lula da Silva drew loud applause from an audience of Chinese dignitaries in Shanghai when he heralded the demise of the dollar. "Every night I ask myself why all countries have to base their trade on the dollar. Who was it that decided that the dollar was the currency after the disappearance of the gold standard?" he asked the delighted crowd. And he wasn't the only one who was asking that question—he was just the loudest in a chorus of rhetoric that had formed among world leaders from Argentina to Saudi Arabia, Malaysia, and India, as each nation came together to look for fresh ideas on how to sidestep the dollar.

Prophecies of the dollar's demise have cropped up for decades. In the early 1990s, some said the Japanese yen was on course to supplant the greenback, while others saw the euro as a potential usurper. Both bets proved wrong. But in the aftermath of a complete fracture of traditional global alliances following Russia's invasion of Ukraine in February 2022, the world is once again wondering if the dollar is losing its power. In the year that followed President Biden's decision to use the dollar as a tool to punish Putin, the United States made apparent the full arsenal of economic weaponry it possessed. Like Brazil's Lula, adversaries and allies alike began to worry what it would mean if they found themselves on the wrong side of Washington, subject to the same kind of financial warfare now being used against Russia, and leaders everywhere began looking for alternatives to the dollar.

Some of the backlash is overt, like the efforts by Brazil, Russia,

India, China, and South Africa (a bloc of nations called BRICS) to expand the alliance and develop a new shared trade mechanism that circumvents the dollar. Other signs are subtle, like the discussions at the world's biggest pulp producer to settle trades in yuan for the first time, following a trend to similarly diversify across commodities like nickel and oil markets. These moves are incremental, but they chip away at the world's vast web of dollarization. In 2001, the dollar accounted for 73 percent of total foreign exchange reserves held by central banks (what amounts to a nation's savings). After two decades of economic sanctions, a financial crisis, and brewing mistrust in America, that has fallen below 60 percent.

Inside economic circles, experts are openly asking if the world would have been a better place if, during a fateful Bretton Woods conference in 1944 to decide a new economic order after World War II, American officials had lost their bid to crown the dollar as king. Is dependence on the dollar worth the trouble? Investors and allies asked the same question after an American-made housing crisis shook global markets in 2008, and again when President Donald Trump began imposing trade tariffs in 2018.

Hand in hand with questions about dollar dominance are questions about American hegemony, pushing the United States into a new and defensive posture. Some of this is subtle: A low-profile hearing in the spring of 2023 called by the House Financial Services Committee to discuss "Preserving the U.S. Dollar's Status as the Global Reserve Currency." A little-known research office that provides impartial reports to Congress releasing a forty-three-page paper about historic patterns that led to previous shifts in currency dominance, dating back to the seventeenth century.

But the most damaging aspect to dollar dominance doesn't stem from outside its borders—it comes from a rolling series of self-inflicted policy wounds, stoking doubts about whether the United States should remain at the center of the global financial system. The global order is shifting for the first time in nearly a century, with a clear coalition coming together to challenge American power. And it's happening just as the United States is coping with internal strife in governance that is chipping away at trust between leaders and voters.

Since being crowned as the world's go-to currency, the dollar has faced several threats, and the arguably small yet significant fractures are becoming permanent.

These assaults can be put into two categories: domestic and foreign. Inside the United States' borders, the dollar has survived an American-made global financial catastrophe that opened up its stewards at the Treasury department to a crisis of credibility. Later, it faced a volatile president who talked repeatedly of weakening the dollar for political gain by aggressively intervening in foreign exchange markets.

Then there's the painful neglect by U.S. economic policymakers of the downsides of owning the currency that rules the world. A policy to support a strong value for the dollar was a key tenet of globalization that emerged in 1990. Globalization, and the high value of U.S. currency, brought in a vast bounty of prosperity for so many people that the nation's leaders overlooked the large chunk of the American populace that was suffering. A currency that was too strong for too long, and economic integration that saw foreign competitors taking market share of made-in-America products, exacerbated a drain on the U.S. manufacturing sector. Americans across the so-called flyover states saw their jobs shipped to China and other parts of the world in the first decade of the century, and they found their ability to climb the economic ladder blunted while those in power celebrated the very cause of their demise. The social and cultural bedlam that erupted from this neglect—from contested elections to the rise of extremist political ideologies in American politics—is emerging as a blight on the central tenets of the nation's democracy.

It's hard to know just when this cycle of self-sabotage began. Was it in 2019, when Donald Trump considered directing his Treasury secretary, Steven Mnuchin, to weaken the dollar? Was it the global financial crisis? Or is it the curdling relationship among lawmakers, with partisanship reaching a fever pitch at two key moments a decade apart—in 2011 and 2023—when U.S. leaders played chicken in fights over the debt ceiling, making investors wonder if Congress might actually fail to reach an agreement to raise the debt ceiling one day? It all makes the U.S. dollar look less attractive, painting a picture of a dwindling superpower with erratic fiscal management. This new image doesn't bode well. And persistent leadership battles—from presidents contesting elections results to unwieldy dogfights to lead the House of Representatives—point to continued instability.

History has demonstrated the link between currency and political dominance over many centuries. In the eighteenth century, the English pound replaced the Dutch florin when Britain gained economic influence. The dollar won in the decades that followed, with America surpassing Britain as the world's largest economy in the mid-twentieth century. The tides might be shifting again.

The consequences of de-dollarization are far-reaching. It would mean that the United States will need to live within its means, or deal with much higher borrowing costs. With less money to spend, a heavily divided Congress will be forced to make tough budget cuts. A drop in the dollar's reserve status would curb Washington's economic statecraft options, ultimately weakening a key channel of influence in global conflicts. The more countries and companies that establish direct trade channels without the dollar, the less influence the buck has.

And in a world that is fracturing under the weight of globalization's failings—manifested through burgeoning protectionism, supply chains broken during the COVID-19 pandemic, and a Russian invasion that could not be contained despite deep global integration—the future of a world order knitted together by a dollar-based system is in question. Nationalistic economic policies are now supported by both Republicans and Democrats, albeit sometimes by a nicer name, like "friendshoring," to denote the desire to boost trade with geopolitical allies. The dollar is no longer there for the greater good but for those who align with America.

A somewhat unipolar global order anchored in the dollar has allowed the country to borrow enormous amounts of debt—$33 trillion as of 2023—at cheap interest rates, all because the world knows nothing will stop the U.S. government from paying its bills. That credit is important, since debt has always been the key to America's economic prowess. So, just as the nation's leaders try to project an ever-constant and strong democracy, they endeavor to project economic strength as well. This also extends to the marketplace for federal bonds—a safe haven for governments, businesses, investors, and individuals in the face of uncertainty, be it war or a pandemic.

A strong dollar derives from a strong and durable economy, and so the story of the U.S. dollar's rise and endurance is the same as the rise and endurance of the nation itself. As Bob Rubin, the renowned Treasury secretary who served from 1995 to 1999, once said, "Faith in democracy and faith in markets go hand in hand."

PAPER SOLDIERS

1.

SURVIVING
DONALD TRUMP

I t was January 24, 2018, and the seventy-seventh United States secretary of the Treasury, Steven Mnuchin, was in the bucolic resort town of Davos, Switzerland. Hundreds of the alpine city's residents had fled to make room for an exclusive group of self-described thought leaders gathered for the World Economic Forum's annual conference. This year, for a weeklong winter camp dedicated to big problems, lavish parties, and cigar bars, the security bill topped $9 million. In attendance was an incongruous collection of people: 53 heads of state, 116 billionaires, and, for some reason, Elton John.

But before Steven Mnuchin could even begin to hobnob with the global elite gathered, the Treasury chief made a faux paus that put the dollar on an immediate weakening streak and momentarily brought the world to the precipice of a full-blown currency war for the first time in more than three decades.

All because of just seven words: "A weaker dollar is good for us."

While there was more to the statement that Mnuchin made to reporters shortly after breakfast, this was the only part that the world's
economic policymakers, business leaders, and investors cared about.
To the untrained ear, it was a dull phrase. But for Mnuchin's constituents in economics and finance, it was scary: secretaries aren't supposed to yearn for a weak value for the dollar.

To world leaders like Angela Merkel, the battle-tested German
chancellor at the time, Mnuchin had just obliterated a rule that
took decades to hone: world leaders do not talk about their currencies. Such chatter amounts to verbal intervention, or "jawboning" in
policy parlance, which is intended to hint at a government plan that
includes a preferred value for its currency. It suggests that the government is willing to use its own cash to jump into foreign exchange
markets, to influence the forces of supply and demand on currency
values by buying or selling dollars. As a mark of sophistication and
commitment to fair economic integration, in recent decades the
world's most influential nations, the Group of Twenty, had refrained
from such activities, a pledge enshrined in dozens of joint statements
and agreements. Mnuchin now appeared willing to defy that.

It would quickly emerge that the Treasury chief had no intention of signaling anything new in U.S. currency policy. But to investors, the comment was a green light to sell the dollar—which is what
they did that day, pushing down its value by 2.1 percent to reach the
lowest level in three years. The remarks fueled an existing trend of
depreciation due in part to an optimistic outlook for European economies, but also to uncertainty about where the United States was
headed now that President Donald Trump was installing an increasingly protectionist economic agenda. Mnuchin's seven words on the
dollar also threw into question the value of investors' stake in pre-

cious American government bonds, called Treasuries. A weak currency erodes the value of trillions of dollars in U.S. debt held by foreign countries, banks, and individuals.

For failing to speak about the dollar without absolute care and caution, Mnuchin faced a barrage of criticism. Christine Lagarde, the head of the International Monetary Fund, said that his seven words amounted to an opening salvo of a currency war. Merkel called the nationalistic policies that Mnuchin's words represented "poison," and another European official, unwilling to be named making such a comment, called the incident an example of "buffoonery."

You could say that Mnuchin had succumbed to a common malady among Treasury secretaries. The dollar must be spoken about with the utmost care, but sometimes in the energetic rush of meetings on Capitol Hill, Wall Street, and around the world, there's the inevitable mishap. It doesn't help that Treasury secretaries are frequently asked to elaborate on their views. After all, the Treasury department's decisions affect so much of our daily lives—our tax burden, spending power, the ability to innovate and operate in a free and fair market, and more. But in reply to persistent questions, all anyone really wants to hear is a boring reaffirmation of a basic tenet of economic order: the U.S. government will not meddle with currency markets, because they should be free and fair, just like a democracy.

But in the Swiss mountain ski resort on that Wednesday in January, the most revealing part of Mnuchin's statement on the dollar was overlooked.

Yes, he boldly said what few predecessors have: a weak foreign exchange rate has some economic benefits. But that's simply a fact. For some parts of the economy, like the manufacturing and services sectors that export goods to those buying in foreign currencies, a weak dollar boosts profits. These companies can sell more at competitive prices, rather than be drowned out by cheaper products made in other countries. Take chocolate, for example: America has Hershey, and Britain has Cadbury. If the dollar is strong against the British pound, then there will be less demand for Hershey's Kisses in England, because their homegrown candy is cheaper. And it makes Cadbury in the United States cheaper and perhaps more appealing than a made-in-America brand.

But it is the rest of Mnuchin's statement that was more revelatory and more reflective of an emerging new era of economic policy, whether the global elite at Davos liked it or not. "A weaker dollar is good for us," his phrase began—but it was what came next that was the most revelatory: "as it relates to trade and opportunities."

In this messy delivery of the president's America First agenda through currency policy, Trump's Treasury secretary was inadvertently conditioning markets to understand that a hands-off approach to the U.S. dollar wasn't a given, especially when its sheer strength in value and the free trade environment that it underpinned were hurting so many Americans.

It was something that Trump had been talking about vociferously since he emerged as a presidential candidate in 2015. The dark vision he conjured of a U.S. economy that was crumbling (despite record economic expansion) resonated with an overlooked part of the electorate. And on November 8, 2016, 62.9 million Americans validated that vision—perhaps because he was the only candidate who acknowledged the pent-up frustration over low wage growth and trade-related job losses that had hollowed out swaths of the heartland. At first glance, the states that voted for Trump represented those Americans who were left behind in the much-celebrated recovery from the Great Recession that lasted from 2007 to 2009. But the pain that Trump found in so-called flyover states had been building for years. Since the 1980s, the decay of steel towns and car factories in the industrial heartland had given rise to a new name for the region that included mostly Midwestern states, like Ohio, Michigan, and Wisconsin: the Rust Belt.

Manufacturing and services jobs, once the backbone of the working-class economy, paid less and less as foreign goods from Europe, Mexico, and Asia were offered at a cheaper price, slashing demand for American-made products. In shops across the nation, MADE IN CHINA or MADE IN VIETNAM was stamped on everything from Victoria's Secret underwear to Cadillacs. Take-home pay for factory workers had been declining since around 1980, but it worsened after China joined the World Trade Organization and the North American Free Trade Agreement took off. In the three decades leading up to Trump's presidential bid, the United States saw 20 percent of its manufacturing jobs disappear. And in the years since the global financial crisis hit, the share of voters considered "working class" (according to their net income) grew by almost one-third.

To be sure, all advanced economies were seeing a decline in manufacturing. But for those who'd lost their jobs across the Rust Belt and American South, the rest of the world didn't matter—their standard of living had plunged. They blamed their leaders for ignoring it, and competitors were often a bogeyman. During a campaign rally in Indiana, referring to China's high number of exports compared to the United States, Trump declared, "We can't continue to allow China to rape our country, and that's what they're doing." This was a politician who appeared to put American needs above any free trade ideology or notion of global leadership.

The concept of free trade as a bad thing was so alien to mainstream policymakers and economists that they spent much of 2017 in shock that Trump had the support of 47 percent of the U.S. electorate. What many didn't understand, or perhaps were unwilling to see, was that as blunt as his words were, he showed the kind of attention that these voters had been craving for more than a decade.

President Trump's plans to fix these deep-seated economic problems were the opposite of the stable and predictable message that the world came to expect from America. He talked of punitive tariffs on imports, a move that amounted to a trade war (something the world hadn't seen in at least half a century), and scarlet-letter treatment for countries found to be gaming their currencies to gain an unfair trade advantage. He also wanted to use the country's national security apparatus to protect certain industries, like military equipment components manufacturers. All of this amounted to the exploitation of American power and the weaponization of the dollar.

And this is where the final part of Secretary Mnuchin's ad hoc statement on that snowy day in Switzerland came into play. With his first seven words, he boasted about the benefit of a weak dollar in a way finance ministers of rich nations aren't supposed to. With the subsequent seven words, he shed light on the plight of a part of the American economy that desperately needed attention. With the very last portion of this extemporaneous dollar talk that day, he reminded the world of the power he and his president could wield to rebalance global trade ties: "Longer term, the strength of the dollar is a reflection of the U.S. economy and the fact that it is and will continue to be the primary currency."

This was the exorbitant privilege that Mnuchin would find himself at times weaponizing—for the sake of the America First agenda that he believed in—and at other times protecting from the president's most dangerous instincts. Like those before him at the Treasury department, for the four years he was in office, Mnuchin was a steward of the almighty dollar. But he would come to work harder to keep it intact for future use than perhaps any of his predecessors ever had because he had to protect it from the U.S. president himself.

During that first official trip to Switzerland, Mnuchin spent most of his time trying to untangle himself from the rhetorical crosshairs of U.S. currency policy.

Those first seven words did not signify "a shift in my position on the dollar at all," he said as he urgently attempted to correct the record that afternoon. "I thought my comment on the dollar was actually quite clear." During a panel discussion the next day, he assured the audience that he believed in currencies being priced in open markets, not at the whim of government policy. His colleague, Secretary of Commerce Wilbur Ross, said that investors were overreacting to Mnuchin's words.

Even Trump weighed in to help with the cleanup, possibly because it appealed to his ego. The ultimate strongman ruler, Trump came to understand that a strong dollar meant he was running the economy well.

"Ultimately, I want to see a strong dollar," he told reporters after he landed in Davos on Air Force One shortly after Mnuchin's flub.

The Trump presidency was filled with a head-spinning range of policies in which U-turns on publicly stated plans became weekly occurrences. Republicans, Democrats, officials inside the administration, foreign allies, and investors were all frequently left reeling from the whiplash. One moment, China was blamed for the "rape" of America's manufacturing sector, and the next, Trump declared that he and President Xi Jinping "love each other." Then there was the wall for the U.S.-Mexico border that he vowed Mexico would pay for, until he decided to force a government shutdown at home in a bid to get Congress to fund the project.

So it's no surprise that his promise to support a strong value for the U.S. dollar would be turned upside down.

By June 2019, Trump was frustrated by the difficulties of renegotiating trade deals to benefit American workers. His administration had just imposed tariffs on $200 billion of imports from China, but it increasingly looked like officials in Beijing were forcing down the value of the yuan by selling loads of it in open markets. (Since a higher-valued currency makes a nation's imports cheaper and makes its exports pricier in foreign markets, countries that rely on an export industry for economic bliss want a weak currency—hence the temptation to force down an exchange rate.) The yuan dropped to a level not seen since the global financial crisis, despite there being no significant change to the nation's growth prospects. It was an action that amounted to the currency manipulation that everyone in Davos just eighteen months earlier had warned the United States not to even hint at.

Trump was angry. He wanted China to promise to buy more American-made products and to stop cheating in currency markets. He directed his team to start plans to impose another $300 billion in tariffs on Chinese imports to the United States, a measure certain to ratchet up the trade war between the two largest economies that was putting the whole world at risk of an economic slowdown.

With burgeoning frustration over the state of his trade war, Trump turned to U.S. dollar policy. Behind closed doors, he started ranting to his advisers that the buck was too strong. He wanted the Federal Reserve to weaken it by lowering interest rates—which have a bigger and more immediate impact than anything the federal government could do.

To say such a move would be devastating to America's superpower status in the world would be an understatement. Aside from interest rates and inflation, the value of a country's currency is a key indicator of economic health (a strong currency means investors see signs of continued economic growth, and a weak one indicates fears of a slowdown ahead as investors look elsewhere for profits). The Fed's policy decisions had ramifications for every nation on Earth. The dollar was on one side of 90 percent of currency transactions worldwide, and two-thirds of international debt was issued in it. Virtually all oil trade is priced in dollars. All of this makes pretty much the whole world beholden to swings in the currency's price and in its management—and now Trump wanted to meddle. It was the kind of undemocratic behavior common in authoritarian regimes, like Turkey, where the president essentially dictates monetary policy.

But Trump's view of the world was colored by such schemes. On June 18, the European Central Bank (ECB) president Mario Draghi signaled looser monetary policy (meaning cheaper credit to spur investment, thus weakening the euro's price) to juice economic growth. The way Trump saw it, other governments were manipulating their currencies with the help of their central banks. Trump's fixation emerged publicly through tweets directed squarely at the United States' central banker, the ECB's Draghi, and others. "Mario Draghi just announced more stimulus could come, which immediately dropped the Euro against the Dollar, making it unfairly easier for them to compete against the USA. They have been getting away with this for years, along with China and others," Trump tweeted on June 18, just hours after the ECB's announcement. "Very unfair to the United States!"

Trump went after his own central banker, the Fed chair Jerome "Jay" Powell, to do what he claimed the Europeans were doing: use monetary policy to target the dollar. By this time, Trump had already flouted economic convention in several ways: starting an unthinkable trade war with the world's second-most powerful economy, and asking White House lawyers to find ways to either sack or demote Powell as head of the Fed, to name a few. But the public heckling of Powell was a shock just the same. It broke with decades of tradition, where presidents refrained from even the mere appearance of meddling with the central bank. Half-jokingly, former Fed chair Alan Greenspan (a giant in monetary policy and financial circles) sent Powell a pair of earmuffs. The U.S. central bank had the support of most of the world in the fight to stave off dangerous political interference. There was speculation that Trump was setting up the strong dollar, and the Fed's unwillingness to intervene, as the perfect scapegoat should he lose his reelection bid.

Publicly, Powell was under pressure to protect the independence of the institution he ran. In a healthy and stable democracy, the Fed needed complete independence to ensure economic stability over the long term, so as not to be impeded by the short-term whims of politicians seeking power. The central bank had fought several hard battles over the past century with White House and Treasury officials to cultivate and maintain autonomy. So he found ways to say no to Trump.

"The Treasury department—the administration—is responsible for exchange rate policy, full stop," Powell said on June 25 in response to a question from the audience about the president's obvious desire to meddle. "We don't comment on the level of the dollar. We certainly don't target the level of the dollar. We target domestic economic and financial conditions as other central banks do."

As the president was starting to run into roadblocks, his preoccupation with the dollar began boiling over. A week after Powell's punt, Trump fired off another Twitter missive: "China and Europe playing big currency manipulation game and pumping money into their system in order to compete with USA. We should MATCH or continue being the dummies who sit back and politely watch as other countries continue to play their games—as they have for many years!"

Trump's desperate attempts to control the dollar had now reached what was perhaps the final line of defense: Steven Mnuchin.

If you ask him what happened next, Mnuchin will probably tell you "nothing at all." One of the president's advisers came up with an idea to address a policy fix that Trump had asked for, and Mnuchin explained to everyone precisely why it was a bad idea, so they moved on.

But when the most powerful man on Earth needs to be convinced not to undermine the foundation of the United States' economic muscle, it's a big deal.

In multiple meetings in the Oval Office, mostly conducted around the historic Resolute Desk, Trump asked Mnuchin and the rest of his economic team how they could "fix" the dollar. It was strong, and that was hurting America's manufacturing sector, the president said.

He got the answer he wanted from a White House trade adviser with a prickly disposition and extreme policy ideas, who had great influence in that room. A PhD economist from Harvard University, Peter Navarro was eccentric, to say the least. He was as anti-China as they get, having penned a book called *Death by China* in 2011. By 2017, he was prowling the corridors of the West Wing, appealing to the president's most protectionist impulses. Trump called him "my Peter." *The New York Times* dubbed him a "Rasputin-like" trade hawk.

Mnuchin, genteel by comparison, never got along with Navarro.

The Treasury chief had gotten into the habit of dashing the 150 or so yards from the Treasury department to the White House to see who Trump was meeting with—by the third year of the administration, everyone had learned that the wilder ideas the volatile president grabbed on to often emerged when the more reasonable-minded officials (the so-called adults in the room, as the media had dubbed Mnuchin and Trump's daughter and son-in-law, Ivanka Trump and Jared Kushner) weren't around to temper bad ideas.

It was during one of these impromptu meetings that Mnuchin missed when Navarro first noted to Trump that there was precedent for the Treasury department controlling the dollar. Navarro laid out how, in the late 1980s, it was commonplace for the U.S. Treasury secretary and the finance ministers of the biggest industrial nations to openly admonish markets for letting a currency strengthen more than they liked. The threat they brandished was the ability to use the combined currency stockpile of roughly $125 billion (some $460 billion in today's money) to sell dollars in open markets and then buy other currencies, boosting supply to lower the price. At the time, the foreign exchange market moved around $1 trillion each day, a sum small enough that government meddling could work. Of course, back then the Fed helped this effort by making calls to market participants to check on the going rate for dollars, a strategy used to remind traders that government intervention was possible.

Once Mnuchin got wind of Navarro's idea, he and Larry Kudlow began knocking it down. "Who would want to work with us? We can't pull anything like that off—our standing around the world is too weak, we're too incoherent," Kudlow, who was the director of the White House's National Economic Council, remarked when Trump wasn't present.

And so Navarro zeroed in on the power that Mnuchin could use without anyone else's involvement—a $94 billion pot of money. It sat in an account called the Exchange Stabilization Fund, designed to do exactly what the name says: soothe currency markets. It was this same mechanism that the agency used in the 1970s, the 1980s, and the early part of the 1990s to influence foreign exchange rates (with the help of the Fed and other countries). The practice had gone out of fashion under Robert Rubin in the Clinton era, who moved toward market-determined rates.

Mnuchin and Kudlow used several negotiating tactics to keep Navarro from fully persuading Trump to direct the Treasury department to torpedo a currency policy the entire world relied on. Mnuchin was on tricky terrain. For the past six months, he had been dealing with the president at a distance. Trump blamed his Treasury chief for recommending the appointment of Jay Powell as head of the Federal Reserve, something he woefully regretted once the central bank started raising interest rates (which amounts to reducing support to the economy as recovery takes hold). Mnuchin had to tread carefully in curbing Trump's interest in Navarro's proposal.

So Kudlow took the lead and gave Trump several reasons as to why it wouldn't work. For one thing, Treasury had only a fraction of the foreign exchange reserves that trade rivals such as China and Japan have that allow them to intervene. That meant that the United States' ability to sell a few billion dollars of reserves would be a mere blip in the global foreign exchange market, which now trades $5 trillion per day. Kudlow also shared examples of past interventions, under very different circumstances. In 2011, the then Treasury secretary, Tim Geithner, had acted in concert with some of the richest nations to stabilize the yen, after it skyrocketed following an earthquake and tsunami. But the last time the Treasury had sold dollars solely for the purpose of driving it down, back in 2000, was part of a broader international effort to buoy the euro when it was first introduced.

And in the rare circumstances when an intervention was conducted, the Treasury department's efforts were worth little without the full cooperation of the Fed. In the last three interventions, in 1998, 2000, and 2011, Treasury and the Fed worked in lockstep, splitting the amount of dollars transacted evenly between them, with coordinated public statements to boot.

Mnuchin and Kudlow carefully explained to Trump that for any move on the dollar to succeed, the Fed would have to not only agree with the policy decision but also clearly communicate its support. Under the current circumstances, with a dollar intervention that had nothing to do with stability but everything to do with politics, the Fed, through mere silence, could undo anything that the Treasury department attempted.

But even investors, far away from Washington and Trump's Oval Office broodings, could sense Trump's exasperation with the dollar. "Could frustration with the Fed prompt the president to take matters in his own hands and weaken the dollar?" one money manager asked his clients, rhetorically, in an email. "Although it would be highly unusual for a U.S. government to attempt aggressive measures to weaken the dollar, it is not beyond the realms of possibility that the Trump administration will try," wrote another.

Meanwhile, the president's obsession was increasing. The only influence a president could have on the central bank was through nominations to the rate-setting Federal Reserve Board of Governors, which includes the chair. In mid-July, as Trump conducted interviews with potential nominees in the Oval Office, he asked pointed questions to determine if they shared his view that the strength of the dollar was blunting an economic boom—the boom that he was counting on to win him a second term as president.

Publicly, Kudlow tried to put the onus back onto the Fed. Speaking on CNBC on July 9, against the backdrop of his efforts to dissuade Trump privately, Kudlow pointed back to Powell: "Price-level stability and a steady dollar is what the Fed should aim for . . . not employment."

Kudlow and Mnuchin both knew this statement was hollow, since such a move by the Fed would be against the Fed's mandate. Congress directs the U.S. central bank to seek maximum employment, stable inflation, and moderate long-term interest rates, not target a level for the dollar. But the president compulsively watched cable news. Taking to the airwaves was the best way Kudlow could speak to Trump.

It was about another month before Mnuchin and Kudlow's work was done. During a Bloomberg News interview on July 18, the Treasury chief, not wanting to steer markets completely wrong and not wanting to stir the ire of a president who was delicately being talked out of an intervention, could only go as far as saying that there was no change in the U.S. dollar policy "as of now." What's true is that the Treasury department never approached the Fed formally or informally to begin coordination on such a move, according to multiple people who would have been directly involved if it had happened. (The sensitivity of dollar talk in any form drove all of these people to request anonymity.)

But those three words—*as of now*—reveal just how uncertain the United States' currency policy had become. It was a phrase that brought on a sigh of relief from investors. For just a moment, the dollar appreciated on those three words from the Treasury secretary.

2.

THE BIRTH
OF A HEGEMON

I t was out of desperation that Abraham Lincoln's Treasury secretary caved to an idea described by many as "immoral."

Salmon Portland Chase, whose height, girth, and dress coat
adorned with large gilt buttons projected strength, was ready to resign
from the president's cabinet. By 1862, he had outlived three wives, but it
was the Civil War that threatened to undo him. His Treasury department had run out of money, and Chase feared total economic collapse.

The economic creed of the era suggested that almighty God himself
had provided man with gold and silver as a standard of value on which
to base the exchange of goods and credit. But Secretary Chase found
his coffers drained of the precious metals needed to finance a war that
was already taking longer than expected to resolve. To keep President
Lincoln's two million Union troops active, Chase needed paper.

Despite what he described as a "great aversion" to a government-
issued IOU, he couldn't avoid reality: "Immediate action is of great importance. The Treasury is nearly empty," he said in a letter to Congress.

The idea of a certificate that offered no interest payments and was not redeemable for gold or silver was, at first, viewed as all but sealing the ruin of a country only just created, and making its stewards look like a "carnival of rogues." What good was paper currency? A mere illusion funded on faith that its issuer held glory worth investing in, perceived as fraudulent and unconstitutional by critics at banks, in Congress, and even inside Chase's Treasury department.

But as soon as the radical idea became law with Lincoln's signing of the Legal Tender Act, the new paper currency immediately lubricated the market for government credit, galvanizing the nation's economy and the Union Army. The universal acceptance of greenbacks (a common nickname for the dollar that emerged during Chase's time for the green ink used on one side, a color chosen for symbolizing stability) made them far superior to notes issued by the South. If anything, the penetration of Lincoln's currency into the South heralded the demise of the Confederacy—everyone was willing to accept bills featuring Chase's broad forehead and chin dimple. Pretty soon, the Treasury chief was using his newfound ability to issue an unlimited amount of money to whip up $2 million in certificates each day.

Despite running a democracy that was not only in its infancy but also facing its first and perhaps most strenuous test, Chase's endeavor to rally government finances during the Civil War put the nation on the path to ruling the world through the power it gives to, and derives from, the dollar. By adopting the once-radical concept of bills representing the promise of payment, American cash became a representation of the full faith and credit of the United States government— not gold, silver, or any other precious metal—just as the nation was set to overtake Great Britain as the largest economy.

Chase's role in the dollar's evolution ends there. His image was eventually removed from the one-dollar bill, with the legacy of that era instead carried on through Lincoln's presence on the five-dollar note we carry in our pockets today. (The Chase name remains ubiquitous, thanks to an old friend who named a bank in his honor.) It would still take another eight decades for the buck to become the cornerstone of the global financial system. That journey includes the creation of the nation's central banking system, a return to the gold standard, and then sudden abandonment of the gold standard.

To understand how in just 250 years the dollar helped the United States come to rule the world—and became arguably the nation's biggest geopolitical weapon against dictators and despots—it helps to understand how the currency was given that power.

Ask any economist in the world about the birth of the global economic order as we know it today and they'll tell you about Bretton Woods. That is a story that begins with the end of another war, and a group of battle-weary officials from around the world gathered in a bucolic ski resort town on America's East Coast. Less than a month after the D-Day invasion of Normandy, France, by Allied forces in 1944 (the turning point in World War II), the United States hosted economic officials from forty-four allied nations in a resort town called Bretton Woods in New Hampshire. More than 730 officials flew in with a clear mission to create a blueprint for multination economic cooperation. They met over twenty-one days at the Mount Washington Hotel, and by the end of it they had reshaped the world.

By 1944, the United States of America was primed to become the most powerful nation on Earth. Referred to by some as "Hercules in a cradle," the country was now ready to take on its geopolitical birthright and use its size, wealth, and productive capacity to rule the world. It had gone from a small collection of colonies fighting to get out from under the weight of the British monarchy to a democracy buttressed by a constitution that had survived a civil war and successfully knit together an organized union of forty-eight states. Not only was it the biggest economy but it also controlled more than two-thirds of the world's gold stores, thanks in large part to the California gold rush. The United States was also the only major power set to emerge from the ashes of two global wars with its domestic infrastructure largely unscathed. Everyone else was in tatters.

This was the leverage that a U.S. Treasury official named Harry Dexter White used to make the almighty American buck the most important currency on Earth.

An agreement called the Bretton Woods System, ratified on July 22, pledged to end an era of economic nationalism that had led to two world wars. At the center of that promise was a nascent global power—the United States—and its currency. White, representing the behemoth that the United States had become, put the dollar at the center of a new structure that would maintain a link to gold. The new system established three key components of the new economic order by creating two multilateral institutions, the International Monetary Fund (IMF) and the World Bank, and establishing an international currency regime.

It was essentially the coronation of the dollar as the world's reserve asset, the go-to currency on which the entire financial system would be based. During the Bretton Woods meetings there were debates about considering whether a better option was to create a unified world currency that wasn't ruled by any one nation alone. But as the men mapped out the postwar financial order, White used the United States' size and the fact that it would provide the most money to fund the IMF and the World Bank's reconstruction efforts to lead the group to crown the dollar as the world's reserve asset. That made gold, which at the time was considered God's gift to civilized commerce, secondary to the dollar. America's large gold holdings gave the dollar strong purchasing power and an ability to anchor itself to the metal, making it the obvious choice to become the new, easily transferable reserve asset for economies to rely on.

The economic officials gathered at Bretton Woods agreed to fix their currencies to the dollar instead of directly to gold. In exchange, Henry Morgenthau, Jr., the Treasury secretary during the Roosevelt administration, pledged to fix the dollar to the price of gold at thirty-five dollars per ounce.

With that, the centrality of the dollar in the global financial system was cemented. The Treasury department was now in charge of drawing together the world's many nations into an interdependent and peaceful economy. The United States would go on to create a global financial and military security umbrella that would make another world war less likely. In return, it would open a vast market of global consumers for American goods and services, traded in dollars.

The U.S. economy exploded in the years that followed Bretton Woods. From the end of World War II until around 1970, the U.S. population grew by more than 60 percent, accounting for almost a quarter of the world's gross domestic product. During the three decades known as the Golden Age of Capitalism, the nation experienced a tremendous improvement in living standards and a growing middle class as Barbie dolls and television sets airing new favorites like *I Love Lucy* peppered nearly every living room in America. The economy was further buoyed by a more than doubling of military spending, solidifying the United States' role as owner of the world's reserve currency and provider of global security. This period fortified the promise of good credit, meaning that Salmon P. Chase's naughty notion of creating a paper currency was a success. This golden age also reinforced Treasury Secretary Henry Morgenthau's implicit vow at Bretton Woods in 1944: that a sound nation would serve as the owner of the world's most important asset. America was the source of economic and diplomatic security, and an enviable example of a democratic government run by officials elected freely and fairly. Key agencies, such as its central bank, were given statutory independence to protect it from political interference.

The nation had shown itself capable of owning the world's reserve asset, intertwining American power and the dollar's primacy.

But turbulence in the 1970s would call on the United States to prove that strength. In 1971, in a battle to tame inflation that would consume policymakers for the next decade and a half, President Richard Nixon jettisoned the gold standard over concern that he no longer had enough gold to cover foreign holdings of the dollar. That pulled the world away from the fixed exchange rate regime established by the Bretton Woods pact, in which official exchange rates were fixed to the dollar, which was tied to the price of gold. With Nixon's change, the world was being pushed toward a floating exchange rate system, meaning markets decided a currency's value based on supply and demand.

It was a significant shift in the postwar economic organization that the men at Bretton Woods had agreed to, and marked the closing of a golden era of growth and prosperity.

The upheaval that began with Nixon's decision, and the subsequent fight to tame inflation, led to a strong value in the dollar that made policymakers not just in the United States but also overseas uncomfortable. In the 1980s, there was another round of tumult that would bring the nation nearer to the peak of its power.

In the five years leading up to 1985, the dollar increased in value by 50 percent compared to four other major currencies of the time (French, British, German, and Japanese), damaging many parts of the U.S. economy, particularly sectors that export to other nations like manufacturing and agriculture. The appreciation of the dollar meant that American-made goods like cars and electronics were too expensive to buy in the face of cheaper products from other countries whose currencies weren't so strongly valued. Take Sony's Walkman: created by a Japanese technology company, it cost roughly 25 percent less than the American-made knockoff in 1985.

Those sectors took a severe beating, with net agriculture trade shrinking by more than half and the country shedding almost a quarter of its manufacturing workforce. From 1981 to 1982, the United States and the world were in the most severe economic recession since World War II.

The dollar soared off the back of high U.S. interest rates, driven by Federal Reserve chair Paul Volcker's tight monetary policy aimed at wringing inflation out of the economy and President Ronald Reagan's expansionary fiscal policy. While Treasury intervened to weaken it, it wasn't enough to tame the protectionist pressures from Congress, despite what one German official at the time called the administration's "benign neglect" of the currency's strength. Reagan didn't see the problem with a strong dollar, at least not right away. Asked about the overvalued currency at a press conference, he said it was "a blessing." But protectionism was raging in Congress. One Democratic senator said Americans would prefer a "wimp dollar" that "wasn't beating their brains out," citing the lost profits and jobs across the nation's agricultural and manufacturing sectors, which had deteriorated over the first half of the decade.

Amid this turmoil, within days of Reagan's second inauguration, James "Jim" Baker was hurriedly sworn in as Treasury secretary in the basement of his home in Washington, D.C., instead of at the Oval Office. The administration's economic team had decided that correcting the strength of the dollar was a key mission, and Baker needed to get to work if Reagan was going to bring the U.S. economy back to life.

James Addison Baker III, who became the nation's sixty-seventh Treasury secretary, once failed an economics exam in college. A ruthless politician with friendships that ran deep in Republican aristocracy, he was a man willing to take defiant steps to preserve power even if it brought him to the brink of flouting legal and political authority. In 1984, while serving as President Reagan's chief of staff, Baker explicitly and secretly directed the chair of the Federal Reserve, the world's most influential monetary authority, to refrain from raising interest rates before the president's reelection later that year. It was a huge gamble. Even the appearance of political meddling in the Fed's work would be dangerous, but Baker was clearly willing to risk everything to secure a second term for Reagan. The chairman, Paul Volcker, ignored that demand.

This was the temperament of the man who became the Treasury secretary in 1985, a time when the dollar was so strong compared to other currencies that it would take a covert gathering of the world's most powerful men to agree to temper it.

In a meeting so secret that most of Reagan's cabinet remained in the dark, Baker met with counterparts from the four richest nations in the ostentatious Gold Room of the Plaza Hotel in Manhattan. Japan, West Germany, the United Kingdom, and France joined to broker a deal to collectively drive down the value of the dollar and reduce the United States' trade deficit. With their central banks working in concert, enough dollars were purchased in the open market to weaken the currency, making American goods more affordable for foreign buyers. It also made it easier for foreign governments to pay down dollar-denominated debt.

The so-called Plaza Accord worked so well that less than two years later the dollar had depreciated by 40 percent and the plan needed to be actively reversed. Choosing the Louvre Museum in Paris as the site of this second secret meeting, the finance ministers of the same group of nations agreed to collectively work toward reining in the depreciation of the dollar (an effort that would take some time).

By 1987, two years into his tenure, Baker had won the battle to tame the dollar. Just as the world was setting up for globalization, he proved that dollar dominance, a concept reflecting its prevalence in world commerce, was so deeply entrenched that it could bring together whole economies to successfully control currency traders. Baker had planted more seeds for an integrated economy driven by free trade and led by the United States that would be cultivated over the next decade. (To be sure, the currency interventions of the 1980s, first to stop the dollar's appreciation and then to stop its depreciation, had damaging effects. Japan was in distress for at least the next decade as it coped with the resulting shift in its export industry.)

But there was one key constituency suffering from all the surreptitious currency actions that would soon start talking back.

A pattern of aggressive and secretive interventions to manage the dollar and other currencies had foreign exchange markets, where all that matters is turning a profit, constantly guessing when the government would meddle and ruin their bets. The Plaza and Louvre agreements revealed that finance ministers had an undisclosed exchange rate target that they were willing to fight for, whether it was through verbal signals to markets that an intervention was in the offing or by actually using currency reserves to manage exchange rates. Traders began overinterpreting every sigh and swoon from policymakers for clues on what governments wanted from their currencies, attempting to front-run another secretive hotel pact that might lead to unnerving swings in global foreign exchange markets.

In one case, Nicholas Brady, who ran the Treasury department for Reagan's final year and then for President George H. W. Bush, accidentally reversed a rally in the dollar's value with a flippant remark on market movements that, to currency traders, sounded like the Treasury secretary favored a weak dollar. Worrying that another multination intervention was in the offing, investors quickly sold dollars, causing it to briefly depreciate.

The ricocheting of currency pricing was unnerving, but Treasury's efforts to stifle this market volatility would backfire for the next several years. While bullying between Treasury and financial experts would go unnoticed by the general public, what ensued would set the scene for economic successes and failures for decades to come.

The decisions made at Bretton Woods during that final year of World War II made the dollar as important and prevalent as the English language itself. It meant that foreigners looking for a safe place to store their cash could forever look to the United States, allowing the government to borrow cheap and spend big on a better future, something that no other nation as heavily indebted as America has persuaded investors to do. It's a power loop that the United States still enjoys today: trust in America's dollar (and its democratic government) allows for cheap debt financing, which buys health care built on the most advanced research and development and inventions like airplanes and the iPhone. All of this is propelled by free market innovation and the superpowered strength to keep the nation safe from foreign threats. That investment boosts the nation's economic, military, and technological prowess, making its economy (and the dollar) even more attractive.

But that power comes with immense responsibility: the world demands from the United States a thriving democracy. Global markets are inextricably linked to the integrity of America's public institutions, governed by a system of checks and balances and rule of law that essentially serve as the arbiters of the world's financial system through oversight of the dollar.

This also means that what the United States owes to the rest of the world is a finance ministry that can successfully wield the often mythic abilities that the dollar carries as a symbol of American soft power and hard currency dominance.

3.

CONTROL FREAKS
AND VIGILANTES

Y ou can't keep a good currency down."
This was the message that foreign exchange traders had
for the U.S. Treasury department in 1989. The trouble was,
policymakers were afraid of a strong dollar.

Nicholas Baker, the diffident Treasury secretary who bridged two
successive Republican presidencies, felt that a high value for the dollar would pose immense problems for the economy. When the dollar
became very strong in the early Reagan years, labor unions and blue-
collar workers in the manufacturing and services sectors began calling for protectionist policies like import tariffs.

Foreign finance ministers, like those in West Germany and Japan,
also preferred a weaker U.S. currency, in part because it made it easier to pay off dollar-denominated debt.

But really, they were all flummoxed by pretty much every sign of
independence in dollar pricing that currency traders showed. In one

incident where the greenback began trending weaker—which usually they said they wanted—several big countries rapidly came together: Japanese officials verbally intervened to bolster it, while Treasury joined forces with the Federal Reserve to buy dollars in open markets, which tended to drive up the currency's value by reducing its supply.

Investors were fed up by the control-freak tendencies of these world leaders. Instead of manipulating the dollar to keep it at a particular level, it was time for a fully free-floating foreign exchange regime where markets determined prices. That meant natural supply and demand, not prices that were artificially induced by government officials—especially since currency interventions were actually in direct conflict with what economic conditions naturally called for. The Fed was maintaining elevated interest rates, which tend to attract foreign investment into the United States because they pay more interest, thus increasing the demand and value for the dollar.

Mostly, traders just wanted governments to stop constantly trying to buck the tides of natural currency flows. But policymakers weren't listening.

Instead, they were constantly demanding "exchange rate stability," despite the fact that they were the ones yo-yoing traders multiple times a week. They treated markets like toddlers: "Be calm, be cautious, and be kind," one White House spokesman said. But currency prices were swinging because of the government's actions. This was a period in which, on some days, up to nine central banks would jump in together to control the dollar—repeatedly. When the amount of daily currency trades in markets was increasing so quickly that they needed more heft to control prices, governments became even more aggressive.

And it was all in some disjointed effort to calm markets down.

"Treasury has become too enamored of intervention and is subject to embarrassment when intervention fails," said one critic. Finance ministers and central bankers were asking for trouble. It would take several years of bickering and, ultimately, retribution from investors for the Treasury department to realize that if they wanted stability, they had to stop butting in.

One such rebuke came just a few years later, and it was a lesson so terrifying that it became economic policy scripture everywhere. After years of aggressive government management of the British pound, a narrative took off among traders that perhaps the currency was worth a lot less than the rate the government allowed. On September 16, 1992 (just as President Bush was on the brink of losing reelection because of the recession), George Soros and a band of fellow investors turned the tables on policymakers, selling enormous amounts of the pound in a short span of time.

The day would later be dubbed Black Wednesday.

It was a bold plan initiated to make money on what Soros viewed as an overpriced commodity. The result was the collapse of the pound's value, ultimately breaking the once revered currency. The $10 billion bet forced the Conservative-led government to crash out of an agreement with Europe meant to unify the continent's economies. Soros's gamble drove the pound down dramatically by almost 5 percent in a single day, earned him $1 billion, and cost the U.K. Treasury £3.3 billion (roughly $10 billion in today's money).

The event eventually pushed the ruling Conservative party out of government. The world saw that not even a rich global power could escape the blight of a weak foreign exchange rate run amok.

It was in this context that in 1993, just a year after the pound nearly broke, the U.S. dollar was firmly on a depreciation streak. A weak currency had just overturned British politics, and Americans wondered if the same could happen on their side of the Atlantic.

It wouldn't be long before U.S. Treasury officials would come to see that trying to control and manipulate markets was detrimental—that it treated the side effect of economic problems, not the problem itself. It was around this time that a new economic doctrine took hold among the Democratic Party: that a strong, healthy economy is backed by policies that target full employment, stable (and thus predictable) growth, and tempered inflation. This meant that governments should create policies that induce business investment and consumer spending (via tax and regulatory policies, budget reduction, welfare programs, etc.), rather than try to cheat in currency markets. If democracy is considered strong by way of free elections and independent agencies and courts, then the nation's currency markets deserve the same autonomy. A truly free dollar—allowed to rise and fall as the forces of supply and demand dictate—would allow the Treasury department to focus on why the economy was weak.

By the time Bill Clinton strode into the White House in January 1993, the U.S. dollar was an unshakable force in global finance and trade. Nearly half of all transactions between multinational corporations and financial institutions were settled in the greenback, with the rest split across more than one hundred others. Poor nations whose currencies were often worth too little to attract investment increasingly used the dollar to sell debt to finance public spending. The price of everything from crude oil to grain and company shares was determined in dollars.

Against the backdrop of so much currency volatility around the world in the 1990s, U.S. currency policy and how it intersected

with markets had never been so important. And that relationship—
between the government and markets—needed improvement.

Despite being the world's most powerful man, in his first year or so
in office, President Clinton was being bullied by a coterie of reckless,
sweaty, and money-hungry members of a boys' club that operated high
up in Manhattan skyscrapers and behind thick sixteenth-century walls
in London, men who measured power and influence only in hundreds of millions of dollars. Their actual names didn't even matter—
they were known by menacing monikers like "Human Piranha" and
told to show up to work "ready to bite the ass off a bear." They worked
at firms like Salomon Brothers and what was then called Goldman,
Sachs & Co. An average workday meant sixteen hours glued to computer screens as these men gambled with billions of dollars. They
operated in a culture of bullying the young, with hazing techniques
reminiscent of a college fraternity—if the pledge leaders had unfath-
omable wealth at their disposal. Some forced underlings to eat pounds
upon pounds of fast food in single sittings. As the author Michael
Lewis described in his book *Liar's Poker*, it was a world where "everyone wanted to be a Big Swinging Dick," and women were kept far
from power.

They were the bond vigilantes. And by 1993, they had amassed
enough power to wield political influence in Washington, D.C.

Bill Clinton's electoral victory over the incumbent George H. W.
Bush delivered him into the White House with a mandate to enact
his "It's the economy, stupid" campaign agenda: an ambitious plan to
lower the tax burden for the American middle class that the new president expected would become law swiftly. His party held a majority in

both chambers of Congress, and the fresh-faced Arkansas Democrat was ready to shake up establishment Washington.

There was just one problem: markets hated Clinton's plan.

Why did it matter in Washington what a pack of gamblers holding court on trading floors in New York and London thought about the president, Congress, and the Federal Reserve? Because investors serve as a daily opinion poll for economic policymakers that reveals, in real time, what policies they think are good or bad for the economy. Those operating in this system go by a variety of names, all colloquially describing the same shapeless species: whether you refer to them in blanket terms like "Wall Street," "traders," or, as one economist in the 1980s dubbed them, "bond vigilantes," they are all part of the same intricate web that stretches around the world, buying and selling anything of value (stocks, bonds, soybeans, hog futures) to turn a profit. The judgment traders render has immense impact: they make a limitless number of instantaneous trades on their computers each day based on assessments made in the mere nanoseconds they often dedicate to parse news headlines, data from government agencies, the Federal Reserve, and the dollar's value against the currencies of other countries. Like George Soros demonstrated on Black Wednesday, in an instant, investors can purchase or dump millions of dollars' worth of bonds and make decisions that can mean the difference between a country or company's survival or doom.

A bond can change hands countless times throughout its life. Each time it is sold and purchased in financial markets, its value shifts and is reflected in a figure that's called the yield, which represents the annual income that an investor pockets on their investment.

Riskier bonds (like those issued by municipal governments in declining Rust Belt cities, or from developing nations) offer higher yields. It's a concept similar to the way that teenage drivers are expected to fork over more annually to an insurance company to offset the increased likelihood they rear-end another car while scrolling through their TikTok feed. And because of the added risk, those bonds are usually cheaper to acquire. Safer bonds (the financial version of the driver who never speeds and always uses their turn signal) pay lower yields and cost more.

But the standard is the 10-year Treasury, a common denominator against which all other bonds are measured.

Since the days of Alexander Hamilton, the U.S. Department of the Treasury has auctioned debt, or taken loans from domestic and foreign investors, to pay for the country's massive military, public works like building highways and bridges, and other government operations. That debt, referred to as "Treasuries," "notes," or "bonds," gives the lender an annual interest payment as income, and they are issued in a range of maturities, from a few weeks to thirty years. As the world's financial system evolved, the ten-year version of those Treasury bonds became the standard against which countless other types of debt are priced. It's the benchmark by which banks lend money to everyday Americans to purchase homes and cars, and finance credit card debt. Broadly speaking, high interest rates on these Treasuries restrain growth and hurt the American middle class, while low rates lubricate the economy.

And here is where the complex cycle of how bonds operate explains why markets matter so much to government policymakers: when the yield for the 10-year Treasury bond is high, so is the rate for other types of debt like mortgages and car loans. As people spend more for their loans, they spend less on household necessities and have even less leftover for luxuries and savings—all of which ultimately stunts economic growth. But when the opposite happens and investors want less interest paid on their investment in the 10-year Treasury, costs come down. People spend less money on their debt, leaving more cash for other expenditures. Meanwhile, the cost for corporations to raise debt meant for investment also becomes cheaper, and that investment from the private sector creates more jobs. Put simply: higher interest rates eat away at disposable income while households pay more for their mortgages and credit card debt, a problem they tend to punish the sitting president for.

By the end of this cycle, the federal government is collecting more in taxes from all that economic growth. That makes investors in Treasuries even more confident in the nation's abilities to manage its finances, thus driving down interest rates.

The result is a huge incentive to keep yields on Treasuries low for those who want the American economy as a whole to do well.

In 1993, the bond vigilantes rejected Clinton's plan to bring the economy out of the doldrums. To Wall Street, Clinton's middle-class tax cuts amounted to a dangerous gambit that would threaten the stability of U.S. debt. They worried it would only add to the nation's already enormous deficit (wherein government spending outstripped what it brought in through taxes and other revenue). And adding to the deficit, Wall Street believed, made their bets riskier since it increased the likelihood that bonds wouldn't be worth as much down the road. For bond traders, the primary worry as Clinton unveiled his economic plan was inflation. To them, it looked like the U.S. government was asking for the equivalent of an investment in a heavily indebted, declining, and directionless business. Obsessed with money and disgusted by what they thought was an unrealistic plan for the U.S. government to spend its way to economic health by issuing

massive amounts of debt, traders were growing reluctant to purchase Treasuries. They wanted assurances that U.S. debt was a safe
investment.

Clinton and his aides viewed these concerns as trivial, petty, or
some combination of the two. The lost tax revenue was simply a
down payment on energizing an anemic economy that had seen just
13 percent growth in the past five years, while 8.4 million Americans were without jobs. But with so much supply and less demand
for these bonds in the market, the government was forced to offer
higher yields—and a higher return on investment—to lure buyers.

From late 1993, when bond traders first started absorbing Clinton's economic plan, until the end of 1994 the yield on the 10-year
Treasury bond went from 5.2 percent to 8.1 percent. In other words,
the "big swinging dicks" of Wall Street were afraid of the risk from
Clinton's agenda and wanted a bigger insurance policy to invest in a
nation that implemented that plan.

It was a harsh lesson for the Clinton team. One of his top political
strategists, James Carville, said at the time: "I used to think that if
there was reincarnation, I wanted to come back as the president or
the pope or as a .400 baseball hitter. But now, I would like to come
back as the bond market. You can intimidate everybody."

And so President Clinton overhauled his economic proposals, with
plenty of input from Bob Rubin, a bond market savant from Goldman Sachs who at the time was the inaugural director of the White
House's National Economic Council. Clinton abandoned promises of
a middle-class tax cut and retrenched on other measures, all because
of the vigilantes in the cutthroat world of moneymaking.

The new, complicated and audacious plan came in two broad
pieces.

The first was to appease the bond vigilantes by rejiggering the proposals to instead reduce the nation's deficit and work toward balancing the budget. The hope was that with the government spending less than the revenue it collected, long-term bond interest rates would be held in check. That meant cheap cash flowing through the economy. If investors rewarded the new plan by pushing down interest rates on government bonds, then interest rates would drop on debt across the economy (like home mortgages and corporate credit). The resulting economic expansion would encourage more investment in the United States, driving up the value of the dollar, which would keep inflation in check because the United States could import cheaper foreign goods. With inflation under control, the Federal Reserve could keep interest rates low, further juicing the economy.

The second piece of this plan was an exercise in public messaging.

Not only did the Clinton team need to take actions that were good for the future of the economy, it also had to remind everyone, again and again, of what it was doing. The message had to be a simple one that projected strength, confidence, and calm.

They needed a new mythology. But the weakening value of the dollar would get worse before it got better.

4.

BOB RUBIN'S
BUMPER STICKER

The first person to serve as Treasury secretary for Bill Clinton would go on to be the most unremarkable member of the administration's vaunted economic team. By the time he became Treasury chief, Lloyd Millard Bentsen, Jr., had been a public servant since 1946, including four terms as a senator representing Texas. He was handsome, he'd been an Eagle Scout as a kid, and he had overseen a squadron of six hundred men in the military during World War II. But in the 1990s, he was outgunned as a policymaker.

The U.S. dollar had a major problem when Bentsen was sworn in as the country's sixty-ninth Treasury secretary. In 1994, the greenback kept plunging, puzzling economists because the Fed's rate increase should, in theory, have driven the dollar higher. But investors were worried about economic growth that remained slow even as the nation had recovered from an eight-month recession. They were also concerned about a potential repeat of the currency crises that had brought about political instability and caused years of damage to the British economy.

Amid all of this, Bentsen exacerbated the weakening trend in the dollar with a statement that was harmless on the surface, but startling for financial experts forever on edge about government intervention or trickery.

"I'd like to see a stronger yen," Bentsen said. What he wanted was to admonish Japanese officials for jawboning the yen toward a lower level to boost its own manufacturing sector. But that brief remark fed perfectly into existing fears and paranoia among currency dealers, who proceeded to dump dollars and snap up the Japanese currency, driving the greenback's value down to the lowest level against the yen since shortly after World War II. They were trying to outrun any possibility that the government was about to launch a wholesale devaluation effort on the dollar, like the Treasury department had in 1985.

While the world's economic overlords of the 1980s met at fashionable Manhattan hotels or Parisian art museums for secret gatherings to manage the dollar, the next shift in the currency regime would take place in a much humbler setting. It was 1994, and Robert "Bob" Rubin, director of Clinton's economic advisory council, would often host Treasury colleagues in his cramped office in the West Wing for strategy sessions on how to induce calm in currency markets—and strengthen the dollar.

For everything the poorly lit, rodent-infested office lacked in grandeur, the participants more than made up for in policy. These gatherings usually included Larry Summers, an undersecretary at Treasury, Tim Geithner, a civil servant for the agency (both would go on to become Treasury secretaries), and Roger Altman, who had taken a pause in his career as an investment banker to serve as a top deputy at Treasury.

The discussions were happening in the midst of currency crises around the world—the United Kingdom was recovering from George Soros's assault on the pound, and a mess lay just ahead for the Mexican peso and Asian currency. Foreign exchange markets were seemingly in constant disarray during that decade due to a mixture of meddlesome fiscal mismanagement and speculative behavior by investors. In the summer of 1994, around the time when Rubin held discussions on currency policy in his tiny White House office, a weak foreign exchange rate conjured the image of a weak country. Governments, including Clinton's, were faced with the prospect that a depreciating currency was reflective of a nation's political and economic health and could even force change in leadership.

But the United States and its allies were running out of traditional remedies to their dollar problem. In previous years, finance ministers would seek to drive the strength of their currency up or down by using the nation's reserves to buy or sell in the open market. But the era of aggressive government intervention was slowly coming to a close. Treasury's currency stockpile, which was deployed to conduct those transactions, was not large enough to compete with the multitrillion-dollar trading flows that now dominated foreign exchange markets. Rubin felt it was best to allow the buck's value to be a reflection of investors' expectations of the nation's interest rates, growth rate, deficit, inflation, and employment.

It was exactly what traders wanted.

But allowing the market to independently price currency meant that U.S. policy was once again at the mercy of the whims and moods of traders on Wall Street. To curb their meddling, Clinton's economic team needed to improve the narrative. If they could convince traders that the dollar should be valued robustly, it would complement the administration's rebooted economic strategy.

There was another important part of the sales job. For the past decade, government officials had maintained a secret, preferred exchange rate target that they oriented policy around. For their gambit to work, the Clinton administration had to convince traders that the game was no longer rigged and that they should take the administration's efforts at face value instead of parsing their words for secret messages and secret meetings.

It was a tough pitch. Geithner, at the time a member of Treasury's apolitical civil service, felt that investors believed Democrats were more likely to game currency markets, using it as a tool for quick bursts of economic growth. That made for dangerous terrain, and even more so with the dollar inexplicably trending weaker despite rising interest rates—the exact type of environment that would, in the past, have caused a politically motivated government worried about horse-race politics and voter approval to intervene. The risk, Geithner warned, was that the slightest comment or movement could send the already jittery markets into a tailspin, as Bentsen had done with his statement that he desired a weaker yen. A message of stability was a key goal.

Rubin and the team wanted to come up with a formulation that was strong enough to help lean against that perception without tying the U.S. government to any particular level. Rubin & Co. labored through a sticky, hot Washington summer in search of a message that would resonate with markets. In the end, it was Altman who came up with the winning slogan: "A strong dollar is in our national interest."

Just eight words—the perfection derived from its simplicity.

Altman's statement had no implicit reference to a specific value for the greenback because there wasn't one. Instead, the phrase simply signaled that a strong rate (whatever supply and demand in markets valued the dollar at) was one way to keep inflation in check. A strong dollar meant cheap foreign imports, giving the American people and businesses unrivaled purchasing power. And a policy consistently and explicitly supporting a strong dollar (and slowing interventions) could help offset concerns about those pesky 10-year Treasury yields. If the government was invested in keeping its currency strong, investors would have more reason to feel confident in bonds issued by the United States.

"It was designed to be a policy for all seasons," Geithner said years later. "It was a statement of broad intent that we were not going to try to artificially engineer a decline in the currency as a tool for economic advantage."

A virtuous cycle would be born. Lower interest rates and a healthy economy would produce higher federal revenue, resulting from a strong economy that increases tax revenue, to pay off debt. All Rubin needed to do was convince investors that this could work.

It was just eight words, but the strong dollar mantra took several months to become ensconced in the economic zeitgeist.

It started on July 8, 1994, in Naples, Italy. While taking questions from reporters after an economic summit with world leaders,

President Bill Clinton revealed the first shading of what would soon become the logic behind Rubin's incantation: "We have participated twice recently in [currency] interventions, and what we see is that sometimes they work for a little bit and sometimes they can make a real difference." But, Clinton said, he believed that the sugar rush of interventions would eventually be offset by economic fundamentals. The best thing to do, he argued, was to stabilize the dollar and other significant world currencies.

"In the last few years we've had some terrible problems with other currencies which massive interventions have not reversed—the best way to do that is to send a signal to the markets that we are working on the economic fundamentals. That we are trying to build the economy." With those words, Clinton told traders that the government was stepping back from its meddlesome behavior in currency markets and focusing on the economy. The nuanced yet simplistic approach prescribed by Rubin and his team of markets men was a notable departure from the freewheeling early days of Clinton's presidency, and proof the young president was learning to speak with nuance.

By evoking "economic fundamentals," Clinton bridged the gap between the often esoteric world of economists and the practical concerns (the strength of the job market, whether prices were rising, and the overall health of the economy) that consumed politicians. Clinton was laying out the intellectual foundation for what would become known as Rubin's strong dollar mantra.

The lesson, as Clinton went on to articulate during that Q and A with reporters in Naples, was that he had learned he needed to focus on the problem, not the side effect. The policy of the United States,

Clinton continued, would be "strengthening the dollar over the long run in a realistic way but also strengthening other currencies as well. . . . I very much want a reasonably priced dollar," he said.

Clinton then made his point impeccably clear: "I'm not for a weak dollar. We have not done this intentionally. No one has tried to talk down the dollar."

Twelve days later, the Federal Reserve joined the new public relations campaign. The chair Alan Greenspan and Larry Summers orchestrated a one-two punch to double down on the president's message. In a routine congressional hearing on the state of monetary policy, Greenspan said, "Any evidences of weakness in [the dollar] are neither good for the international financial system nor good for the American economy."

Translation: the Fed did not want a weak dollar.

The very next day, on July 21, Summers was on Capitol Hill for testimony of his own. Once a top economist at the World Bank, he was now the undersecretary for international affairs in Secretary Bentsen's Treasury department, a senior position that included currency policy in its remit. On the back of Greenspan's comments, Summers unveiled for lawmakers a carefully prepared statement: "The administration believes that a strengthening of the dollar against the yen and the [German] mark would have important economic benefits for the United States."

Translation: Treasury did not want a weak dollar.

A stronger dollar, Summers continued, "would restore confidence in financial markets that is important to sustaining recovery. It would boost the attractiveness of U.S. assets and the incentive for longer-term investment in the economy, and it would help to keep inflation low." Moreover, he argued that other members of the Group of Seven—the collection of the world's wealthiest and most influential nations—agreed that a further weakening of the dollar would be "counterproductive" to a global economic recovery.

Translation: a strong dollar is good for America.

Over the next five months, the greenback appreciated as investors warmed to the administration's strategy. Lloyd Bentsen would announce his plans to retire from public office, noting that his time as secretary of the Treasury had been the capstone of nearly a half century of public service. The task of getting full buy-in for the new narrative would fall to the strong dollar policy's intellectual father, whose political influence was swelling like the dollar itself.

And so it was Bob Rubin—the native son of Miami Beach, Florida, who played a key role in the painstaking development of the president's entire economic agenda—whom Clinton tapped to take over at the Treasury department.

The nomination set up a high-stakes confirmation hearing before the Senate Finance Committee, where lawmakers would be weighing not only Rubin himself but also Clinton's entire economic platform.

Rubin came into the January 1995 hearing well prepared. The nominee had gotten to know the senators who oversaw Treasury during the first two years of the administration as he coordinated economic policy from his perch at the White House. Rubin's schedule during that period had been a flurry of meetings with lawmakers from both parties as he sought to deepen his understanding of the part of Washington he knew the least, Capitol Hill.

He was nothing if not obsessive about it. Sensing his own vulnerability, he solicited advice readily and regularly. He kept a book describing the inner workings of congressional appropriations committees on his desk at the White House for easy reference and won plaudits from Democrats and Republicans alike for his outreach. In fact, during his time as a White House official, Rubin had built up enough credibility with the senators that ten minutes into the question-and-answer portion of the confirmation hearing as Treasury chief that Senator Bob Packwood, the Republican chair of the panel, revealed to the public that the committee had already approved Rubin's nomination, although they expected him to stay and answer questions.

That announcement didn't rob the next two hours of drama.

As Rubin sat under the crystal chandelier in room number 215 in the Dirksen Senate Office Building, for the first time he delivered the strong dollar mantra: "A strong dollar is very much in this nation's economic interests."

U.S. economic policy would never be the same again.

The line would go on to be a motto that Rubin and his successors would be expected to recite almost on command over the next twenty-five years. It was an edict for investors worldwide, delivering reassurance in the strength of the U.S. economy, and the message that investing in it (building a business or buying government debt) was a safe bet. By another measure, the policy had to do with promoting a strong foreign exchange rate, meaning that a dollar can buy a larger amount of a foreign currency. The advantage can be as simple as the benefit an American tourist gets while grabbing lunch during a trip abroad. If that tourist decides to buy a Big Mac, he might be charged £3. A strong dollar means that the American might need to pay only $3.50 to buy the British pounds she then needs to purchase the burger. But if the dollar is weak, that same £3 could cost the American $4, or more.

The phrase was an emollient for investors after the recent currency crises in other parts of the world. They rewarded Rubin for the new so-called strong dollar policy: the dollar began an upward march in 1995, rising roughly 16 percent in the four years he was Treasury chief.

The chain of events that Rubin had prepared for began to materialize. Clinton worked with Republicans in Congress to slash government spending, trimming the federal budget deficit even as the economy began its resurgence. The yield on the 10-year Treasury dropped from somewhere around 8 percent at the beginning of Clinton's presidency to 4.16 percent in 1998. The bond vigilantes were just investors, nothing scarier, and currency markets began to calm—a calm that had evaded policymakers for more than two decades.

Bob Rubin's staff was used to seeing their boss padding around the high-ceilinged third-floor corridor of the Treasury department without shoes. With his shiny cuff links and his tie still knotted, the millionaire was often dashing out of office 3330, the secretary's suite, and down the building's large black-and-white-checkered hallway in his socks.

Beneath the surface of Rubin's modest, aw-shucks demeanor was a market-savvy economic guru. At the age of fifty-six, he came to lead President Clinton's economic team with decades of experience at the Wall Street behemoth Goldman Sachs. He had the perfect pedigree to manage the nation's finances and fuel the fulfillment of the American dream. For Rubin, taking the reins as Treasury chief meant that he largely gave up beloved hobbies. He would trade sedate weekends saltwater fly-fishing for chartered government flights to Beijing and Kuala Lumpur to trumpet investment in the United States. He would race across the marble floors of Capitol Hill to warn lawmakers of the dangers of a ballooning federal deficit. He would drive heroic measures to contain the financial crises of Mexico and Asia.

From the moment Rubin took office, currencies loomed large on his agenda.

The world's economies had become increasingly interwoven in the postwar period as a burgeoning middle class began buying goods from all over the world. Those trends only accelerated in the aftermath of the Cold War as the United States emerged as the dominant force of a capitalist system that now ruled the globe. The capstone of that new global outlook was a signature policy of the Clinton administration: the North American Free Trade Agreement, commonly referred to as NAFTA, which took effect in 1994. The deal reduced or cut tariffs on trade between Canada, Mexico, and the United States, with the resulting giant free-trade zone setting the stage to incorporate Asian nations into similar pacts (including China's nascent entry into the World Trade Organization).

With the United States a leader in these efforts, it was up to Rubin to establish norms for a modern economic order centered around globalization. The bounty of this deep economic integration was predicted to be immense: prosperity for everyone, a larger middle class, a lid on inflation, and cheap imports, not to mention the cultural benefits of being able to move and trade easily across borders. To ensure its success, stability and fairness in foreign exchange policies was imperative. Everybody needed to play by the same rules, especially when it came to currencies, since their rates directly affected whether a company could make money selling goods overseas.

Rubin's work began immediately. His wife, Judith, had barely set down the Bible on which he placed his left hand for his swearing in on January 10, 1995, when the Oval Office was cleared so the newly minted Treasury secretary could walk Clinton through a $25 billion bailout necessary to stabilize the Mexican peso.

But Rubin's management of the dollar, in particular, would dominate much of his tenure. Perhaps for that reason, Rubin kept a daily reminder of its importance on a sign near his desk at Treasury: "The buck starts here."

So what does Bob Rubin's strong dollar policy mean, and how was it different from previous wisdom and policy? To Rubin and his acolytes like Summers and Geithner, the mantra symbolized one component of a broad economic agenda often referred to as Rubinomics.

This fiscal theory, meant to describe Clinton's economic policy, goes like this: A balanced federal budget (or one that at least works to cut deficits) spurs economic growth because it keeps inflation in check, which then keeps a lid on long-term interest rates. Federal spending should be financed through tax revenue as much as possible to keep America's debt load in check. Rubinomics also sought to protect the trillions of dollars that foreign investors poured into U.S. government bonds in order to encourage more investment in America.

Put all that together and you have a policy that maintains dollar supremacy.

"The dollar moved quite high against the yen today, what do you make of that?"

When William Murray of *The Wall Street Journal* posed that question to the Treasury chief on April 7, 1997, Bob Rubin was in a hotel conference room in Hanoi, Vietnam, with a large round wooden Treasury department seal pinned to the podium that stood between him and the press. He had spent the three-day swing through the country meeting with Finance Minister Nguyễn Sinh Hùng and Prime Minister Võ Văn Kiệt to sign a pact for Vietnam to repay $146 million of an old wartime debt that would clear the path for better trade ties with America.

With his salt-and-pepper hair spilling over his forehead, Rubin shook hands with schoolchildren in Ho Chi Minh City and enjoyed a cultural performance in Hanoi, even letting one artist put a mushroom-shaped straw hat on his head.

The trip was intended, and so far had succeeded as, a ground-breaking moment of reconciliation with a nation whose economic and political circumstances had become the flash point of one of America's bloodiest wars, inexorably shaping an entire generation. But Murray, who had traveled with Rubin from Washington to report on the trip, wasn't concerned with any of that. Investors had only just lived through dramatic currency crises that had broken the pound and nearly eviscerated Mexico. Murray knew what they wanted to hear from the Treasury secretary.

"My view on the dollar," Rubin began, as he somewhat begrudgingly chuckled, "is pretty well-known, but let me restate it . . ." He knew his comments were sure to overshadow his efforts as the highest-ranking American economic official to visit Vietnam in decades. But Rubin knew what he had to say.

"I think the strength of the dollar that we have had for quite some time now has served to lower interest rates, keep a lower rate of inflation, and therefore promote job creation and growth in the United States."

To a layman the talk was, at best, hard to decipher. But to financial experts the impact of Rubin's words was unmistakable. The Treasury chief wanted to convey that he was not particularly concerned by cheap imports or, by extension, the fact that domestic manufacturers might suffer because other markets found U.S. goods too expensive. It would send a clear signal to investors and multinational corporations that strategized based on a predicted value of the dollar against other currencies, since that value directly influences revenue and profit margins.

Each time a reporter asked about the dollar, the real goal was determining whether the secretary was preparing to unleash funds from Treasury's Exchange Stabilization Fund (ESF)—the only stockpile of money that a Treasury secretary has authority over (under the auspices of the president, of course). Dating back to the 1930s, the ESF is made up of several types of assets, including dollars and Japanese yen, to help the Treasury department manage exchange rate policy and provide financing to foreign governments. The amount of money in this pot fluctuates, but during Rubin's time it hovered around $40 billion.

In anticipation of the ESF's use (which would certainly move markets), any change in tone or tenor in a secretary's commentary on the dollar could prompt speculation among traders that a currency intervention was in the offing. Investors were right to worry about Rubin tapping this fund because of Treasury's well-documented addiction in the preceding years. While the ultimate goal during the Clinton years was to reduce such activities, the United States bought or sold dollars on six occasions during the administration, with two of those interventions lasting more than a day. But each of those occurrences proved how futile government meddling was because the dollar's value only shifted briefly. The global foreign exchange market was too large to be influenced by a few billion dollars from Treasury and the Federal Reserve.

It would take time for traders to accept that a new regime had truly begun. And because they parsed each word the Treasury chief used as they made decisions on dollar pricing, Rubin was highly disciplined in the delivery of his mantra. Traders around the world kept a log of each time he made the statement: how many words he used to deliver the message, what order the words were in—anything to measure how different or similar it was to the time before. If Rubin inadvertently flipped his delivery from "a strong dollar is in our national interest" to "it is in our national interest to maintain a strong dollar," those traders bought some of their dollar assets, pushing down the currency's value, a move that usually lasted just a passing moment.

Because of such sensitivity, when *The Wall Street Journal*'s William Murray asked Rubin to comment on the dollar's value during that press conference in Vietnam, he bolted from the room to quickly reach the telephone that sat in the corridor to call his editor with what Rubin had just said. That editor sent a headline to broadcast to traders all over the world, who would then allow no more than a nanosecond to parse Rubin's words before making their next trade.

Treasury staffers in the room chortled when Rubin called out to Murray just as he was dashing out. "Bill, I don't know what you're going to make of that. . . . Anything you make of it is not correct."

That was the thing about Rubin's mantra. He never explained the reason for his words, no matter how loudly reporters hounded him with questions. That was because one goal of Rubin's strong dollar bumper-sticker phrase was to induce boredom. He hewed strictly to a repetitious and tedious delivery of the mantra so that eventually markets would stop caring what the U.S. Treasury chief had to say about the currency. Refraining from moving markets except in the rarest of circumstances was key to his credibility, he believed. For the entirety of his career, drawing on his training as a lawyer, he weighed each word he uttered in public with extreme precision. One errant word had the potential to shake global financial markets, and Rubin knew the damage that could be done by mishaps in public relations around the dollar and the economy. If he misspoke, it could irreparably damage his credibility as Treasury secretary, making it harder to stave off future crises and calm jittery markets with verbal intervention.

For him, dollar questions from reporters had become his own version of *Groundhog Day*, the popular film featuring the comedian Bill Murray in which a grizzled weatherman named Phil Connors relives the same day over and over again. But unlike Connors, who at least got to spend his days persuading a character played by actress Andie MacDowell to fall in love with him, Rubin's loop was merely a rotating cast of singularly focused reporters and harried traders.

The sheer repetitiveness of the task would become a quandary for Treasury secretaries for decades to come. Paul O'Neill, President George W. Bush's first Treasury chief, fielded a question about the dollar when visiting Kyrgyzstan in 2002. His immediate successor, John Snow, faced it while holding three stuffed teddy bears he had just purchased for his grandchildren after touring a Build-A-Bear store in Independence, Missouri.

"Journalists would like to get the secretary of the Treasury to say something different or interesting or stupid, it's natural," said Tim Geithner, who served as secretary from 2009 to 2013. The world is always watching, always listening to a Treasury chief's every utterance. One slip could spur a sell-off in almost any currency in the world, or influence the price of American debt, a vast market with tens of trillions of dollars at stake.

Rubin would go on to cast a long shadow over the job of Treasury secretary. His early involvement and influence in the policies he later came to personify as Treasury chief, and his market savvy gathered from his time on Wall Street, allowed him to redefine the role of the nation's chief economic spokesperson.

On the news of his resignation during Clinton's second term in 1999, the reaction from Wall Street and across partisan Washington and economic circles was to "lionize [him] like a retiring sports star," one profiler wrote at the time. Rubin was behind an economic recovery that stemmed, in part, from an eight-word incantation that he would forever be associated with—usually for its genius, occasionally for its hollowness. Larry Summers would step into the Treasury secretary job for the final eighteen months of the Clinton administration, carrying forward the torch of Rubinomics that he had helped create and that the country—and the world—now relied on. Rubin weaned Treasury and other finance ministries from its controlling tendencies in currency markets, massively curbing the pace of interventions in the dollar after 1995.

Helped in large part by the Federal Reserve, the Clinton era became synonymous with economic bliss. The United States embarked on the longest period of economic growth at that time: GDP expanded an average of 4 percent each year with the median family income up by around $10,000. More than twenty-two million jobs were created, leaving the unemployment rate at 4 percent (a healthy level according to most economists), and inflation had reined in from faster than 4 percent to a comfortable 2.5 percent.

On top of that, there was what Rubin himself called his single most important accomplishment: a balanced budget for the first time in a generation. When Clinton departed government, he left a $230 billion annual budget surplus, the third consecutive one. With the economy growing at a healthy clip, it created room for Americans to spend even more, further fueling growth with purchases of homes and cars.

But that was the view from Wall Street. In middle America—the Rust Belt states of manufacturing and farming—trouble was brewing.

5.

THE BAD DOLLAR

In 2001, most Americans could find a piece of Weirton, West Virginia, in their kitchen pantry. Every fourth can of tuna, sliced pineapples, or crushed tomatoes was created out of tin that was rolled and pickled in acid at a Weirton Steel facility. "We make tin plate for the tin cans that make life so much more convenient for you," read one magazine ad from the 1960s, the height of the company's production.

Launched by Ernest T. Weir in 1909, Weirton Steel found early success and became the lifeblood of the local economy, a quintessential tale of the American dream. Not long after its launch, Weirton became the world's second-largest producer of tin plates, featured on the cover of an issue of *Life* magazine with photographs depicting a vibrant rendering of Smalltown, USA. Children raised in this company town grew up with the ethos that if they worked hard enough, their lives would get better, and scars from working in the factory inferno were seen as a badge of honor—proof of your labor.

But by the late 1990s, the city and its 20,000 inhabitants had come upon hard times. The workforce of the local mill, run by Weirton Steel, was down to 3,500, roughly a quarter of the peak employment. Unemployment averaged about 9 percent in the region. While the preceding decade was celebrated for aggregate growth, broad economic indicators hid the harsh reality of trade deals put together by both the George H. W. Bush and Clinton administrations. NAFTA, along with other similar pacts, led to a difficult period that would hurt the whole town that the steel business supported. It would amount to a class war between what Wall Street wanted from the U.S. government and what the rest of the country needed.

As Bob Rubin and his colleagues led the nation in a march toward a policy that was paving the way for globalization, the governments of China, Japan, and other foreign countries were breaking the rules of fair trade by subsidizing their steel companies' expenditures through tax breaks and other measures meant to encourage production. There was enough product in the market to drive down the price of the metal to such a cheap level that American companies would lose money if they matched those prices. It was no accident— the point of "dumping" is to capture market share and then, once the competition has withered away, raise prices so that buyers have nowhere else to turn.

So while Wall Street was winning big bets in markets that counted on Rubinomics to keep the private sector spending, factory workers at American steel companies—in a microcosm of the entire domestic manufacturing sector's troubles—saw the price for steel around the world plunge to twenty-year lows, making "Made in America" too expensive.

The whole scheme was supposed to be against global trade rules, but the U.S. government seemed to willingly look the other way. Lessons from the calls for protectionism of the Reagan years had faded away.

It wasn't necessarily good for all parts of the economy. From 1997 to 1998, the domestic steel industry's operating income dropped by half, a stark contrast to international competitors that were enjoying a period of record sales. Their steel was far cheaper than anything American companies could produce, and that led to cutbacks at domestic factories. The situation was aggravated by outdated production methods and machinery, while international competitors had the cash flow to invest in the infrastructure of their factories.

In the four years leading up to George W. Bush's election, a whopping thirty-one American steel companies entered bankruptcy proceedings. Thousands in the town of Weirton marched across the streets shouting, "Save our steel!" They wanted the government to know just how frustrated they were that those in power kept ignoring violations to global trade laws, violations that took away their livelihoods.

"It's time for a new dollar policy," Tom Palley of the AFL-CIO federation of labor unions said at the time. "[The United States] needs to stop this strong dollar rhetoric and replace it with a sound dollar policy."

In the six years since Rubin codified the strong dollar mantra, the focus on the greenback by industry and lawmakers reveals the extent to which U.S. currency policy had become the poster child for where globalization went wrong. What this simplified view ignored was the larger picture: the deindustrialization (driven somewhat by technological advancement) of rich nations had eroded a cornerstone of the blue-collar job market, which for several decades had been factory work. But that was the nuanced view. Targeting the dollar gave protesters a bogeyman, and they used it with all their might.

What companies like Weirton Steel wanted were punitive tariffs (higher import taxes on foreign-made steel) to encourage buyers toward products made in America. President Bill Clinton's rescue efforts, which included asking Congress for tax breaks, were largely panned by the industry. Other efforts, like the threat of punishment for dumping products with the goal of driving down prices, led some nations to export less steel to the United States.

For the most part, nothing changed. Wall Street had bullied policymakers in Washington for so long that everyone had forgotten how a strong dollar could hurt parts of America. Five years later, Weirton Steel filed for bankruptcy and the jobless rate in the region the company served soared.

Before long, the town of Weirton was practically empty and made up of haggard shopping centers, strip clubs, and poker bars. Over in New York, traders were enjoying a more than 17 percent increase in one of the best gauges for how American stocks are faring, the S&P 500 index. The inhabitants of Weirton, and other towns like it, were left feeling duped.

One damaging side effect of a stated policy desiring a strong dollar was that it meant that the government was choosing winners and losers in the economy, a betrayal that rarely amounts to good policy. The demise of Weirton reveals the cost paid by American workers of a policy preference for a strong exchange rate and the principles of free trade that authenticate it. Much like Weirton, American manufacturing towns from Pennsylvania and Ohio to Kentucky and Indiana shriveled up because their goods were too expensive to sell. The toll of "Made in China" and "Made in Bangladesh" was starting to cost hundreds of thousands of American jobs.

This also posed a national security problem because the U.S. military couldn't access enough homemade steel. Such products are key components of the nation's military operations. The Pentagon has programs that require the acquisition of steel or aluminum for the U.S. military for missiles, jet aircraft, submarines, helicopters, Humvees, and munitions, making trouble in the steel industry an issue of patriotic importance.

On the political front, Democrats paid the price at the polls.

On Election Day in November 2000, George W. Bush won West Virginia for Republicans for the fourth time since the Great Depression, buoyed by surprise victories in areas like Hancock County, where Weirton is located. (Since then, the county has voted Republican in every presidential contest, while West Virginia went on to become a heavily Republican state. By 2016, Donald Trump won the state with around 69 percent of the vote.)

As President George W. Bush was stepping into office, the plight of America's factory workers was bubbling up in Congress. It was one of the rare times that Bob Rubin's name came up as a villain in those days.

John "Jay" Rockefeller was arguably the loudest critic in early 2001. The great-grandson of the famous oil tycoon of the early 1900s, Rockefeller was a Democratic senator from West Virginia. He blamed

Rubin and the rest of the Clinton economic team for putting globalization ahead of everything, including the health of the domestic steel
industry that provided work to countless Americans. By the senator's measure, the United States was facing a terrible crisis and he
didn't want investors to decide who would emerge victorious in this
battle: Wall Street or American workers. The Montana Democrat
Max Baucus went one step further, warning president-elect Bush's
incoming economic team that a "big backlash" against globalism was
coming from people who felt they're not part of the deal that globalization offers, instead becoming a catalyst for economic nationalism.

Labor unions and manufacturers would go on to lobby the Bush
administration for a weaker dollar, saying that the currency was
overvalued by as much as 30 percent, a reference to the amount it increased against the currencies of the largest U.S. trading partners in
the eighteen months through March 2002. That ebullience, achieved
over a short span of time, accounted for a $140 billion plunge in U.S.
manufacturing exports and hit hundreds of thousands of households
whose incomes fell away with the resulting job cuts, according to the
National Association of Manufacturers, a Washington-based organization that serves as the voice of its industrial member companies
before the U.S. government.

The group warned the Bush administration that it would see more
calls for protectionism if the government didn't weaken the dollar, as
they had in the past. The Big Three automakers (who were heavily reliant on steel) were already frustrated, saying that the Japanese government was deliberately pushing down the yen to give their country's
manufacturers a competitive edge. The "overvalued" dollar had driven
up the average cost of U.S. auto exports by $3,700 per car, while the

Paper, Allied-Industrial, Chemical and Energy Workers International Union blamed it for the loss of ten thousand jobs in the past year.

No one in the political establishment in Washington or the investor community wanted to hear these warnings from manufacturing that globalization—and the strong dollar—could hurt anyone. The economic zeitgeist of the era was all about shared global prosperity, increasing the free flow of people and new ideas, and open borders. But the concept of a country putting its own economic needs before that of the rest of the world, or protectionism, was reemerging for the first time since the 1980s. As Senator Baucus had already warned the Bush administration, it was time to "understand that Americans come first."

Looking back, the frustration with Rubin's strong dollar mantra at the turn of the century as the balance of power in government shifted parties was significant. The interests of Wall Street and Main Street were colliding: one was driven by sheer greed while the other— the average Joe, living in Smalltown, USA—was looking for his share of the American promise of prosperity. And with the dollar as the lingua franca of global commerce, these downsides were particularly painful, planting the seeds for weaknesses in the very foundation of the dollar empire.

It would be another fourteen years before the unlikeliest of presidential candidates descended a set of golden escalators with a battle cry that sounded very similar to the warning the folks of Weirton had issued and everybody had ignored. It would be another fourteen years before anyone talked, in a significant way, about putting America first.

But before any of that could come to the fore, another flaw in Bob Rubin's plan would plague his successor.

The powerful mythology around the dollar that Rubin had created had taken on a life of its own. On the one hand, the strong dollar mantra added to the United States' role as the world's organizing power. Not to mention the benefit of a massive economic expansion that widened the American middle class. But financial markets had grown obsessed with Rubin's dollar rhetoric, changing it from a mantra grounded in sophisticated economic and financial philosophy that helped redefine fiscal management to a mere catchphrase. Take what happened when President-elect Bush unveiled an unknown aluminum tycoon as his pick for Treasury secretary—when the obsession among the investing class over that one phrase, "a strong dollar is in our national interest," morphed into another round of bullying from investors.

Paul Henry O'Neill was a blunt man. He spoke in public the same way he did in private—no airs, whether he was talking to his boss, President George W. Bush, or one of his many grandkids. A Midwesterner of humble roots (he was born in a St. Louis home without electricity or water), O'Neill was unafraid to speak his mind or express his values. In 1987, the year he became CEO of industrial giant Alcoa Corporation, he canceled a corporate membership at a golf club in Pennsylvania because it didn't admit Black people or women (an unusual stand in a time that came decades before the concept of progressive corporate governance emerged).

For the thirty-one days leading up to him becoming the nation's seventy-second Treasury secretary, O'Neill had Wall Street's support. In fact, he had garnered the most widespread praise of any of Bush's cabinet nominees. Democrats, Republicans, the Federal

Reserve chair Alan Greenspan, who had a godlike status in economic circles—everyone was impressed with O'Neill's extraordinary career. Sure, he was a curious choice to oversee the nation's public finances considering his complete lack of financial sector experience, but everyone thought it was refreshing to have an outsider running the Treasury department.

Bush chose O'Neill for his top-notch industry and government experience: By the time he was sixty-five and preparing to join the new administration, O'Neill was a self-made man with a $60 million fortune. He had government experience from the Nixon and Ford administrations, but had spent most of his professional life as an industrialist in a career that culminated with thirteen years at the top of what was, in the 1990s, the world's largest aluminum producer. His efforts put him a class above the hundreds of stock and bond traders who made themselves out to be luminaries for minting millions when the broader market was already rising. O'Neill had stepped in as CEO of Alcoa when its stock was worth five dollars and aluminum prices were trending downward, and by the time he retired the stock price was at around forty dollars a share.

There seemed to be appreciation for a man who, as he put it himself, had spent his career "out there in the world that makes things" (as opposed to dabbling in esoteric financial instruments), which meant he understood an important part of the U.S. economy that his predecessors did not.

But O'Neill's honeymoon with investors ended before he was even sworn in, all because of Wall Street's hypersensitivity to currency talk and the prospect that a new administration would revert back to trying to aggressively control the dollar's value.

On the eve of his confirmation hearing in January 2001, one

sentence at the very end of a two-thousand-word article set off a panic across global markets: "As an exporter he would be expected to favor a weaker dollar, but he has made no statements on this question." The story was on the front page of *The New York Times*, and it wreaked havoc for O'Neill.

Investors immediately threw a tantrum and dumped dollars in the market, with the sell-off amounting to the biggest one-day decline the greenback had experienced in a month.

Traders were suddenly worried that the same nonmarket experience they had applauded would lead O'Neill to prefer a weaker dollar once he became Treasury chief out of sheer habit built up over decades in the manufacturing industry. Back when the United States struck the Plaza Accord in 1985 with the sole purpose to drive down the dollar, O'Neill was helping run a paper company that benefited immensely from the weaker greenback that resulted.

Based on that logic, traders fretted that with him at the helm, Treasury would jettison the strong dollar policy. It was pure speculation— O'Neill hadn't said a word in public since his nomination was announced. But investors didn't know what to do with an industrialist as America's top economic spokesman. He was a break from, as they put it, the "market-based" secretaries, someone from their own tribe. And now they wondered whether the dollar policy created a division between investors and the working class.

Anxiety was so high that Wall Street analysts began advising investment clients to adjust trading strategies around the expectation that O'Neill would intervene to forcibly weaken the dollar once he took office. Thousands and thousands of financial experts in financial hubs from Tokyo to London and New York wanted to hear O'Neill say just one thing: *A strong dollar is in our national interest.*

"As long as he keeps the 'U.S. desires a strong dollar' mantra, he shouldn't get into too much hot water with the markets," said one economist. To them, Rubin's catchphrase characterized the pledge to propel economic integration, so that American consumers continued to feast on cheap foreign products and keep capital flowing into the economy.

Markets are often the clearest indicator of whether an administration's policy has credibility or not, serving as an opinion poll that government officials keep an eye on. The incoming Bush administration's economic team felt that it was imperative that O'Neill won the trust of Wall Street, even if he had to pass what amounted to a silly test in public relations.

And so the scene was set for O'Neill's confirmation hearing, broadcast live to investors and finance ministers around the world, to serve as an exam on O'Neill's intentions for the dollar. Because so much of that boiled down to dollar talk itself, O'Neill and his aides concocted a plan. As he prepared for his hearing in sessions that in Washington parlance are called "murder boards" (where nominees are cross-examined by a team pretending to be hostile lawmakers), they decided that the future secretary's very first words should address Wall Street's biggest question: Is Paul O'Neill for or against a strong dollar policy?

At 9:30 a.m. on Wednesday, January 17, 2001, three days before Bush's inauguration, Paul O'Neill entered a hearing room inside the Dirksen Senate Office Building on Constitution Avenue in Washington, D.C. He took a seat at a heavy wooden table covered in a dark green tablecloth, situated right in front of his personal cheering section of kids and grandkids. Before him, crouched on the floor, was an assortment of photographers whose camera shutters let loose a thousand chirps per second the moment O'Neill started speaking.

The multimillionaire metals tycoon was ready to prove himself worthy of the highest level of public service to the fifteen or so lawmakers on the Senate Finance Committee, which oversees Treasury. The senators sat on a horseshoe-shaped dais that was raised at least two feet above everyone else in the room, meaning they looked down upon their target.

In that moment O'Neill was not a wildly successful corporate chieftain. He was on a job interview where anyone who wanted to could listen in.

Rather than beginning with the customary introduction of his wife and family, O'Neill, as practiced the day before, got straight to the point. With his elbows resting on the table and without any notes to read from, he casually picked at some lint on the tablecloth and, in what was his third sentence spoken publicly since being nominated, said: "I've noted in the last few weeks since my nomination was made lots of media attention to a couple of issues, and I thought in the interest of not wasting a lot of television footage, I should say from the very outset: I am in favor of a strong dollar. I can't imagine why anyone would think to the contrary."

A gang of reporters fled from the scene, rushing to telephones outside of the hearing room to file that quote to their editors. Within seconds, headlines flashed across the Bloomberg Terminal, which feeds information directly to traders. "Dollar Rises to Near 1 1/2 Year High vs Yen on O'Neill Remarks," read one. It was a clear sigh of relief from investors.

With one swift statement, O'Neill had made Rubin's strong dollar mantra bipartisan.

But the battle between O'Neill and financial markets had only just begun. The Treasury chief would spend the next twenty-three months in prolonged conflict, while struggling to remain loyal to a president who counted on him to successfully stand behind the strong dollar policy, along with other key pillars of Bush's economic plan.

During O'Neill's time in office, the dollar fell 8 percent, due almost entirely to forces outside of his control. He believed that the dollar's value would reflect economic fundamentals, and as Treasury chief, he sought strong fundamentals for the American economy. Unfortunately, that led to his falling out of step with the president's policies, which did not necessarily have the fiscal discipline that O'Neill himself thought would lead to the kind of hearty economy that rallied the dollar.

What investors overlooked, and what O'Neill didn't manage to convey, was that Bush's economic agenda was one that would naturally lead to a weaker dollar, but without design. Bush and O'Neill stepped into power as the United States was nearing the end of a decade-long economic expansion. By March 2001, about two months into Bush's tenure, an eight-month recession had started and the unemployment rate started to edge upward. To jump-start the economy the Bush administration looked to an economic policy tool that came naturally to a Republican Party keen on a smaller government: tax cuts. The peacetime plan, before 9/11 upended everything, was predicted to cut the nation's tax revenue (used to finance spending) by over one trillion.

The dollar drama that O'Neill faced was essentially a game: Investors wanted to hear the Treasury chief talk about the dollar and enjoy the blip of volatility that created, making room for quick-kill profits. By egging on reporters, they created a Chinese finger trap for

O'Neill where truth and accuracy only made things worse. The damaging effect of Wall Street's obsession played out over most of the Bush presidency and eventually came to reveal some of the strong dollar policy's obvious flaws. But even as Bush's chief economic spokesman tried to educate reporters and investors on the hollowness of the strong dollar policy as it had evolved into the early 2000s, all anyone wanted was the robotic parroting of Rubin's eight-word incantation.

O'Neill went on to become so frustrated with the land-mine hopscotch that dollar talk had become that one day, when he was yet again asked if he had a secret desire for a weak dollar, he told reporters that they would know if he had made a change to U.S. currency policy because if he ever did, he would rent out a baseball stadium from which to announce the new plan. It underscored just how central the tension over dollar policy had become—O'Neill was untrained in the subtlety of delicate policy signals. After that, reporters chasing O'Neill as he traveled to Ghana, to Brazil, and around the United States were prone to shout at him: "Have you hired Yankee Stadium yet?"

O'Neill didn't find it funny.

In the words of one former Treasury official, who didn't want to be named making this comment, during the Bush years the strong dollar mantra would become "devoid of intellect."

6.

A WAR OFFICE
FOR TREASURY

The Imperial Hotel in the Hibiya district of Tokyo boasts a private tea ceremony room and an elaborate sauna for guests. It is described as an "oasis of luxury and comfort." For Secretary of the Treasury Paul O'Neill, it was the final destination after a week of back-to-back meetings in Shanghai and Beijing, followed by a four-hour flight to Japan's capital. He was looking forward to nothing more than calling his wife to wish her a happy birthday and then stretching out on a king-size bed. It was September 11, 2001.

When he arrived at the hotel at 10:00 p.m. in Tokyo (thirteen hours ahead of Washington, D.C.), O'Neill turned on the news as he undid his tie. He was shocked by what he saw. Perched on the edge of his bed in the opulent hotel room, he watched harrowing scenes unfold on CNN and, like most Americans back home, tried to convince himself that air traffic controllers had made a terrible mistake. What else could explain how a commercial airliner flew into a Manhattan skyscraper on a cloudless, sunny morning?

The answer came slowly amid the confusion of the initial reports, but by midnight in Tokyo it was clear that America was under attack.

With his eyes glued to the television, O'Neill watched in horror as two people jumped from one of the World Trade Center buildings, holding hands. Tim Adams, the tall, soft-spoken Kentucky native with a light southern drawl who was O'Neill's chief of staff, popped in and out of the secretary's hotel room, while the rest of the traveling entourage (including the press) watched together down the hall. Adams knew what he had to do: cancel meetings with the Japanese finance minister and Bank of Japan governor, and then find a way home.

Terrorists that day had targeted the heart of the United States' economy. The World Trade Center was home to thirty-two brokerage firms, thousands of financial industry workers, and extensive market services operations. They were also just six blocks away from the New York Stock Exchange. The first plane struck at 8:46 a.m., forty-four minutes before trading should have commenced. Needless to say, American markets didn't open that day. Or the next six. The closure precipitated a sharp plunge in stocks throughout the rest of the world, ultimately wiping $1.4 trillion of markets that week. The S&P 500 index fell another 14 percent over the next week. Stock traders from London and Bangkok to Osaka halted their work as the world wondered what else the terrorists had planned, and what it meant for the rest of the United States and its economy.

The assets of the world's largest and most powerful economy have traditionally been a haven in times of turmoil. But in the days after 9/11, when American stock markets were shuttered abruptly for the first time since the Great Depression, that refuge was looking weak. "Opposing forces are acting on the U.S. currency," one markets strategist said. "Its traditional safe-haven role is competing against the fact that the attacks are specifically directed at the U.S."

O'Neill released a statement to reassure investors and to defuse speculation that the dollar could spiral downward: "In the face of today's tragedy, the financial system functioned extraordinarily well and I have every confidence that it will continue to do so in the days ahead."

The next morning, the U.S. embassy in Tokyo sent cars to collect O'Neill, Adams, the economist John Taylor, who was the undersecretary of international affairs at Treasury, Michele Davis, the agency's top spokesperson, and a few others (the rest would return to Washington later). For essential workers like O'Neill, the federal government had arranged transport via C-17 military jets, the kind made to move cargo to areas of conflict.

It was a frigid twelve-hour flight. The military aircraft the team flew on that day was designed to hold tanks and had a cavernous, twelve-foot-high echoey belly that was almost windowless. The only place to sit was on a row of straight-backed jump seats bolted along the metal wall or the cold, bare aluminum floor. Visions of a city ablaze flashed across everyone's minds and the group fought off thoughts of what other nightmare might be lurking in the sky.

The Treasury secretary spent the night either in fitful sleep on that icy metal floor with just a small woolen blanket and a pair of earplugs to drown out the noise of the unpressurized cabin, or plagued by thoughts of the cruel and cold calculation with which terrorists stormed the cockpits of four commercial airplanes. As he worked through his raw emotion, O'Neill's patriotism persevered. The assault on American soil failed to "understand that the genius of our system is in the hearts and minds of the people—not in the buildings we work in," he said later, revisiting his thoughts during that eerie plane ride.

To get back to Washington faster, the pilots did an aerial refueling, rendezvousing with a tanker jet as they flew over Alaska. Once they reached mainland America, the radar screen was mostly blank—no commercial flights were allowed. When they landed at Joint Base Andrews, a military facility fifteen miles away from the Treasury department, Michele Davis looked out and saw hundreds of members of the armed services surrounding their plane, machine guns in hand. Neither she nor Taylor ever expected to be on the front lines of war when they signed up to work for George W. Bush's Treasury department.

America had changed.

What happened next revealed to the world just how strong a force the U.S. dollar could be. And this time, it wasn't about the exchange rate. It was about the dollar as a weapon to punish miscreants, pursue American foreign policy goals and global security objectives—and keep Americans safe. Thirteen days before American forces launched any real war weapons against Al Qaeda and the Taliban, Bush would begin the war on terrorism by unleashing the power of the U.S. Department of the Treasury.

At 9:35 a.m. on September 24, 2001, President George W. Bush stood on a set of risers in the White House Rose Garden behind a podium bearing the presidential seal. It was a blustery morning, the gray skies heralding some half a dozen dangerous tornadoes that would touch the region that day. But as Bush stood on the platform, he projected the full strength of the United States: he was surrounded by half a dozen American flags, and the glass-paned east doors leading to the Oval Office and distinguished exterior of the White House were visible just behind him.

With O'Neill and Secretary of State Colin Powell at either side, Bush announced that "with the stroke of a pen" at 12:01 that morning, the war on terrorism had begun. He told the world he was attacking "the financial foundation of the global terror network" by using the dollar's power to punish the nation's enemies. Using a combination of legal authorities for national and international emergencies, he issued an executive order that immediately gave Treasury the ability to block and freeze U.S. assets and transactions with individual terrorists, terrorist organizations, or those known to associate with them. To further starve them of money, he created the Foreign Terrorist Asset Tracking Center, which would work across several federal agencies to identify sources of terrorist funding and freeze that money before another attack could take place.

Bush's executive order also provided the names of twenty-seven different entities that had been blocked from the U.S. financial system—meaning they could no longer access the dollar. "We will punish you for providing the resources that make these evil acts possible," O'Neill said after Bush's announcement, as if he were speaking directly to the terrorists.

On that windy September day in the nation's capital, the supremacy of the U.S. dollar that had emerged over the course of three massive conflicts—the American Civil War and both world wars—and the dogma that Bob Rubin had created allowed the president to make global finance a linchpin in foreign policy during one of the darkest hours of the country's history. Bush had put sanctions on steroids and was now using the power of the world's reserve asset to punish enemies and protect the democracy he led.

In the days following 9/11, O'Neill had several tasks to manage at once. The Treasury department sat right beside the White House, with the two buildings separated by 150 yards and a twelve-foot-tall replica of the Liberty Bell, putting O'Neill's agency at risk from an attack on the bigger target next door. Military tanks stood outside both Treasury and the White House, a constant reminder of the threats that loomed. The federal government created contingency plans in case the Treasury building was wiped out, including evacuation routes for the staff managing the Treasury's Exchange Stabilization Fund in the event of an attack on Pennsylvania Avenue. Protecting the ability to deploy the ESF (which had around $30 billion in it at the time) was vital since it would be crucial if another shock caused the financial markets to become disorderly. In those days, such events seemed just around the corner.

The fear that permeated stock, bond, and currency trading floors in those early days was that the terrorist attacks had seriously damaged the plumbing that undergirds the vast American financial marketplace. Hundreds of thousands of phone lines and four hundred million data circuits had gone down, compromising trading in key financial instruments like equities, bonds, futures, and options. Data that was critical to communication and trading had been lost since the North Tower of the World Trade Center backed up its computer records in the South Tower, and vice versa.

There was also the matter of the New York Stock Exchange (NYSE), which remained closed for nearly a week after the attacks. But destruction of Lower Manhattan meant that the physical foundation of the $3 trillion market of U.S. Treasuries, known as the "govvie" market (as market insiders call government debt), had also been hit. It was a market that was (and remains) the most critical in global finance, made up of the most extensively held debt instrument. Because the securities are issued by the Treasury department, O'Neill's Office of Domestic Finance needed to get into the trenches of reopening operations in New York. That unit, along with the Securities and Exchange Commission (as the independent federal regulator charged with protecting investors and maintaining efficient markets), would play a large role in helping the NYSE reopen.

The stakes were high. O'Neill had told the president that they had one shot to reopen markets successfully if they wanted to display American strength and endurance. Failure would undermine efforts to shore up America's image at a time of huge vulnerability, but it was a task riddled with emotional and logistical complexities. Every person who worked at the NYSE had friends and lunch buddies who had just died. Nearly three-quarters of those who were killed in Manhattan that day worked in finance. The smell of burnt rubber, the smoldering pit that was once the site of twin skyscrapers, and the heavy police presence gave the world's most powerful financial district the feeling of a war zone.

With fears of a run on banks (when a large number of customers rush to withdraw their money from savings and checking accounts all at once) across America making headlines, the government needed to take strong actions. Within a day or so, the Federal Reserve announced it was "open and operating," ready to meet liquidity needs of investors. The Federal Deposit Insurance Corporation, which backs the money of everyday Americans in their checking and savings accounts, proclaimed during that period that everyone's "money is safe."

The NYSE worked around the clock, with the help of the SEC, private sector engineers, and Treasury officials including Peter Fisher, the undersecretary for the unit overseeing debt management (often seen in those days carrying a hard silver suitcase and holding a secure phone).

They stood up new phone lines, found temporary office space, and dug into the information their data centers managed to save to start reconstructing trades that had been issued but were either never completed or weren't recorded on 9/11. Investors were skittish—there was no guarantee that once opened, the patched-up market would make it through the day. A technical glitch could prove disastrous to morale, an important component for investors. Everyone was braced for a massive sell-off. U.S. stocks were predicted to drop 10 percent in anticipation of an economic recession, driven by airlines, since passengers avoided flying, and weak consumer confidence.

The government explicitly urged everyone to remain calm. Investors like the billionaire Warren Buffett, whose business interests took a $2.4 billion hit from the rout in markets following the terrorist attacks, went on television one day before the NYSE's reopening to promise the American public that they wouldn't sell stocks when markets opened. "If you own a piece of American business that you felt good about a week ago, it would be crazy to sell [now]," he said.

O'Neill appeared on ABC's *Good Morning America* in the hours before the NYSE would open—opting for a mainstream show over the usual financial networks—with a message for investors to "buy America." "If I could buy stock, I'd be buying a whole lot," he said. (His influence over the economy as secretary precluded him from actively trading stocks.)

To further shore up investor and consumer confidence, one hour before the stock market bell would ring on Monday, September 17, the Fed chair Alan Greenspan lowered the central bank's lending rate half a percentage point to 3 percent. By then, O'Neill's motorcade was already approaching 11 Wall Street in Lower Manhattan, where the classical revival building that housed the NYSE stood.

The New York senators Hillary Clinton and Chuck Schumer, the NYSE head Richard Grasso, and members of the city's police and fire departments joined the Treasury chief for two minutes of silence on the trading floor. Standing together in the 16,000-square-foot arena, surrounded by large screens flashing stock tickers and prices, the group sang "God Bless America," cheering as they rang the opening bell at exactly 9:30 a.m. O'Neill waved a small American flag in his hand.

U.S. stocks tumbled in early trading, with the Nasdaq Composite index and the S&P 500 index both down roughly 5 percent, but it was far less than the worst-case scenario the government had feared. "Our economy is strong. . . . We're going to be fine," O'Neill said, surrounded by traders, police officers, and firefighters, the red and white stripes of a large flag visible in the background. "We're going to show the world resilience and what resilience means, and we're going to get those rotten people."

The Bush administration went full throttle in its use of laws such as the USA PATRIOT Act of 2001 in a bid to tighten national security. The law would eventually become controversial for allowing the government greater authority to conduct surveillance, which alarmed privacy advocates. But a less controversial part of it gave the Treasury department the ability to thwart future terrorist attacks by drying up cash flows and following money trails to trace terrorist activity.

To foil future large-scale destructions, following the money was key. As Juan Zarate, who worked in Bush's White House and Treasury department, wrote in his book *Treasury's War*, while one suicide bombing might cost a terrorist group $1,000 to carry out, it still requires sophisticated training and even pension money for the families of dead soldiers. Moving money always leaves a trace: banks have paper trails as they communicate among themselves to transfer money, details that include the time of money transfer, amount, names of banks, and account holders. Each of these steps is an opening for Treasury's gumshoes to track the movements of bad actors.

The nineteen men who hijacked United Airlines flight 175 and American Airlines flights 11 and 77 used wire transfers, cash deposits, and travelers checks placed in U.S. accounts to fund the attack to carry out the mass murder of three thousand people on American soil. Roughly $300,000 flowed through their accounts in the United States in plain view for anyone to see—if they bothered to look. They used their real names to open a handful of bank accounts in the United States, like at SunTrust in Florida, and to shift around the mere $400,000 needed to finance their attack. Sums of anywhere from $5,000 to $70,000 were moved to and from these banks, and some in Germany and the United Arab Emirates, as the men applied for American visas, enrolled in flight training schools in Florida, and then purchased their tickets from American and United Airlines for those final deadly plane rides.

It turns out there was enough information stored across the various databases available to the U.S. government to have stopped that plan, had the dots been connected. It was an unsettling thought for those who ran the country.

Using intelligence and evidence drawn from investigations into how 9/11 was financed, the Treasury department created a public list of terrorists and related entities and ordered U.S. banks to locate and freeze those accounts. To stop it from ever happening again, the Treasury department put pressure on financial institutions to heighten their compliance calculus. Failures would mean scarlet-letter treatment for banks and financial institutions—and big fines.

Bush needed allies in his financial war. On that front, O'Neill's undersecretary for international affairs, John Taylor, was ideally placed. Already a recognized global expert on monetary policy, Taylor was known for designing an eponymous economic rule in 1992 that, at the time, revolutionized the way central banks think about monetary policy. But 9/11 had turned him into a financial warrior, and he dutifully set aside monetary and macroeconomic theories to work with the world's richest and most influential economies, called the Group of Seven. Together they pledged to share financial intelligence and other information, expanding their Financial Action Task Force for money laundering to add terrorism financing to its mandate, with a dedicated "war room" to boot.

Treasury was now part of the national security apparatus that dealt with real-life threats to the American public, and the dollar was one of its weapons. It would take another few years for Treasury's war office, where economic sanctions are created, to hone the weapon the dollar had now become. The final step—building the unit that would go on to wield this power—led to the largest expansion in the agency's 215-year history, when in 2004 the U.S. Treasury department became the first (and for decades the only) finance ministry in the world with an in-house intelligence operation. As part of President Bush and Congress's whole-of-government response to

9/11, Treasury's small enforcement office became the Office of Terrorism and Financial Intelligence (TFI). The new unit included the Office of Foreign Assets Control (OFAC), as well as a new Office of Intelligence and Analysis (OIA, referred to colloquially as "oya"), a division focused on terrorist financing and financial crimes, among other related units. Treasury went from having two main units (domestic finance and international affairs) to having three, each with its own undersecretary.

With the creation of TFI, Treasury now had an anti-terrorism division and more enforcement capacity. The office helped foreign counterparts develop similar capabilities to TFI and worked diligently to convince economic officials in the G7 and G20 clubs, the International Monetary Fund, and the World Bank that finance ministries were on the front line of the financial statecraft necessary to win the war on terror.

It was not all about making Treasury bigger. The new national security infrastructure called for a great deal of reshuffling among the hidebound institutions of Washington. This meant that Treasury, which had been the home of U.S. Customs and Border Protection since the time of Alexander Hamilton, lost one of its oldest agencies—the Secret Service—to the newly created Department of Homeland Security. While its primary mission is to protect the president, the vice president, and their families, Abraham Lincoln initially created the Secret Service to investigate counterfeit dollars, a pervasive problem after the Civil War. (The Secret Service continues to protect the Treasury chief, who is fifth in the line of succession to the presidency.) The Secret Service was perhaps the most glamorous part of the Treasury department—its role as the protector of presidents has been romanticized by Hollywood, like with Kevin Costner's role as a former agent in the 1992 hit film *The Bodyguard* alongside Whitney Houston. While some of the changes in the building were welcome, the departure of the Secret Service (or "guns and badges," as some former officials called it) was a big loss. It made Treasury look as if it was being dismantled, which hit morale at a time when officials were already coping with the challenges of economic warfare. This new type of battle was taking the stewards of the dollar to dark corners of the web that the financial system had become.

Put the concept of weaponizing the dollar on steroids, and you've got American sanctions. For decades when diplomacy failed, war was the only next option for escalation. Economic sanctions throughout the 1900s were largely in the form of countrywide trade bans, like with Cuba, which lacked precision and, therefore, effectiveness. But the centrality of the dollar in the global financial system enabled Treasury to sharpen the sword. The dollar was on one side of almost all the world's currency transactions, and the price for virtually all oil trade—the most important source for energy—was settled in dollars. That pervasiveness gave American politicians the leverage to exert their foreign policy goals over the rest of the world. It's a power that only one country has. And in the early years of the 2000s, that meant fighting terrorism.

Block off billions of dollars intended to fund terrorism, trigger a stock-market crash, or deliver a financial death penalty on an individual or a company—from billionaires and oligarchs to mega-yachts—the U.S. Treasury department could now do all of this and more.

7.

THE CRYSTAL BALL
OF TERROR

After terrorists hijacked four commercial airliners in a once unimaginable plot, the nation's 285 million residents were wondering what other threats loomed. "Biological and Chemical Terror—How Scared Should You Be?" one magazine headline blared.

Americans living in high-rise buildings were buying parachutes. Some used rubber gloves to open their mail or started wearing bulletproof vests and gas masks. Others directed their anger at men with bushy, dark beards and olive skin, or any resemblance to the Al Qaeda terrorists whose photographs flashed across the evening news almost daily. Everyone was learning how to pronounce the name of Osama bin Laden, the then-suspected mastermind behind the attacks. In Manhattan, the foul odor of burnt plastic that emanated from the wreckage of the World Trade Center brought back horrible memories of men and women jumping from buildings. It was, as *The New York Times* put it, the smell of "unsettled souls."

In the months following the attacks, this raw terror that had drenched the American public stayed with David Aufhauser, the Treasury department's top lawyer, on half a dozen secret missions to a tightly guarded building located on the outskirts of Brussels. Braced for something else to fall from the sky, the government and financial industry were coming together to punish terrorist groups, weaponizing the global networks these terrorists relied on.

Treasury's aggressive financial intelligence collection campaign, which the president launched just days after 9/11, brought Aufhauser to an idyllic wooded estate in La Hulpe, Belgium. That's where headquarters for a banking cooperative called the Society for Worldwide Interbank Financial Telecommunication (SWIFT) is located. Created in 1973 to replace radio dispatching and telegraphs, SWIFT is not a bank. It doesn't hold any assets or have any accounts. But as the system that financial institutions use to talk to one another, it delivers secure messages for 10,000 financial firms in over 200 countries. In 2001, it saw $6 trillion in payments each day, tracking orders and confirmations for payments, international trades, securities settlements, and foreign currency exchanges. It was a treasure trove of financial data.

"If you want to stop a bomb going off in Berlin, Brussels, or Boston, you need human intelligence, signals intelligence, and financial intelligence," said Leonard "Lenny" Schrank, the Brooklyn native who was SWIFT's chief executive officer from 1992 to 2007. "If you want to stop a bomb, you need more than just spies on the ground. You need financial intelligence. It took money to pull off an attack like 9/11," he said. "SWIFT was the nexus for all of that financial data."

Behind the concrete facade of the expansive main office of SWIFT in La Hulpe, the Treasury department could find out which banks terrorists were using to access money, the names and contact details of the account holders, and the precise date and time of transfers. Since all of that was a prelude to an attack, that data was, effectively, a crystal ball for Al Qaeda's next move.

SWIFT, overseen by a group of central banks including the Federal Reserve, the Bank of Japan, and the Bank of England, is by nature supposed to be a neutral player in geopolitics. That means it's averse to allowing its data to be used to achieve foreign policy goals, which tend to be politically motivated. But 9/11 had altered the global landscape. "We were always an international organization, but after 9/11, we were all Americans," Schrank said years later, recalling how even the Queen Elizabeth of England sang "The Star Spangled Banner."

The speed at which the United States U-turned from ignorance to obsession with terrorist financing reflects the deep pain of the attacks. In 2001, neither the FBI nor the Department of Justice had a single unit focused on terrorist financing. Just two months prior to September 11, Secretary of the Treasury Paul O'Neill had talked of easing the U.S. regulatory regime to "depend on international cooperation rather than threats of sanctions for combating money flows." September 11 would force the government to do the opposite. The Treasury department would have to move beyond just looking for illicit proceeds of crime—Al Qaeda didn't try to hide the cash they used to fund their attack. "We needed to start looking for the clean money that was intended to kill," according to Aufhauser.

The shift was fast. At first the Central Intelligence Agency considered covertly accessing the data they wanted to dig through from SWIFT. They had tried to do so years earlier, but Treasury officials found out and prevented it—such a move could damage the world's faith in the free and fair dollar-based global financial system. In the fall of 2001, the CIA repeated that message. And so Schrank got the call he had been anticipating since the moment he watched the World Trade Center go down in his old hometown.

He appreciated that Treasury didn't take an aggressive approach and immediately subpoena SWIFT. Instead, he got a call from senior leadership at Treasury. Like millions of Americans, Schrank remembers exactly where he was when the World Trade towers were struck: eating a sandwich in a conference room in Ireland as he met with SWIFT's Irish members.

Schrank explained to Aufhauser, Treasury officials, and others that SWIFT's data was the most private and sensitive commercial data on the planet. Its board of twenty-five bankers from nineteen countries would take its responsibilities very seriously, regardless of patriotic emotions.

Fed chair Alan Greenspan was apprehensive. He felt that "gentlemen shouldn't read gentlemen's mail," as one person explained it.

It was up to Aufhauser to win the trust of SWIFT's board to allow the U.S. government to access the financial data it had. The team came up with five examples, all classified, to present to SWIFT. The goal was to explain how Treasury, the State Department, the CIA, and the FBI would use the precious financial data to disrupt terrorism. Then, in early 2002, he flew to Brussels with a fellow government agent—handcuffed to a briefcase filled with highly sensitive documents—to make the case to create what would soon be referred to as the Terrorist Financing Tracking Program.

It was a bland name, considering how innovative it was and how vital it would become to safeguarding the lives of millions of people.

America's ability to be persuasive was tied to the fact that the dollar is at the center of the world's financial system. For SWIFT to give any government so much access was a huge leap of faith, and it was a leap that was built on personal relationships. Treasury officials including Aufhauser worked with Schrank to create a program that would allow SWIFT to remain apolitical, and also maintain its role as an impartial messaging system for the financial system. They would protect the data of its members while allowing the United States access, with elaborate guardrails to prevent its abuse. For each tranche of financial data, Treasury would lay out its case through subpoenas to be reviewed by both SWIFT and external auditors.

Treasury could have the information it wanted on terrorists but, as Schrank put it, "not one bite more." Information from SWIFT for any other purposes was forbidden. If the subpoenas yielded information the United States didn't need, officials deleted it from their systems and honed future requests to be more targeted in scope. Schrank called it "the gold standard for balancing national security with data privacy and civil liberties."

Though officially called the Terrorist Finance Tracking Program, its secret code name until its revelation was "turtle" (the opposite of "swift"). It's hard for any former Bush-era official to quantify exactly how effective the program was, though one former Bush cabinet officer asserted that it "saved lives." Secrecy was key—the moment Al Qaeda or any other bad actor found out that the U.S. had access to real-time financial transaction data, they would find other ways to move money. (The program was revealed to the public by *The New York Times* in June 2006, but remained a somewhat potent mechanism for the government.)

Many of the plots disrupted by the Treasury-SWIFT alliance remain classified, but government officials over the years have publicly confirmed that the program provided thousands of leads, helping thwart terrorist attacks in America, Germany, Spain, and the United Kingdom. It yielded useful information on the bombings in London in July 2005, and more than 1,500 other valuable leads for the British government. It also led to the capture of Al Qaeda operative Riduan Isamuddin, considered to be the architect of a 2002 bombing in Indonesia; and disruption of a 2007 plot to blow up John F. Kennedy International in New York.

In those first few weeks after 9/11, when the American public was overcome with the chilling fear of unimaginable threats around each corner, President George W. Bush assured the public that the government would "follow the money as a trail to the terrorists." Treasury's work with SWIFT, conducted through deep coordination with the intelligence community, was one key component of his plan.

For decades, the national security apparatus included a small number of major players such as the CIA, the FBI, the Pentagon, and the National Security Council. After the terrorist attacks, this exclusive club added a new member, one of the oldest institutions in the federal government: the U.S. Department of the Treasury. Treasury, along with the State Department, would run the economic sanctions and terrorist financing show. One former Treasury official describes the sanctions team he was once part of as "guerillas in gray suits" who managed the more than two dozen related programs. The dollar continued to serve as the world's safest asset, allowing the country to have a massive amount of debt on which to rely on for growth, while geopolitically it allowed the United States to export its foreign policy agenda. Financial institutions, companies, and businesspeople around the world were put on notice that access to the dollar comes with expectations: loyalty.

With 9/11, the United States' dollar dominance had reached its pinnacle of power.

And with that power, the men who sat atop Treasury had an even tougher job. Not only could a missed verbal cue send markets into tumult, but now, a Treasury secretary had to guard how the dollar was used to protect America. The pressures of the job were only getting higher.

8.

A SECRETARY'S DOWNFALL, IN TWO ACTS

P aul O'Neill was hunched over a jewelry stand in a crowded outdoor street market in Ghana, his head foggy with jet lag. It was May 22, 2002, and the Treasury secretary was helping a little girl pick out a necklace. Tieless and in formal gray slacks, blue shirtsleeves rolled up to his elbows, O'Neill was weathering humidity and 90-degree temperatures in the city of Accra that afternoon. The child standing beside him was shy about which trinket she wanted him to buy her, so Bono helped decide.

It was a trip that everyone had dubbed the "Odd Couple Tour of Africa." One was an Irish rock star who dressed in all black, the other a buttoned-down politician. Both were superrich, but for very different achievements. Together, they visited local businesses, AIDS clinics, schools, and towns where thousands lived in poverty in Ghana, Uganda, Ethiopia, and South Africa. MTV had sent a camera to film the U2 front man, who had just won four Grammy awards, as the pair toured on a chartered plane nicknamed U3.

It's common for the U.S. secretary of the Treasury to travel the world to meet with top economic officials in developed and emerging market nations and talk over how federal aid is distributed and how global commerce can work better. But this was the first time a music icon was present. It was the kind of trip where the chord progressions for U2's hit song, "I Still Haven't Found What I'm Looking For," hung in the air throughout the trip—Bono frequently broke out into an a cappella rendition for his fellow travelers.

If you had to pick a moment when it became glaringly obvious that President Bush's economic team was falling apart, O'Neill's eleven-day swing through Africa was probably it. By the time he was donning multicolored Ghanaian ceremonial robes with Bono and borrowing the rock star's iconic sunglasses, the Treasury chief's credibility had already taken several hits.

In May 2002, instead of focusing on Bush's economic plan, O'Neill was diving headfirst into a public persona of a compassionate philanthropist braving scenes of human misery, worrying about access to safe water and the state of orphanages across Africa. That trip illustrated just how far he had drifted from his job description, setting the table for his eventual firing a little over six months later.

The Treasury secretary's job is to grow the U.S. economy and create jobs. Since the agency's inception, the public relations component of that role has been key. A successful secretary exudes confidence, has deep markets knowledge, and is a loyal spokesman for the president's economic vision. The post-9/11 era added a new wrinkle to the remit: maintain the dollar's superior status even as a weapon of war.

From day one, a Treasury secretary must be prepared to face down disaster because the department is on the front lines of any economic crisis. A key part of the assignment is to ensure stability in currency policy for an orderly and risk-free government debt market. This including the personal integrity and gravitas of the Treasury secretary. Somewhere between off-the-record asides that Bob Rubin's strong dollar policy was "a bunch of crap," and chowing down street food in Uganda with Bono, O'Neill had lost investor confidence.

And when a U.S. Treasury secretary falls from grace, it risks putting a chink in the pristine status of the dollar, which happened during the Bush years with two different Treasury chiefs. O'Neill was fired for trying to do things his own way—a mismatch in Treasury leadership and the demands of the job. His immediate successor (who departed on his own terms but still under the shadow of not being able to fill Rubin's shoes) was seen as an economic cheerleader, not a maker of policy. In both cases, a misconception of how currency policy works was at the center of the problem, and in both cases, the headwinds to the sanctity of the dollar came from within the empire.

"Credibility is a crucial asset for any Treasury secretary given that financial panics or crises can come suddenly and the secretary's words can come to be needed for reassurance," Larry Summers, who held the job from 1999 to 2001, said in an interview. "If such a moment comes, a secretary will regret previous false claims, highly political forecasts, or unsound assertions."

Paul O'Neill's tenure was riddled with some of these very opinions.

For one, he made fun of his biggest constituency. Not one to soliloquize on the abstract nature of markets, at times he openly discredited the work of stock, bond, and currency traders, saying they just "sit in front of flickering green screens" as they trade money from their desks. That glib remark, made in the early days of his tenure, was a harbinger of the complete lack of trust that Wall Street would have for him throughout his incumbency.

O'Neill also alienated another important stakeholder: the lawmakers who decided on fiscal spending and whose buy-in he needed for any significant economic proposal. While his storied predecessor, Bob Rubin, had worked hard to develop and maintain ties with congressmen and senators, O'Neill demeaned the work they did as "show business."

President George W. Bush's stumbles as he tried to create a viable economic team during his first term underscored the pitfalls of having an ineffectual Treasury secretary. Felled by undisciplined remarks and the cutthroat dynamics of the Bush White House, O'Neill lasted just twenty-three months on the job.

He also proved unable to comprehend that he was the steward of another, more powerful man's vision.

Compounding O'Neill's stylistic quirks and distrust of traders was the unenviable task of championing an economic agenda that he didn't fully believe in. From his perspective it was the presidential campaign that wanted the tax reduction program, but since he was never part of that, he appeared to have decided that as CEO of the Treasury department he could do as he pleased. He argued privately (and hinted publicly) that the administration should abandon some of the tax cuts it had proposed, citing concern for the ballooning federal deficit. He also took on initiatives that were outside the sphere of the Treasury department, triggering head-scratching among colleagues when he talked as if he still sought to reduce injuries on a factory floor where laborers worked with metals at 1,500 degrees and machines with the strength to rip an entire arm off. Workplace safety was important in government, too, he said repeatedly to white-collar Treasury employees spread across cubicles in Washington, D.C. Perhaps in his mind he was still the chief executive officer of Alcoa, the aluminum giant that he ran for more than a dozen years.

As Bush wrote in his autobiography, *Decision Points*, he and O'Neill "never clicked. He didn't gain my confidence." This was obvious to anyone who knew Bush. With his penchant for nicknames, when the president switched from affectionately referring to O'Neill as "Pablo" to the slight irritation with which he'd say "Big O," everyone saw the change in the Treasury chief's fortunes on the horizon.

The president also retrospectively acknowledged that his first economic team, which included the ex–Federal Reserve official Larry Lindsey and ex–Treasury official Glenn Hubbard, was a "personnel mismatch." The dynamic undermined O'Neill's chances from the start: in the customary White House power grab, someone routinely blocked him from joining key White House senior staff meeting where agendas were set. On top of that, some of his market-sensitive memos to the White House were leaked to the press.

Without being a trusted insider within the economic policymaking cohort of the administration—which required an alliance with colleagues, access to the commander in chief, and loyalty to the goals on which the president won election—O'Neill's efforts to run Treasury were hobbled.

So Bush fired him. But not before finding a replacement.

By 2002, Bush had become the most popular U.S. president among voters since John F. Kennedy after the nation rallied behind his vision to fight back following 9/11. But Bush had a problem: among the investor class, he was the least popular in nearly a quarter of a century. An overtalkative Treasury secretary with a penchant for moving markets by accident was one complication. But worse, the U.S. economy was looking a lot like it did in 1992 when Bush's father failed to win a second term. Growth was anemic, eking out 1.5 percent annually, and unemployment was edging up. The threat of war had pushed the S&P 500 stock index down 23 percent in 2002, in what was the biggest slide since 1974 when President Gerald Ford was battling double-digit inflation. The dollar's 8.5 percent drop was the worst since Bush Sr. was in office.

The fate of his father's presidency made Bush acutely aware of the danger that economic malaise posed. What Bush needed now was a new secretary of the Treasury, one who had the panache to coax lawmakers to back his plan to boost economic growth, create jobs. He needed someone to persuade investors that widening budget deficits were not always a prelude to doom.

What he needed was a Republican with a Rubin-like magic touch with financial markets.

One thing was clear to the White House: this new Treasury chief should be the opposite of whatever Paul O'Neill was. Being in lockstep with the White House was imperative if Bush was going to win another term.

It wasn't as easy as simply turning to Wall Street. Bush's friendship with Kenneth Lay, the chief executive officer of Enron (which collapsed spectacularly in late 2001 amid one of the greatest accounting scams in history), had become a political liability and also set a narrative that was derogatory toward corporate chieftains. Still, Bush's team was tempted to recruit from Wall Street. Behind the scenes they had been eyeing Charles Schwab of the Charles Schwab Corporation and Hank Paulson of Goldman Sachs.

In November 2002, under the guise of needing someone to lead the Securities and Exchange Commission, Bush invited the chairman of the nation's third-biggest railway system, John William Snow, to the White House. It had to remain a secret—in fact, even Snow didn't know during those initial interviews that he was being considered for the Treasury job. In the middle of an administration, a mere whiff of change in that particular agency could move markets, so the White House's interviews had be done in a clandestine fashion. At times like these, candidates are snuck into the East Wing, away from the prying eyes of reporters who work from inside the West Wing. Within a few weeks, Snow landed Secretary O'Neill's job.

Vice President Dick Cheney had asked O'Neill to lie and say that he had offered his resignation, but he was unwilling. "I'm too old to begin telling lies now," O'Neill said, according to *The Price of Loyalty*, a book on the Bush presidency by the Pulitzer Prize–winning reporter Ron Suskind. (Published in 2004 amid controversy around its veracity, the book was primarily based on interviews and documents provided by O'Neill.) He told Suskind that no one would believe it if he announced he decided to resign from the Bush administration.

"People who know me well would say that it wasn't true. And people who don't know me well would say, 'O'Neill was a coward—things aren't going so well, and he bailed out on the president.'"

On paper, John Snow and Paul O'Neill were hard to tell apart. Both men were from the Midwest, were in their sixties, and had been CEOs of large industrial firms. They had also known each other since they were colleagues in the Ford administration in the 1970s, and both had maintained ties with George H. W. Bush.

Neither had deep knowledge of financial markets, which many saw as a requirement to becoming Treasury secretary. "Oh, good, just what we need, a railroad guy," one top Wall Street banking executive said of the nomination. "If you want an army that's going to win wars, you want a general with training. The same principle needs to be applied at Treasury."

Just like with O'Neill, investors were not shy about illustrating how nervous they were to have another Midwestern industrialist running Treasury: stocks fell between 2 and 4 percent on major indices the day Bush revealed Snow's nomination. Investors had sniffed out that the change was symbolic, not substantive.

Critics said that Bush lacked an economic agenda altogether and that Snow's selection revealed continuity of the current vision (whatever that was), but with a better salesman. Still, Snow came with close ties to most of the senators on the finance committee that oversees Treasury's work. And to address the lack of credibility the Bush administration had with Wall Street, the team went back to Bob Rubin's old stomping grounds and chose Stephen Friedman, who had been cochairman of Goldman Sachs, to be director of the White House's National Economic Council.

Snow was also given advice that his predecessor perhaps never received: his job was not to set policy, but rather to implement the vision of a democratically elected president. That lesson was instilled during Snow's first week as secretary, when George Shultz, a former Treasury secretary, visited him at his new office at 1500 Pennsylvania Avenue. They had a conversation that essentially summed up why President Bush needed a new Treasury chief.

"John, you're going to get asked: 'Mr. Secretary, what is your policy on the dollar? What is your policy on taxes . . . on IMF gold reserves?' Whatever the question, the answer is, 'Let me tell you what the *president's* policies are . . .'"

Known for his bushy and emotive eyebrows and Midwestern charm, John Snow grew up Toledo, Ohio, a working-class industrial town that was steeped in the prosperity of the post–World War II golden age. Scores of locals studied mathematics and engineering in high school or at a vocational college and went on to become wealthy as tool and die makers. Those highly skilled craftsmen facilitated the mass production of cars in Detroit, just eighty miles north on Interstate 75, on the other side of Lake Erie. But Snow's parents, who had deep roots in the region, were not part of the manufacturing trade. He describes them as intellectuals: his father was a lawyer and his mother a high school teacher. Snow would later give up a place at Harvard to study economics at the University of Virginia under two Nobel laureates, and would become a professor, a lawyer, and, finally, a railway man and public servant.

He was also a PhD economist. But despite his training, the dollar trap that had haunted many Treasury secretaries—how to talk about the buck without stirring the pot—ensnared Snow within three months of taking the top Treasury job.

All he wanted was to offer intellectual substance when he talked about U.S. currency policy, and all he got was the dollar falling 1 percent here or there for a few moments, damaging his credibility in the process.

He found it annoying.

One of those sitcom-style mishaps unfolded in 2003 in the coastal French town of Deauville, where reporters traveled with Snow and the Treasury team for a G7 meeting between the finance ministers of the world's richest nations. It was an auspicious locale. Deauville is just twenty-seven miles from where the D-Day landings took place in 1944 a few weeks before the Bretton Woods Conference met to crown the dollar as king.

As the G7 meetings were set to begin, Snow sat down with Simon Kennedy of Bloomberg News and his cohort at the Hotel Le Royal Deauville, and launched into a homily on the dollar policy. In the off-the-record meeting (meaning not one word could appear in news reports), Snow talked with half a dozen reporters about the relationship between exports and the exchange value of currencies, and how the currency is a store of value determined by markets. To the jovial economist with a penchant for academics, it was just a lesson in how terms of trade and currencies work in order to explain a recent depreciation in the dollar. To Kennedy, the U.S. secretary of the Treasury had just killed the strong dollar policy.

Not that anything he had said was inaccurate. But simply by elaborating beyond Rubin's eight-word prescriptive statement on the dollar, Snow was charged with revealing a queasiness over the strong dollar policy during a time when traders were not yet convinced that the Treasury department was no longer active in foreign exchange markets.

Huddled together under the lavish tapestries and lush sofas in the lobby of their hotel in Deauville a few hours after their lecture from the world's most powerful finance minister, Kennedy and the rest of the journalists traveling with Treasury tried to figure out how they could possibly report that the secretary had redefined what foreign exchange markets saw as Rubin's storied dollar policy. They decided to try to get Snow to repeat what he said in the off-the-record setting during a press conference (transmitted live and therefore fully reportable) that was scheduled as the G7 meetings wrapped up.

"Can you define what you mean by 'strong dollar'?" Kennedy asked during a press briefing, his tape recorder rolling.

Snow gave a response that was more verbose than what his public relations team ever wanted from the Treasury chief, whose every word was dissected by traders and policymakers around the world.

"You want people to have confidence in your currency. You want people to see the currency as a good medium of exchange, you want the currency to be a good store of value, something that's willing to be held."

Kennedy sat in the front row of the makeshift briefing room in the hotel, his pencil scurrying across his notepad. As Snow answered more questions, he revealed to the reporters that the dollar's 21 percent drop against the euro over the past year was "fairly modest."

Add it all together and it looked to Kennedy as if the United States was all of a sudden happy with the recent weakness in the dollar. If the trend stayed, it would be a win for manufacturers, since their goods would be cheaper overseas, increasing the value of global sales that were then converted back into dollars.

"The market had been wondering whether the strong dollar policy was real—it's pretty clear it's not," one currency trader said. Rubin's mantra, which according to investors was intended to keep the dollar strong in exchange markets, had just been "abandoned," according to another.

Bloomberg's headline over Kennedy's story was a nightmare come true for Treasury's public affairs team: "Snow's Redefined 'Strong Dollar' May Extend Currency's Slide." *The Wall Street Journal* took it further: "The Bush administration has abandoned the eight-year-old U.S. strategy of verbally supporting a 'strong' dollar in foreign exchange markets, Treasury Secretary John Snow indicated during the weekend."

Both articles portended that the "new strategy" for the dollar could lead to a sell-off in the already weakened greenback as traders absorbed the prospect that Treasury would not take action to strengthen the currency. It could keep capital away from the United States, possibly lowering the value of stocks and bonds, subsequently hurting the private sector's capacity to invest in the economy.

The news stories also featured a line that Snow's spokespeople had repeated hundreds of times while at the Bush-era Treasury department: "There's no change in dollar policy."

It was a denial that few believed.

The scene in Deauville, much like the one Rubin experienced in Vietnam and others that played out countless times, illustrates the immaturity of the strong dollar policy. Asked about it decades later, Snow suggested that financial reporters and currency traders were in cahoots. "Reporters love to hear a Treasury secretary say something that is out of kilter with predecessors, and the financial markets love it because it sends shivers through the market," he said in an interview. "They don't care if it goes up or down but as long as it's got volatility, they're happy." (The up and down in the price of anything was a chance for traders to place a bet and turn a profit.) While the subject was a sore one during his tenure, eventually he was able to laugh at the thought of the dollar trap that investors and reporters put him in. "There's a symbiotic relationship there."

Trust between financial markets, which play such an influential role in the dollar's status, and a Treasury department had never been so vital. In the wake of 9/11 the buck had become a full weapon of war and remained the linchpin to almost every kind of commerce conducted in an increasingly integrated world economy. The man (and, many years later, the woman) serving as caretaker of this asset needed to intuitively appreciate market forces if they were to win their respect.

Working with his chief of staff, Chris Smith, and others, Snow held strategy sessions to try to create a credible, repeatable strong dollar mantra. To simply stop talking about it would exacerbate concerns, since markets were certain that Bush wanted to weaken it. It didn't help that currency traders, eager to make a buck, egged on journalists to ask Snow about the dollar. Despite attempts at rigor, Snow was unable to telegraph the strong dollar mantra with the robotic precision that Rubin and Larry Summers had conditioned traders to expect, and instead kept leading to accidental market moves.

"In the past it has usually been the Treasury secretary who soothes markets when a president moves the dollar with an off-hand comment. On Friday, President Bush issued the calming words after Treasury Secretary John Snow sent the greenback down by saying the dollar's recent decline has been 'orderly' and that the dollar was still at historically high levels," wrote *The Wall Street Journal*. It had been just one hundred months into Snow's tenure after one of his many dollar policy mishaps.

Despite being taken in by the circus around dollar policy, for the most part President Bush got what he asked for when he hired Snow: a cheerleader for his economic plan. That November, voters were choosing between a second term for Bush, or sending Democrat John Kerry to the White House. The seventy-third secretary of the Treasury visited half of the states in the nation in 2004, eschewing most foreign travel. Snow went to Missouri, Ohio, Oregon, Montana, Maine, and North Dakota to talk about the state of the economy and "promote President Bush's economic agenda," according to Treasury press releases.

Snow spent his time on the road touring construction sites and dropping by schools, local senior centers, hotels, and even a Build-A-Bear shop. His job was to put a positive spin on what a second term for Bush held, from Florida to Nevada, where he told an audience of local business leaders how the state of Nevada had recently created 3,800 new jobs and promoted federal provisions to help hotel owners and others get terrorism insurance. During his downtime on those trips, he played basketball with reporters and Secret Service agents.

That didn't mean he escaped the dreaded dollar question.

When a student in a school gym in Cleveland asked Snow his view on the strong dollar policy, Snow turned and glared at the reporters he had in tow, assuming they had put the student up to the task of asking the question he most hated.

The campaign-style tours only solidified Snow's reputation as a salesman for Bush rather than a policymaker. He was a team player, selling a product he had no hand in making rather than serving as an innovator of policy. Political and financial circles pilloried Snow over the fall in his stature from Treasury chief to messenger. They saw him with diminished influence in the Oval Office and on the fringes of the president's inner circle where decisions were made. At the time, William Dudley, an economist at Goldman Sachs during the Snow era (he would later go on to become head of the Federal Reserve Bank of New York), said that on Wall Street "there's a strong presumption that the primary economic strategy doesn't rest with Treasury." It didn't help that Snow kept failing the test that reporters put him to.

That wasn't good news. On rare occasions, the U.S. secretary of the Treasury's voice was essential in calming jittery markets. Paul

O'Neill never had that power. And by 2005, Bush was discovering that Snow had also drifted away from the core job description for the U.S. Treasury secretary.

The biggest reason that Snow never fully commanded the trust of investors and Congress was that he succumbed to the same market-moving gaffes that bedeviled O'Neill's tenure.

Rubin's shadow loomed large even years after his departure.

As rumors spread that President Bush wanted to replace Snow, it was the job of Salvatore Antonio "Tony" Fratto, a consummate public relations guru, to assure the world that Snow was remaining at Treasury. He found himself fighting headline after headline that cast shadows over Snow's future prospects. "Treasury's Snow, Embraced by Bush, Still Faces Doubts," ran one in November 2004. Fratto's battle with the media would continue for eighteen months.

It didn't help that the president's public show of confidence in his Treasury chief was feeble. Unnamed administration officials were cited in *The Washington Post* and *The New York Times* saying the president wanted a new leader at Treasury within months. In one particularly painful episode, the White House waited an alarming ten days before dispelling news reports that Bush was ready to dump Snow. News pundits said that Snow's credibility had been damaged by the period of uncertainty. Fratto recalled, "How could Snow negotiate with [lawmakers] and the G7 if everyone thinks his days are numbered?"

The president himself was now playing a role in leaving Treasury's stature utterly diminished before the world's finance ministries, investors, and lawmakers. It went on for months.

But behind closed doors big changes were in the offing: Bush was actively looking for Snow's replacement. The Treasury chief had privately indicated he was eager to return to private life, and the president accepted. The next dollar steward would quickly find himself as the commander during a financial crisis so deep, so devastating, that only innovative policymaking would go on to help save the entire economy from outright calamity. No one knew this at the time—but Bush was aware he needed a strong Treasury chief.

The problem was, the man who was perfect for the job kept saying no.

9.

"JUST CALL
ME HANK"

Since his days as a somewhat small offensive tackle on Dartmouth College's football team, Henry Merritt Paulson, Jr., had run toward problems, not away from them.

In the late 1960s, when he donned his green and white number 76 football jersey to throw the full force of his 198 pounds at his opponents, he knew what was coming. With his powerful tackle and unwavering team spirit, he usually emerged with the dirtiest uniform. But he was unapologetic about the bruising style with which he protected and aided his quarterback, earning him the nickname "Hank the Hammer." Over his four years at Dartmouth, Paulson lost just four games, a feat that placed him among sports legends at the Ivy League university.

Four decades later when he would put on a dark suit and tie for his first day as Treasury secretary (a more solemn uniform reflecting the work he now did), his old habit of running toward problems would come in handy.

In 2006, Wall Street was in a profit-making arms race. Banking behemoths and financial institutions were developing complex instruments to turbocharge the ways that money could be made on the back of an unusually powerful credit boom in the American housing and auto sectors. From December 2003 to the end of 2006, the U.S. stock market had risen 28 percent, adding tens of thousands of dollars to the retirement accounts of millions of Americans (at least on paper). Buying a home and fulfilling that consequential piece of the American dream that led to richer futures had rarely been easier.

And the bankers behind it all were building immense personal and corporate wealth. As the head of Goldman Sachs, Paulson's annual income around that time was a whopping $37 million, with the bank's share price at an all-time high. From the perspective of Paulson, who was the envy of all of Wall Street, life could not get any better.

Treasury secretaries tend to be a stolid bunch. Their enormous responsibility requires them to weave through political thickets of ideological bickering and get into the weeds of the plumbing of the global financial system, and of lawmaking. We want the U.S. Treasury department to be run by people who understand economics and finance, and understand the importance of stability and predictability in anything that relates to America's money and debt. If any policy gets in the way of that stability and predictability, we need a secretary who can put their personal credibility on the line to protect the nation's most valuable asset: the dollar.

But it is exactly when the country demands the most from a Treasury department—when the country's economic articles of faith are in peril—that the job suddenly necessitates someone who is willing to think creatively, push the limits of power, and move as quickly as an offensive tackle down a football field. Even if, in the end, he emerges muddier than anyone else on the team. Few private sector jobs can prepare someone for the unique demands of leading Treasury, but running Goldman Sachs comes pretty darn close.

A Wall Street darling with a 150-year history, the multinational investment bank prides itself on influence only matched by its revenue, and a reach that extends to every part of the globe. Its pedigree in cultivating public servants is unprecedented: Australian Prime Minister Malcom Turnbull, Italian prime ministers including Mario Draghi, once head of the European Central Bank, and, of course, Bob Rubin. Goldman has churned out more congressmen, presidential economic advisers, White House chiefs of staff, and central bank governors than you can count, earning it the moniker "Government Sachs."

Over three decades climbing the ladder to the top rung of this venerable behemoth, Paulson had acquired, practiced, and honed all the tools of the trade that Goldman had to offer. Much like when he was Hank the Hammer at Dartmouth College, he was both feared and admired. He adopted the bank's culture of making all clients feel like the most important client under the sun, and understood the importance of paying attention to broader policy needs to ensure economic health—like using his perch as a chief executive officer to encourage China to open up to private enterprise. Paulson was also behind Goldman's transformation from a private partnership to a public company that posted the largest quarterly profit in the history of the securities industry until that time. It didn't hurt that he had maintained an athletic build, with his more than six-foot-tall stature garnering immediate respect.

Paulson's deeper history reveals someone who understands what it means to work hard to change your fortune. A native of America's heartland, he grew up in the late 1940s and '50s on a farm in Barrington, Illinois. He had a crow and a raccoon as pets, and cows to provide the family milk. He was an Eagle Scout by the time he was fourteen years old, and in a family that often scraped by, he churned cream to make butter.

All of that made him the perfect salve to a cabinet-level irritant that plagued President Bush throughout his presidency. Bush had fired his first Treasury secretary, and his second one, John Snow, was doing exactly what the White House had wanted: serve as a ceremonial booster for policy set by staff at the White House. It turned out that approach didn't buy much trust in financial circles. The Treasury chief should be more than an economic spokesman: he needs to drive and set economic policy. Bush had chosen men who, one after another, were rejected by the global investor community whose buy-in was a necessary component to a successful economic agenda.

If the parable of billionaire investor Warren Buffett (dubbed by some as "Mr. Market") was right, that "in the short run, the markets are a voting machine," then Bush needed a Treasury secretary with instant gravitas with Wall Street. The department's work in the market for federal debt, or Treasuries, had only gotten more important: that market had grown by over 25 percent in the past two decades to nearly $8.2 trillion.

America's chief bond salesman now had a much bigger job than any of his predecessors.

By 2006 the world was running on dollars, its web reaching nearly everyone in the new hyperintegrated world economy. The United States was enjoying the heights its power had reached, supported by democratic government, rule of law, and independent courts. That the United States was too big, too important to stumble without dragging the world down with it was an economic creed.

Paulson was, in some ways, an unlikely candidate. For one, despite being a titan of finance, he didn't play the part of Wall Street royalty. Most conversations he had, whether it was an important client or an intrepid reporter, began with: "This will be a lot easier if you just call me 'Hank.'" In dismissing formalities around the formal titles he'd held, he instantly conveyed that knowledge was more important to him than rank.

More importantly, he kept refusing a job that most men in his milieu would eagerly step into. Part of the reason was that the offer wasn't entirely appetizing: By the spring of 2006, President Bush had squandered the bipartisan approval he enjoyed in the aftermath of 9/11 with his insistence on pursuing a war in Iraq that Americans increasingly saw as folly. And as if the missing weapons of mass destruction Bush went to Iraq in search of weren't enough, the bungled response to Hurricane Katrina had badly damaged his already poor standing. A Gallup poll showed that 59 percent of Americans disapproved of the job that Bush was doing. It was one of the reasons Bush picked Josh Bolten, a motorcycle enthusiast who once played in a band called Deficit Attention Disorder, as his new chief of staff that March—he needed a fresh perspective.

As Bolten began evaluating the administration's top advisers, the economic team stood out like a sore thumb. It had been riddled with intense personality clashes from the early days of the presidency, and Bolten worried they were poorly prepared for the unexpected. Bush's presidency had already faced several once unimaginable disasters: airplanes knocking down Manhattan skyscrapers, a devastating natural disaster, not to mention two corporate scandals and an economic slump. It left Bolten pondering Murphy's Law—if something could go wrong, it probably would. And financial troubles seemed like the only thing left.

With the fifth anniversary of 9/11 approaching, the dollar was now a full-blown weapon of war that also empowered the United States to compel the rest of the world to accept its foreign policy goals. The new brand of financial warfare harnessed the full force of the currency and its indispensability in global commerce. Now, any time that diplomacy failed but the United States was not ready for kinetic action, Treasury was prepared with innovative financial techniques. Around 2006, it was tracking tens of billions of dollars that belonged to Iraq's Saddam Hussein.

But Paulson was wary of the diminished Treasury department that Bush had cultivated and skeptical of how much he could accomplish in the final years of a two-term administration.

It would take some creativity to get him to change his mind. The winning effort drew on help from an old Treasury hand who, after having served in three different cabinet-level positions in as many administrations, had become an eminent force in Washington: Jim Baker, the Treasury chief from the 1980s who had managed to persuade the world to weaken the value of the dollar. In a meeting, Baker addressed Paulson's concerns head-on, suggesting Paulson lay out the conditions on which he might accept the job. His advice for success was to ensure that the secretary was treated with the deference and autonomy of the top economic principal for the president of the United States. (With that in mind, Paulson would eventually demand, and be given, regular access to the president, the freedom to choose his own staff, and the leeway to say no to taking on the kinds of political junkets that had tripped up John Snow.)

Bolten also continued the pressure campaign to recruit Paulson, who continued to demur. How would he break the news to his family? They were all fervent liberals (his mother cried when he eventually told her he would join Bush's cabinet). But besides that, Paulson was being pragmatic. Giving up his position among Wall Street royalty to join an administration heading into the lame-duck period of a two-term presidency, with laughably low approval ratings to boot, would be a stark contrast to his life at Goldman. His annual income would go from tens of millions of dollars to below $200,000, with scrutiny coming not indirectly through share price moves or company proceedings held behind closed doors but under the public spotlight and from Congress.

So Bolten devised an intellectual honey trap to lure his reluctant target. The White House sent him an invitation to attend a formal lunch with the Chinese president Hu Jintao—the perfect event to woo Paulson, who had made dozens of trips to China as Goldman's chief executive and built close relationships with Chinese leaders.

Bush hosted the lunch under the three immense crystal chandeliers of the White House's East Room, among the most auspicious locations in the residence. The largest room in the Executive Mansion, it features late-eighteenth-century-style architecture, decorative trimmings on the ceiling, an oak floor, and a full-length portrait of President George Washington. Seven presidents who died in office have laid in repose in the grand room. It is the where the Civil Rights Act was signed and where President Barack Obama would later announce the death of Osama bin Laden. But on Thursday, April 20, 2006, it was the venue for a lunch in honor of a Chinese dignitary—and for President Bush to pay court to Mr. and Mrs. Paulson.

Part of an elite guest list of about 150 people, the couple enjoyed a Nashville bluegrass band, wild-caught Alaskan halibut, and ginger-scented dumplings. It was a grand affair that caught Paulson's attention. As he wrote in his memoir *On the Brink*, after lunch he and his wife, Wendy, took a short walk over to the Treasury building next door to enjoy Washington's famous cherry blossoms in full bloom. As they strolled, he wondered if he had made a mistake in turning the job down. "Do you really want to be seventy-five and telling people 'I *could have been* Treasury secretary'?" a close friend had asked him.

After President Hu's high-profile state visit to the White House, critics were disappointed that Bush hadn't made more progress on the massive trade imbalance that persisted between the United States and China. But the day wasn't a total loss, for it was the day that Bush won Paulson over.

It would still be a few weeks before Paulson accepted the job. His reticence put him in a great bargaining position—Paulson told Bush he would take the job only if he was truly in charge of economic policy and had direct access to the president. Bush knew that from a guy like that, the administration would have someone loyal to the economic agenda that was already in place, and a varsity player ready on day one for an all-out battle.

Bush agreed to all of Paulson's conditions.

Around 11:20 a.m. on Monday, July 10, 2006, Chief Justice John Roberts helped break a hex that Wall Street had seemingly cast on Bush's economic team. The ceremony was broadcast on live television as Hank Paulson was sworn in as the nation's seventy-fourth Treasury secretary. Bush, who had walked over from the White House for the occasion, told the world that his new hire would be the "principal spokesman" for his administration's economic agenda, describing him as "a man that every American can have faith in." The lessons learned after two secretaries that had struggled with investors were clear when Bush touted Paulson's "intimate knowledge of global markets." In what could be read as a message to the rest of his economic team, which had spent the previous six years undercutting both of his secretaries, the president said that the "Treasury secretary is the leading force on my economic team and the chief spokesman for my economic policies."

Paulson was inheriting a strong U.S. economy. It was growing at a fast clip of about 5.6 percent, with 5.4 million new jobs created in the preceding three years, bringing the unemployment rate down to 4.7 percent—a level that most economists say reflects a healthy economy. Paulson's peacetime agenda (for the battle to rescue a flailing economy would begin with a shock eighteen months later) included a heavy focus on encouraging the international community to maintain fair trade policies and cutting taxes. But on that hot July day, the president made a promise that, in hindsight, sounds ominous: "The American economy is powerful, productive, and prosperous, and I look forward to working with Hank Paulson to keep it that way."

Every promise that Bush had made to Paulson that would allow the new Treasury chief to reestablish the luster and power of the agency was about to come into play at a time when the country needed a strong

Treasury and mastery in its dollar stewardship the most. Paulson knew that one of his first tasks would be to restore the credibility of the agency before markets, Washington, and the world. Through the regular and easy access that he had negotiated before taking the job, Paulson made it clear that he had a strong relationship with the president. Everyone knew who the top economic adviser was. "Treasury would no longer take a back seat in administration policy making, waiting for the White House to tell it what to do," he remarked later.

When Paulson spoke, investors, lawmakers, administration colleagues, and international counterparts all listened. Like during the Rubin era, the Treasury department rarely triggered accidental market moves under Paulson, and he was willing to do whatever it took to maintain that. Paulson used his first big economic speech to restate the Treasury department's allegiance to the strong dollar mantra, saying: "I believe that a strong dollar is in our nation's best interest and that currency values should be determined in open and competitive markets in response to underlying economic fundamentals."

He delivered a line that had sunk O'Neill and Snow time after time, without markets questioning his intentions. Reflecting on the new secretary's first big speech, one investor at the time said Paulson was "cautious and he said all the right things." After all, he came from the same habitat as those investors, which in effect silenced all the consternation from markets on the dollar.

Wall Street could finally stop pining for Bob Rubin's return.

Walk down the black-and-white-checkered marble floors in a third-story corridor of the Treasury department and you might mistake it for an exhibit on two hundred years of white male couture. There are oil paintings of men in colonial wigs and silk ascots, men standing in lordly postures amid rich red velvet draperies and thick columns familiar to the Greek Revival style of the building. Some are wearing the ditto-style suit popular in the 1800s, consisting of a waistcoat, a knee-length frock coat, and trousers. All of these larger-than-life-sized portraits feature men striking majestic poses: Seated in a mahogany and leather armchair with a stack of papers, the glimmering gold chain of a pocket watch visible. Or perhaps one elbow perched on a windowsill, a smoking pipe in the other hand, and, in a clear sign of Treasury's proximity to the nation's power center, a view of the White House. Almost all the men displayed are wearing a full suit and tie.

Then there's one of a tall, slightly unkempt bald man with glasses and no suit jacket, his hands shoved in his pockets and a hint of stress and agitation etched across his face. It's as if the painter had to stop his hurrying subject on the way back from the men's room and implore him to strike a quick pose, his shirttail sticking out. In lieu of any real scenery is a neutral mossy-green impressionistic backdrop.

This image of Secretary Paulson is reflective of the energetic and urgent economic policymaking and diplomacy that defined his tenure, and the humility with which the man who preferred that everybody just call him Hank did his job.

Paulson being chosen, lobbied, and finally persuaded to accept the job may be the most fortuitous development of the era for the global economy. Within a year and a half of his taking over from two predecessors who lacked hands-on market experience and the gravitas needed to lead economic policy, Paulson was in the throes of the worst financial crisis in a century. He would go on to convince his colleagues in the administration, and fellow Republicans and Democrats, that the ugly and politically risky options he had concocted were the only ones that had a chance of getting the nation—and the world—out of an utter mess.

For each stately oil painting of the men who have led the U.S. Department of the Treasury, there are dozens of unheralded heroes and heroines who have worked to build, nurture, and wield the dollar. While they are largely unknown to those outside of diplomatic and economic circles, the roughly 80,000 staffers that work for Treasury at any given time perform the essential work that maintains the dollar's stability even as the gears of the bureaucratic apparatus shift back and forth between Republican to Democrat administrations.

Take Mark Sobel, for instance.

In his forty years working at Treasury, he had barely uttered two extemporaneous words in public, adhering strictly to the rules that leave political appointees to do most of the talking. The bespectacled career bureaucrat, hired during the Carter administration in his twenties, held many jobs throughout his career. His titles were absolute mouthfuls, like "deputy assistant secretary for international monetary and financial policy." Dollar Guru might have been more fitting. "There was no one in the U.S. government that knew more about [currency policy] and backed it up with sound analysis than Mark Sobel," Paulson once said.

Sobel, who cites both St. Louis and Tallahassee as his hometowns, is a humble, private man with a dry sense of humor. He's worn the same black Casio watch for years and he doesn't like to share details about his private life, except that he likes cats and college basketball.

For years, he kept up the tradition of giving new parents at Treasury a onesie or bib in the garnet-and-gold colors of his favorite team, the Florida State Seminoles. The men he worked for at Treasury were usually multimillionaires who came from Wall Street and had gone through the Senate wringer to get confirmed as secretary or assistants to the big boss. But no matter how large a figure these political officials cut, Sobel had the power of institutional and cultural knowledge from years of American economic diplomacy, and the tested courage of a man who had proved resilient over seven administrations. He also knew which secretary was known to throw childlike temper tantrums when they didn't like a speech an aide drafted, stomping all over the paper copy. (You'll have to try him directly if you want that name—a good civil servant never leaks.)

By the description of multiple officials reflecting affectionately on their time working with Sobel, he was a bit of a "curmudgeon" or an "acquired taste," but also an uncompromising and effective negotiator for the United States at G7 and G20 meetings. Perhaps that stemmed from his candor and the fact that he was never intimidated by the bigwigs that often join administrations. The pride that Sobel had in his achievements as a bureaucrat in the very heart of American policy is illustrated in the story he shares as the highlight of his career. When the then Treasury secretary Tim Geithner introduced Sobel to President Barack Obama, Geithner called him "the mandarin's mandarin—the outstanding bureaucrat." Geithner joked that he meant it as both a compliment and an insult.

Sobel drew on this mastery at a crucial moment in the nation's economic history. In the spring of 2008, the outlook for the U.S. economy was perilous, especially after the investment banking behemoth

Bear Stearns went bankrupt that March. To stanch further calamity the Federal Reserve was slashing rates, which weakened the dollar. Foreign economic officials grew alarmed at the dollar's rapid slide, particularly those in France and Germany. The United States was pilloried in public and private by European officials for not caring about a spiraling currency. What these nations were worried about was the damage to their own economic outlooks, because a weak dollar would stymie their exports to the United States (since Americans would find foreign goods pricier).

It was during a private conversation with a group of Europeans that Sobel heard a worrying phrase. One of these government officials used the term "benign neglect" to describe the United States' currency policy. Though it's a phrase with little meaning to the public, Sobel found it triggering: it's a term that harks back to the Nixon years, around the time when the currency regime established at Bretton Woods in the 1940s fell apart (the United States abandoned its peg to gold). According to Sobel, it "conveys the image that we aren't mindful of the rest of the world and has a pejorative connotation." And since the United States had caused the financial and economic crisis that most of the world was now stuck in, it was an especially sensitive topic.

This was a time when currency intervention was no longer standard practice. In fact, Treasury officials had not intervened to buy or sell the dollar since Bush took office in January 2001. The obsession around dollar talk had been largely neutralized, thanks to Rubin, Paulson, and the sheer size of global foreign exchange markets making the concept of a successful intervention laughable.

But the dollar's sharp drop of almost 13 percent in the twelve

months through May 2008 had Treasury and Federal Reserve officials concerned. Not only were U.S. allies annoyed, but it was also
bad for domestic inflation because it was driving up the cost of oil.

Sobel, working with Nathan Sheets, an economist at the Fed (who
would later oversee international economic policies at Treasury),
made an unorthodox suggestion to top officials at the two agencies:
it was time for the Federal Reserve chair Ben Bernanke to make a
clear break from tradition and talk about the dollar.

By this point, Sobel had served in more than half a dozen different
roles at Treasury. Drawing on his three decades of experience, he saw
an opening to give what newspapers later called a "rhetorical lifeline"
to the dollar. For one thing, the Fed was set to hold interest rates
steady, temporarily ruling out the possibility that they could cut
them (therefore drive down the dollar) just as officials were talking
the dollar up.

Second, the Europeans and the United States were clearly in a
shouting match over the downtrodden dollar. A show of unity was
necessary to maintain what little expectations there were that the
country's economy would recover quickly. It was a tenuous time for
the world economy, and jawboning the American currency was a cheap
fix. To have just Secretary of the Treasury Hank Paulson talk up the
dollar felt like standard operating procedure—markets were somewhat immune to that. So Sobel concocted a one-two punch to rally
the dollar in a way that would eventually draw cheers from European
officials, and from markets.

Here's how Sobel's plan unfolded: On June 1, during a speech in
the United Arab Emirates, Paulson delivered an old Treasury chest-
nut (the very one that had tanked his two immediate predecessors),

but an amped-up version: "I have repeatedly stated that a strong dollar is in our nation's interest."

The dollar started strengthening on those words.

He continued: "The U.S. dollar has been the world's reserve currency since World War II and there is a good reason for that." He cited the nation's giant economy and safe capital markets, and then reiterated his commitment to policies that would strengthen the U.S. economy.

Then he continued with an even more dramatic statement. "The long-term health and strong underlying fundamentals of the U.S. economy will shine through and be reflected in currency values."

The second punch came from Bernanke. It was crafted with meticulousness by both Fed and Treasury officials, with Sobel quietly at the helm. "In collaboration with our colleagues at the Treasury, we continue to carefully monitor developments in foreign exchange markets," he said, speaking via satellite to a conference in Barcelona, Spain. Bernanke went on to acknowledge difficulties in the U.S. economy and called the subsequent drop in the dollar "unwelcome."

The message got through. In the coming weeks, Sobel's idea to clobber markets with dollar talk sparked a rally in the dollar's value and muted the volatility that had plagued currency market for weeks. During a fragile moment for the American economy, when the Fed and the Treasury department needed a quick fix to a burgeoning problem of instability in the dollar, it was Sobel who stepped in with the idea to protect the nation's currency.

But ask him what his favorite story from the "Hank era" is, and he'll tell you a different dollar story. That one is about the time he was in South Africa with Paulson, who was preparing to speak to reporters after a G20 summit. Sobel asked the Treasury chief if he was ready for a reporter to ask the inevitable question about his views on the dollar. Paulson said he was ready—and then broke out into Johnny Cash's song "Ring of Fire": "*I fell into a burning ring of fire/ Went down, down, down, and the flames went higher . . .*"

No one laughed as hard as Paulson did.

That was the thing about Sobel—right up until he retired at the age of sixty-four at the start of the Trump administration, he was always there to protect the dollar, especially from the culprit he blamed the most for the strong dollar policy run amok: reporters. "Reporters are always trying to elicit or provoke commentary because they know it will move markets and they get lots of attention. It gives them something to write about," he once said. "That is why people like me are always there, hovering around."

By September 2008, U.S. presidential elections were in full swing—and so was the global financial crisis. It was a race between Barack Obama and John McCain, who had to navigate the tricky terrain of distancing himself from the often nasty financial solutions his fellow Republican, President Bush, had to embrace to stave off an actual economic depression. Around the same time that McCain and Obama faced off in their first presidential debate, the crisis reached its climax: Lehman Brothers went belly-up, and the federal government was forced to take ownership of mortgage giants Fannie Mae and Freddie Mac.

Everything that was happening in Washington was controversial. Secretary Hank Paulson was urging a $700 billion government bailout of Wall Street, a move despised by a populace seeing homes and life savings disappear. The plan meant using use taxpayer money to purchase toxic assets and equity from financial institutions. The goal of the purchasing facility, called the Troubled Asset Relief Program (TARP), was to stabilize a rapidly deteriorating financial sector. Nobody liked the idea, but, as Paulson explained it, it was the only way to save the nation from total economic destruction.

That was a point that he was able to successfully telegraph to Bush, and the very reason that Paulson was so fervently courted for the job in the first place.

"When the financial crisis hit there probably was no more important relationship maybe in the world than between the president and the Treasury secretary," Josh Bolten said about Bush and Paulson. Speaking together on a podcast more than a decade later, Bolten told Paulson: "You had developed the confidence that you were able to tell him, 'We have to do something dramatic in the next two hours and you gotta trust me, it's the right thing.'"

Ugly problems with dreadful, imperfect solutions—that's what Paulson was constantly talking about with his president, with Congress, and with the American people. "Plan beats no plan," was one of his mottos as he was forced to make hasty decisions, where the time necessary to gather all the facts was a luxury he couldn't afford.

One moment in particular stands out as an example of his charisma and confidence. In September of that year, Paulson was trying to ratchet up the necessary congressional support to pass TARP, but he was struggling to demonstrate to lawmakers why such an abhorrent plan was the best option to save the global financial system. Bush gathered congressional and party leaders in the White House's Cabinet Room. The group included presidential hopefuls John McCain and Barack Obama, Speaker of the House Nancy Pelosi, the House

Republican John Boehner, and Senators Mitch McConnell and Harry Reid. And a disheartened Paulson.

"If money isn't loosened up, this sucker could go down," President Bush told the group, referring to the U.S. economy.

Democrats were prepared to deliver the votes necessary to make TARP law, Obama said during the meeting. But Republicans were refusing to sign on, and the meeting dissolved into a verbal brawl that a disconcerted Bush ended abruptly when he stood up and declared, "I've clearly lost control of this meeting. It's over." Paulson was stunned that his own party could be the roadblock.

Once the Cabinet Room had emptied, Paulson walked down the hall to the Roosevelt Room, where the Democrats that Bush had invited were angrily commiserating in a huddle around Obama. Paulson found his way to Pelosi and stood in front of her for just a moment before doing something that both made him laugh and surprised him: he dropped to his knees. "Don't blow this up," he implored, looking up at her. She reminded him that it was the Republicans who were doing that.

The moment was intended as one of levity for the Treasury chief— and it worked. Pelosi held the line on Democratic support, giving Paulson time to bring around enough Republicans to pass the Emergency Economic Stabilization Act of 2008, authorizing TARP.

Paulson won over a fiercely oppositional Congress and won their trust on the back of the stature and gravitas that he was known for. Until the Bush administration ended, Paulson took controversial actions to stanch economic paralysis as pieces of the global financial system went bankrupt, bringing down some of the nation's largest and oldest financial institutions. That included working with J.P. Morgan to acquire Bear Stearns, injecting hundreds of billions of dollars into Fannie Mae and Freddie Mac, and letting Lehman fall apart. It was a time that barely needed dramatization in Hollywood's block-buster adaptation of Michael Lewis's book *The Big Short*.

Paulson has faced as much criticism as applause for the rapid-fire decisions that he made during the crisis. Some say that Hank the Hammer moved swiftly to take consequential actions that served to save the world economy. Others gave him a new, pejorative moniker, "Mr. Bailout," for doling out taxpayer money to the very institutions that created the problem in the first place. Polls revealed that *TARP* was the second-most unpopular word in America, following *Guantanamo*, the detention camp that the U.S. military controversially used to torture suspected enemy combatants tied to terrorism. Critics say that Paulson was out of control, particularly in September 2008 when he put the troubled government housing finance vehicles Fannie Mae and Freddie Mac under government control (together, the two served as the guarantor of more than half of all mortgages in the United States). To this day, it's considered an open sore that the Treasury department continues to cope with.

But what Paulson wielded was a finance ministry with its power revved to the max. His policymaking and financial prowess were tested in a way no predecessor had ever been tested. He rehabilitated confidence in the agency in the nick of time, just before American economic institutions and the dollar were put to the test. And while the world suffered from a financial crisis brewed inside the dollar empire itself, the currency's power didn't wane—it strengthened. It was a safe haven throughout the knock-on crises that cascaded through the world, with investors confident that the United States would survive with its democracy, and therefore the power of the dollar, intact.

It turned out that President Bush's third and final pick for Treasury secretary was the best man to navigate the calamity that he walked into. Paulson presided at a time when the dollar's power faced formidable threats. His leadership and the efforts of those who worked alongside him, across the administration, Congress, Wall Street, and the Federal Reserve System, weren't mistake-free but they were heroic. Paulson was able to traverse the obvious threats—the homegrown financial crisis and the political brinkmanship that came with it—with clear success. The less obvious one, the nascent strength and influence of an Asian powerhouse that was exacerbating the slow drain of the American heartland, is perhaps where he faltered.

10.

CHICKEN FEET IN
OHIO AND CHINA'S
1,000-YEAR HORIZON

Spend a day in Moraine, Ohio, and you'll see firsthand how much the American heartland suffered from a government policy that supported a strong value for the dollar. All around you are those who the strong dollar mantra left behind—globalization's casualties. For more than half a century, glassmaking served as a key source for jobs to the local economy of this southwestern Ohio hamlet, supplying some 13,000 jobs. Celebrating the post–World War II boom, Moraine started out making home appliances for Frigidaire, stocking microwaves and refrigerators in homes across the nation. In the 1980s and 1990s, its factories joined the auto industry, producing chassis for car lines as American as apple pie: Oldsmobile, GMC, Chevrolet, and Buick.

But somewhere between the trade agreements of the Bush and Clinton presidencies and China's ascent into the World Trade Organization, Moraine reached its pinnacle and then crumbled—all within one generation. It was a fate that played out across American manufacturing states like Wisconsin, Michigan, Pennsylvania, and West Virginia, where swaths of Americans were living paycheck to paycheck, unable to find jobs that paid enough for even life's most basic necessities. Some of those troubles can be traced back to the global financial crisis. The Moraine plant, which eventually employed 24,000 workers, was unable to withstand it, and two days before Christmas in 2008, the factory closed.

Many of Moraine's problems can be traced back to the strong dollar. American economic policymakers failed to effectively navigate, or even fully recognize, the dark side of open trade borders: foreign competitors. Domestically there was a financial crisis borne of the excessive risk-taking in the United States that spread to the rest of the world. That was accompanied by benign neglect of the economic pain of Americans left behind by globalization.

But the other threat emerged from the Far East. Since the late 1970s, China had been slowly transitioning away from a "command economy," in which economic decisions are made by an authoritarian government, and toward a free-market system determined by supply and demand. It was a massive undertaking for a country that has grown so rapidly, and it has been micromanaged by the government. A look back to what happened in Beijing in 1989 helps explain China's resolve to maintain stability, even at a sloth-like pace from an international-relations perspective.

In the years leading up to the Tiananmen Square Massacre, millions and millions of citizens were being asked by their government to leave the farming life. To do that meant they would leave a familiar environment for the uncertainty of urban life. The shift boosted household incomes and improved the daily lives of ordinary citizens.

But the inflation that resulted, and lack of preparedness of those entering the workforce of a new economic system, was socially destabilizing. Corruption at the highest levels of China's government added to the rancor. In June 1989, thousands began gathering in Tiananmen Square, the centuries-old former gate to the Imperial City now located in the heart of Beijing, for protests and hunger strikes. The nearly six-week event (often referred to as a massacre for the hundreds of lives that perished in the protest) ended only when martial law was enforced. Since then, China's political leadership has sought to maintain social stability through authoritarian rule and economic growth. The bedrock of public order that the Chinese have held on to is a grand bargain of sorts between the Communist Party and its citizens: the politicians keep their monopoly on power in exchange for improving the standard of living.

It's an important history lesson that reveals what drove China to protect its economic success as it participated in the newly globalized country. China's leaders continued to modernize the economy over the next decade, and in 2001, the nation became a member of the World Trade Organization. Over the next fifteen years, America watched as its manufacturing sector was decimated, going from 12 percent of the workforce to less than 9 percent, while in China the sector grew from close to 15 percent of the economy to 20 percent. The fortunes of the Chinese were shifting. The nation's global share in the manufacturing sector went from some 4 percent in 1991 to nearly a quarter of it by 2012. In the resulting economic turnaround, millions of Chinese were lifted out of poverty.

Meanwhile, the economic shock from two landmark shifts in global trade policy (the North American Free Trade Agreement and Beijing's entry into the WTO), which further opened trade with

Canada, Mexico, and China, was reverberating in America's heartland. According to the economist David Autor, whose groundbreaking research revealed the deep scars of globalization, China's rapid evolution in manufacturing created a "seismic shock" in middle America, accounting for 40 percent of the manufacturing job losses from 2000 to 2007—roughly two million jobs. Few were replaced. And the federal government failed to find a way to ease the pain. Wage insurance or value added tax might have leveled the playing field for imported versus domestic goods. And, as Autor's work lays out, the shift scarred an entire generation of blue-collar families. This was happening as economists held steadfast to the view that open markets and free trade would lift everyone's fortunes, and those left behind could easily be retrained for new careers. It was an idea flawed from the very start, for the simple reason that you can't teach an old dog new tricks. Autor described it best: "Trade grows the economic pie . . . but it typically shrinks the slices received by some citizens."

Look at Moraine, for example. The big factory that shut down over Christmas in 2008 remained closed for seven years. The local economy wilted. When the factory reopened in 2015, the once all-American plant was to be run by a Chinese company with Chinese managers. It was their prerogative, really, since they poured around $460 million to purchase and then jump-start the factory.

In its heyday, when the plant was run by American car maker General Motors, workers at the plant earned upward of $125,000 a year (a figure adjusted for inflation for over time). But Fuyao Glass, one of the world's largest auto-glass suppliers, took over and started paying roughly half that. The staff included a few hundred Chinese nationals, speaking halting English, who taught Ohioans how to assemble windshields. If they started to miss home, there was a new restaurant nearby that served chicken feet.

The threat that China posed gave the American electorate a villain that was conveniently overseas. But there were problems within America, too, if one listened carefully to the blue-collar workers in the so-called flyover states.

The 1990s policy preference for a strong dollar as the lodestar for globalization was bad for some American workers. It made American industry less competitive and allowed other countries to manipulate their currencies (essentially cheat their way out of parts of trade deals) to boost their own exports, to the detriment of the American worker.

Here's how the currency manipulation was conducted: to depreciate the value of a currency, a country sells its own currency and buys another (usually dollars). The laws of supply and demand make the country's currency less attractive, pushing down its value. This runs afoul of almost every bilateral and multilateral trade agreement because it makes the manipulator's exports artificially cheaper, eventually drowning out competition.

Much of China's alarming pace of growth stemmed from this kind of activity.

All of the trade deals that world leaders had signed meant nothing if nations turned a blind eye to currency manipulation. And under Paulson and his successor, the U.S. Department of the Treasury pulled punches. For one, it refrained from intervening in currency markets to help domestic manufacturers. That wasn't surprising since Treasury's own currency reserves weren't large enough to influence a multitrillion-dollar-per-day foreign exchange market. But the bigger punch that was never delivered was to publicly name and shame the nations that were manipulating their currencies, even when Congress was clamoring for it.

That's where the Chinese currency, called the renminbi (a unit of which is referred to as the yuan), came in. China was a poor nation as it started its economic transition. Until the 1970s, the government kept the yuan massively undervalued as part of a strategy to reduce dependency on foreign goods. Once the shift away from a command economy began, the government was forced to look for growth opportunities through exports rather than consumer spending. The bit-by-bit transition away from an economy planned and controlled by the government has led to painstakingly slow changes in foreign exchange policy. In the 1990s, it involved a dual currency rate system and the gradual expansion of markets for foreign exchange. If it was a market-determined currency, then shifting economic factors should have pushed the yuan higher at times. But the central bank, called the People's Bank of China (PBOC), which unlike the Federal Reserve is not independent from government and politics, managed the peg by using newly printed yuan to buy or sell as many dollar assets as necessary to eliminate demand for its currency, and keep the rate low to buoy the export sector.

In stark contrast to how U.S. policy and markets function, in China it was up to President Hu Jintao to determine the yuan's value overseas. It's for this reason that China's currency policy is considered a "sovereign matter" for the highest level of government to make final decisions on, not just economic officials.

The PBOC maintained its peg through July 2005 when, succumbing to pressure from global trading partners, it moved to what is called a managed peg. That allowed the currency to move within a price-band determined by the Chinese government, bringing the nation one step closer to an open economy. In the eight years that followed, the yuan rose by 34 percent against the dollar, the proof that seemingly no one needed to know just how out of whack the yuan's pricing had become while juicing a rapid economic expansion.

Here is where it becomes easy to blame the erosion of American manufacturing on Washington. Union workers, industrialists, and the like prefer a weak currency to boost demand for their exports. But by the mid-1990s, Rubin's strong dollar mantra (along with economic policy that backed it) had taken hold and the greenback was on a tear. Blue-collar workers declared that Washington cared more about what Wall Street wanted—a strong dollar to protect the value of their burgeoning wealth—than what the real economy needed.

The United States and China have a deeply intertwined and fraught symbiosis. The two countries in many ways are polar opposites, yet can simultaneously inflict great pain and fulfill each other's needs. One is a young, constantly evolving democracy driven by idealism. The other is an autocracy that lives by directives rooted in centuries-old traditions and acts out plans made with thousand-year horizons. The two countries have the most significant relationship in geopolitics today—a bond that is at once perilous and self-serving. The fortunes of the United States and China (which by 2023 accounted for a combined 34 percent of the global economy) are tethered to each other through a colossal credit cycle in which China's weak currency-driven export boom has enabled an exceptionally high national savings rate. It has then invested back into the United States. That investment has financed trillions of dollars in public spending in the United States and underwritten mortgage loans to millions of Americans.

Put another way: the Chinese government's actions to subsidize its export industry through a weak yuan have, essentially, subsidized American living standards. Had the yuan's value been left up to market conditions to determine, China would have less money to invest in U.S. government debt.

This mutual addiction isn't all bad. It proves that the United States remains an attractive haven for foreign investment, reinforcing the dollar's superpower status. Since President Richard Nixon's dinner with Chinese leaders in Beijing, during what he called "the week that changed the world," there have been moments on the brink of outright confrontation with China, with U.S.-China policy a rare point of consistent bipartisanship for American lawmakers. In 1972, after twenty-five years of diplomatic isolation, Nixon and his cohort dined with five thousand Chinese dignitaries inside the Great Hall of the People, officially drawing China into the fold and to the surface of the American psyche. On December 14, 2006, this monument once again became the scene of unification between the East and the West.

At 9:05 a.m. in Beijing, Secretary Hank Paulson opened the inaugural U.S.-China Strategic Economic Dialogue, later dubbed just SED, on urgent issues that were hurting the trade partnership of the two nations. President Bush had anointed the creation of the forum as a channel for formal talks to connect economic officials at every rung of the two governments, with Paulson given "super cabinet"–level designation in his very first year in office so that the Chinese saw him as the official envoy.

The stakes for the forum were high: Paulson needed to save American jobs from China's unfair trade practices. At the time, Congress had nearly thirty pieces of legislation aimed at curbing Chinese imports. The one with the most momentum proposed a whopping 27 percent tariff on Chinese goods coming into the United States. The secretary had spent his first few months at Treasury persuading American lawmakers, investors, and factory owners that the best way to get the Chinese government to open its economy was through discourse, not sanctions and tariffs.

On that Thursday during Paulson's first trip to China as a public servant, in opening remarks that lasted just seven minutes, he stated three concise goals for the two-day meeting. His brevity reflected his desire for a "frank and energetic" meeting that produced "tangible results" for the American people he served.

His Chinese hosts had something else in mind. They launched into a loquacious presentation starting with events that took place more than a thousand years ago. An American delegation that included many of Bush's cabinet officers, the Federal Reserve Chair Ben Bernanke, and dozens of staffers and translators listened to a lecture on the subjugation of China by the West. The slide show presentation included an oil painting of an old British frigate, the kind that aggressively captured the port of Dinghai during the First Opium War in the 1840s.

The so-called opening remarks went on for hours. Tim Adams, a southerner with a warm smile who served as Treasury's undersecretary for international affairs, sat in the Great Hall with a new appreciation for two vastly different cultural spheres. While in the United States policy can shift every two to four years, due to midterm or presidential elections, China is an authoritarian state with a centuries-long outlook. They weren't motivated to tinker with it just to appease the impulses of America's two-hundred-year-old democracy.

As Paulson's first SED kicked off, lawmakers reminded the Treasury chief of the importance of coming home with concrete results. Adams and his team needed to return to Washington in two days with "deliverables" to show skeptics on Wall Street and Capitol Hill that Paulson was on the right track. One of those deliverables was directly related to foreign exchange rates, an issue central to Americans.

In a public letter addressed to Paulson on December 14, just one day after he walked into the Great Hall of the People in Beijing, Senators Richard Shelby and Chris Dodd told him they blamed China for the loss of three million U.S. manufacturing jobs. Thousands of taxpayer dollars were spent on flying half the president's cabinet to China, most of whom would return to the Grand Hyatt Hotel in Beijing that night to assess what promises they could secure from China that would portray a successful trip.

But after that first morning, Adams couldn't see how they would go from lessons on trade during the Han Dynasty 2,000 years ago to an agreement for a 3 percent appreciation in the yuan in the coming months. "It was a remarkable education, but I realized in that moment that the new economic forum with China was one hell of an undertaking," Adams said.

China was already the most populous nation, though it had not yet overtaken Japan as the second-largest economy (that would come four years later), and the American government thought it was time for it to start playing by the same rules as everyone else. The Chinese market was a lucrative target for multinational companies around the world, especially in America (Apple Inc.'s CEO Tim Cook would soon be eying the country, where the best-selling music device the iPod was already being produced, for a much-needed revenue boost). Paulson did not speak Mandarin, but he saw it as his job to leverage the relationships he had built in China over seventy trips to the country as a Goldman Sachs executive, and to coax officials toward the kind of global leadership that demands transparency and fairness.

Participating in such a closely coordinated effort with the United States forced the Chinese to create a staffing org chart that matched the Treasury's and gave American policymakers at all levels deeper insight into how they were viewed from the other side of the globe. The engagement resulted in press briefings, 7,000-word joint statements and "family photos" reminiscent of grade school class pictures with everyone organized in rows, hands clasped before them as they displayed practiced smiles. It was a show put on so that the top officials from each side could celebrate what they had in common even if they were miles apart on more substantive issues. And the Chinese benefited from an alliance with the world's superpower on full display.

Through the SED, Paulson sought to bring order to the relationship between the two most influential countries in the world. That the two countries disagreed on everything that was most important made the talks even more crucial. In drawing together economic officials at all levels with their counterparts from the other side of the world, Paulson used the twice-a-year gatherings to consistently address issues with China's currency policy and its integration into the global economy. Each side learned exchange rate perspectives in the broader context of the other nation's politics and domestic economy.

This structure ensured that the U.S. government would speak to the Chinese with one voice and on a regular basis. "The more fundamental your disagreements, the more important it is that there be some form of communication. . . . An ongoing channel to manage potential crises is key," Larry Summers, who served as Treasury secretary under Bill Clinton, said years later about the dialogue that

Paulson started with the Chinese. He'd learned that from the creation of the Group of Twenty block of nations during the Clinton administration that brought together influential economies to work toward global financial stability, helping face down disasters such as the 2008–2009 financial crisis and the Iranian nuclear threat.

The SED dialogues, hosted in turn by China and the United States, left no issue untouched no matter how difficult. Americans proselytize free market economics, urging Beijing to free its financial markets and allow more foreign competition by allowing the protection for intellectual property and expanding financial products to hedge against risks. But the biggest point of contention for those watching was always the urgency with which the United States wanted the Chinese government to relax currency controls.

It certainly helped that American officials had stopped currency interventions—without that, they couldn't hope for any change at all from China (or any other country for that matter). While the dollar policy continued to be a talking point during Paulson's time—it was, after all, part of Treasury's remit to manage it—it was no longer the *Tom and Jerry* chase it once was for investors, reporters, and the secretary of the day. Paulson's gravitas with markets helped to successfully shift the debate away from foreign exchange policy and to trade policy, financial regulations, economic statecraft, and, perhaps most importantly, the nation's economic ties with China.

Hu Jintao's final edict for the Chinese people, issued as "Eight Honors and Eight Shames," was intended for China's youth: "Honor to those who uphold plain living and hard struggle, and shame on those who wallow in extravagance and pleasures." As head of the People's Republic of China (and direct descendant of the Ming Dynasty that ruled for three centuries), Hu saw it as his job to rein in the wild moral compass of a new generation that had grown too enamored with the economic liberalization of a reformed China.

His final commandment, published just a few months before Paulson was sworn in at Treasury, may as well have been a forewarning that the Asian powerhouse was not ultimately willing to forgo a culture of state capitalism for the consumer-driven domestic economy the rest of the world wanted it to be. Relying on the consumption of goods was to "wallow in extravagance and pleasures," as Hu said.

And for China, currency policy that requires full control of the foreign exchange rate was a key tenet of its brand of state capitalism.

While Paulson badgered the Chinese for moving toward a freely traded currency too slowly, he felt that the most persuasive argument was to drive home the benefits to China's own domestic agenda. Their currency interventions were complicating the nation's economic picture, undermining key monetary policy goals such as controlling inflation.

Together with the Fed chair Ben Bernanke, Paulson urged China to allow the yuan to strengthen because it would improve the lives of ordinary Chinese by raising living standards, controlling inflation, boosting domestic demand, and helping to ease global trade imbalances—an all-around win for China, as the Treasury chief explained it. He suggested that if the Chinese would widen the band within which its currency is allowed to fluctuate, it would then develop more mature capital markets and instruments to help businesses and financial institutions cope with that volatility. American officials also encouraged China to boost its domestic demand by encouraging more consumption and spending on services to curb its reliance on exports for growth. For a high-saving society this would also be an evolution that involved a cultural shift—the kind that President Hu's Eight Honors and Eight Shames advised against.

To the leaders of China's central bank, a shift toward a market-determined exchange rate was inevitable, but it was equally imperative to protect domestic growth as it developed instruments to allow the yuan to be traded freely without damaging economic activity. Paulson made the case that the risks were higher to China's own domestic bliss if they moved too slow. But currency exchange reform was a sovereign matter for the Chinese, which meant that any shift would be slow.

One of Paulson's first steps in 2006 when he first took office was to begin diluting the emphasis on the yuan's value in U.S.-Sino engagement. In a speech devoted almost entirely to China, he said that the foreign exchange rate had become a "symbol of unfair competition." Currency manipulation is a simple concept for Congress and the American public to grasp in a quick news bite, making China and the yuan an easy target for all global trade fears. But Paulson believed that a stronger yuan would not single-handedly fix distortions within China or cut its trade surplus. The second, more potent point was that he believed China's interventions were not malicious. Rather, they were done to deal with larger structural problems related to a growth model that was heavily reliant on exports, a sharp contrast to the consumer-driven economy of the United States. Households in China were compelled to save in order to overcome the lack of health insurance and pension benefits.

China rewarded Paulson for his deep understanding of the currency issues. As he spoke at the start of the first economic dialogue in Beijing's Great Hall, China's central government allowed the yuan's price to increase to the strongest since the end of a dollar link in July 2005. The gain appeared to be "a reaction to Paulson's arrival [in Beijing]," one currency trader noted at the time.

While the Treasury secretary did urge China to switch to a flexible currency regime, by the time he had checked into the Grand Hyatt Hotel in Beijing in December, he had also persuaded Senators Chuck Schumer and Lindsey Graham to drop a bill imposing a 27 percent tariff on Chinese imports, and even soften their bald criticism of yuan intervention. The senators were willing to give "strategic engagement" a try. They would soon come to regret it.

What happened days after that first SED in Beijing represents how the U.S.-China dialogue would go on for almost another decade: A Treasury secretary eager to keep the peace, unsatisfied lawmakers channeling the anger of their constituents, and China sticking to its thousand-year planning horizon.

Shortly after the first SED concluded, Paulson released a routine report to Congress in which he chose not to formally designate China a currency manipulator, though there was evidence to the contrary. Not only that, he softened the Treasury department's criticism of China's foreign exchange policy. Lawmakers immediately attacked Paulson, and labor unions and manufacturers chimed in on the browbeating. China's manipulation was "the worst kept secret in the world," one critic said, adding that it "betrayed the American middle class."

Paulson led a total of five strategic meetings with China. Each had some two hundred American government officials, with participants usually seated in rows of tables facing their Chinese counterparts in ornate conference rooms for formal yet friendly meetings. No one spoke unless they flipped over their name card first, and everything required a translator. Agendas for each session, no matter how large or small, were agreed upon in advance and each ended with a concrete list of what progress needed to be made ahead of the next summit in six months. The teams worked through the preceding year to manage the logistical challenges of such large, publicity-driven retreats. There were working lunches, Chinese acrobats performing over dinner, and fulsome professions of cooperation. In his two and a half years as secretary, Paulson's U.S.-China Strategic Economic Dialogue yielded accords on food safety, energy, and environmental cooperation.

But just under the surface of the showmanship, the process and polite talk, there was discord. Fearful of protectionist rhetoric coming out of the United States Congress and the American electorate, Beijing frequently turned to threats of retaliation. They were somewhat unconvinced that Paulson's speeches at home and abroad to resist protectionism—"trust me, it doesn't work"—were genuine.

The Chinese believed that by managing the supply and demand of the yuan they were allowing their currency to be "market determined." Under intense pressure from the United States, the International Monetary Fund started to address this misconception by ramping up its monitoring of exchange rate regimes. Managing director Rodrigo Rato rammed through a new set of procedures that mimicked what the United States had been asking for all along. The IMF was finally taking a close look at China's currency regime which, according to Treasury, was clearly designed to give the competitive edge to Chinese exporters, damaging terms of trade for the rest of the world.

Building on those efforts, Paulson used his Strategic Economic

Dialogue to make forceful connections between China's inflation problem (it accelerated 8 percent in the first half of 2008) and its currency scheme. He was able to point to some strengthening of the yuan as a measure of success: over 2007, it rose about 6 percent, followed by another 8 percent through mid-2008.

But the reviews of Paulson's influence on China's currency regime were mixed. During the 2008 presidential election season, candidates Barack Obama and John McCain openly accused the Bush administration of coddling China, implicating Paulson's efforts to bring the relationship between the nations to an even keel. Meanwhile, investors, American manufacturers, and unions felt that China had ignored the United States' calls to set the yuan free. They pointed to modest progress in the opening of Chinese financial markets, saying that the nation had used arcane regulations to keep out American products.

The dollar was at the zenith of its clout, which was still not enough to bully or charm China into following the rules. But this problem would be set aside once the 2008 U.S. housing crisis hit, and during a protracted fight to stave off a global depression that demanded a tone of equals between the United States and China for half a dozen years. During this period, U.S. policymakers would instead find themselves reminding the world that the American-brewed financial crisis did not mean that the dollar was any less potent.

TIM'S CASH
ROOM CRASH

At half past six on the morning of January 27, 2009, Timothy Franz Geithner entered the U.S. Treasury department, and marched across the white-and-black-checkered marble floors as he had thousands of times when he worked there in the 1990s. But that wintry morning in Washington, D.C., was different—where once Geithner was an apolitical civil servant and privately registered as a Republican, now he was secretary of the Treasury for a Democratic administration. This time, he had a code name from his Secret Service detail: Fencing Master. One could imagine a sense of glory as he emerged on top after the hard climb up through the ranks of public servitude, but as Geithner later described his moments, "There was no thrill in it—I was so worried and so burdened by the dark challenges still ahead."

It would be a rough start for him.

A little after 11 a.m. on an unseasonably warm February morning, a split-screen image on CNBC painted a grim picture. On the right side of the screen, a newly minted Treasury secretary was standing in front of a row of American flags delivering his first live speech. On the left was a rolling list of stocks that were losing more and more value with every word he spoke.

Standing beneath three enormous brass chandeliers in the gilded two-story Cash Room of the Treasury department, Geithner was swaying. It was the only way he could cope with the two teleprompters he was reading from. The problem wasn't that he flubbed the lines. But the speech that one day earlier President Barack Obama had hyped-up as "terrific" turned out to be impersonal and devoid of captivating stories or mentions of American families struggling to make ends meet. Geithner wanted to lay out the new administration's plan to save the economy, but rather than use soothing words, he spoke in short, halting phrases that portrayed a dour outlook.

"This strategy will cost money, involve risk, and take time. . . . We will make mistakes," he said. Wearing a baby blue shirt and a deep red tie with an occasional crack in his voice betraying his nerves, Geithner looked, as one investor put it, too young and too scared to be in charge. "We will go through periods where things get worse and progress is uneven or interrupted," he went on, using jargon that made little sense to the panicked American public, like "borrowing costs have risen sharply" and "banks are reducing lending."

It was not the message of hope that Obama had campaigned on.

The most devastating moment occurred about fifteen minutes into the speech when he admitted to investors that he had no specifics to offer. "We will announce the details of this plan [*long pause*] in the next few weeks."

With that pause, traders watching the speech on the floor of the

New York Stock Exchange walked away from the television screens, horrified. As Geithner wrapped up, almost every market had slumped (even the tiny market of Ukrainian government debt dropped 30 percent). What the world heard was that a new president who launched into the White House less than a month earlier on a message of change was out of ideas. "Now we know there's no magic bullet," said one money manager a few hours after Geithner's now infamous speech. Everybody was disappointed in the lack of details, according to another.

Geithner had personally chosen the historic Cash Room, with its grandeur and seven types of marble, as his venue. It was the site of the inaugural ball for President Ulysses S. Grant in the 1860s. A hundred years before that, the room had a row of counters to handle cash bills and coins given over to Treasury for storage from commercial banks. Back then, Americans could visit the Cash Room to invest in their own future and the nation's by purchasing American government bonds. Now Geithner was trying to get Americans to invest in his vision of a way out of the financial crisis. Standing alongside gold accents and designs of wheat and corn to reflect the wealth of what was formerly an agrarian economy, he was supposed to light the way forward for a nation in the midst of a dark and rolling crisis that left educated, professional Americans jobless and homeless.

But markets—that pesky blob of money managers and traders who can express discontent with the click of a button as they price their investments—were disappointed. By the end of the day, financial stocks had tumbled 11 percent.

The state of the U.S. economy was in a calamitous position when Obama was inaugurated. The nation had led the world into the worst recession in at least a quarter of a century, domestic unemployment had rapidly risen to 7.2 percent—the highest in nearly sixteen years—but what was even more frightening was how hard it was to know just how deep the economic hole was. Within six months of the administration's start, the toll of the pervasive meltdown that had started in mid-2007 would leave a whopping ten million Americans without jobs.

The tale of economic demise that unfolded across the country was familiar no matter which of the fifty states you zoomed in on: The story of a small business owner who went to the bank for a mortgage to buy a house in, say, 2006, egged on by the lender to take out an even larger loan. A bigger, fancier house was a better investment because the value of that property could only increase, the banker would say—you'd never have to move again if you bought your dream house now. But in a year or so the value of that home would plunge and the economy would slow, bringing the new homeowner, perhaps with his second child on the way, to a financial precipice. He should have listened to that little nagging voice in his head when he and his wife signed their home loan agreements, that voice that said they were overreaching. His small business began to wilt and she had just gotten laid off, leaving the family without health insurance. Before they knew it, they were evicted, having missed one too many mortgage payments. With their life savings drained, they swiftly went from a comfortable middle-class life to near poverty. The family of four moved into her parents' basement—the grandparents would be handy as babysitters, anyway, because the college-educated mom and dad needed to work three jobs each (delivery drivers and unskilled health care workers were still of use) to make ends meet. Still, at least this couple had a family to turn to. His old college roommate, she'd heard through the grapevine, was sleeping in his car with his dog.

All eyes were on the new American administration to lead the world out of the crisis. Obama had vowed to do whatever it took to counter the worst economic crisis since the Great Depression, with an $850 billion tax cut and spending boost the centerpiece of his plan. When Geithner took the job, he was pretty sure that it was a no-win situation for him—after all, he was signing up to be the face of the most unpopular economic rescue efforts the government would launch in almost a century. His tenure was filled with what he later described as "communications failures," foreshadowed by his now-notorious Cash Room speech.

While the withering punditry that followed the speech was savage (one commentator said he looked like a shoplifter), Geithner was equally as tough on himself. In his memoir, using his characteristic bald language, he said his speech "sucked" and that he had "botched the theater."

It was a lengthy fall from the stature he came in with. Wall Street had expected Geithner to be a savior, rewarding the forty-seven-year-old with a 6.3 percent boost in the S&P 500 when his nomination was first announced three days before Thanksgiving in 2008. He was described as a "boyish technocrat" who had won confidence in 2007 and 2008 working as head of the Federal Reserve Bank of New York, when in tandem with Hank Paulson and the Federal Reserve chair Ben Bernanke he spearheaded the rescue of Bear Stearns and the government takeover of insurance giant AIG.

Geithner was no stranger to Washington, either, having worked at the International Monetary Fund and the Treasury department under Bob Rubin, when he helped create the strong dollar mantra.

He had also studied Japanese and Chinese, and had lived in East Africa, India, Thailand, China, and Japan.

But that morning in February 2009 was what happens when a Treasury chief can't match the moment. The man or woman charged with the stewardship of the dollar needs to inspire calm and confidence, convey prowess and control. As Bob Rubin put it, "Having somebody who is viewed as possessing some measure of credibility with respect to markets and economic matters speak in a calm and thoughtful fashion . . . probably does contribute positively to the psychology of a volatile situation." Take, for example, October 27, 1997. Investors, jittery over developments in Asian currencies, had driven down U.S. stocks to a level that alarmed policymakers, with the Dow Jones Industrial Average falling more than 7 percent, a record under the trading volumes that day. Taking advantage of the majestic setting right outside his office, Rubin invited a gaggle of reporters to the front steps of the Treasury department (with the White House visible just to the right) and issued a terse 150-word statement that sought to calm investors. With Buddha-like composure, he told the world: We know it's wild out there, but we looked into the plumbing of financial markets and everything is working just fine. We'll keep an eye on markets, but rest assured the U.S. economy is strong. It was an effort that didn't cost a dime, and it worked simply because of the magic touch of the man who delivered the statement.

But klutzy delivery of assurances scarce in detail from the person who signs the almighty dollar can tank markets, especially when they're already facing economic and financial upheaval.

Geithner's first speech as secretary struck a raw nerve with an American public that had voted for Obama on a message of prosperity. A few weeks later, *Saturday Night Live* opened with a savage takedown of the Treasury chief. The comedian Will Forte played Geithner, reeking of desperation as he offered $420 billion to the first person who called and provided a plan to solve the banking crisis and bail out the new administration. It wouldn't be the last time Tim Geithner would be jeered at on *SNL*.

His tenure came at a time when everyone touched by the dollar empire was being burned by it. Efforts by Geithner, Paulson, and Bernanke to paste the global financial system back together were loathsome to the public: multibillion-dollar rescues of the very financial institutions that caused the crisis, and their CEOs departing with "golden parachute" exit packages worth tens of millions of dollars, while the average Joe struggled to pay for their groceries and faced a generation of economic setbacks.

What made selling the emergency measures as successes even more difficult was that there was nothing to boast about: the government demanded that the public accept nasty compromises to stave off a full-blown depression, but millions of American families were still dealing with the devastation of a severe recession. The dilemma of trying to brag about counterfactuals was best described by Barney Frank, the pithy lawmaker from Massachusetts: to say "it would have been worse without me" ain't much of a bumper sticker.

About two months into the job, Geithner saw global stock markets reach the lowest point in more than a decade. On March 9, the S&P 500 (a benchmark for America's stock market health) was down 57 percent from a peak in 2007. By Halloween that year, with the U.S. subprime mortgage market's collapse jamming up the plumbing of the entire the global banking system, the nation's unemployment rate would hit a crisis peak of 10 percent. The world economy was projected to shrink for the first time in half a century, driven by an unholy trinity of economic problems: a dearth of credit, mounting job losses, and home foreclosures. Nearly every business in the world headed into survival mode. People were running out of money, and no one could stop the bleeding. Bernie Madoff had been arrested for a $50 billion Ponzi scheme, reinforcing the view among voters that the federal government had thrown away billions of dollars of taxpayer money to help the bad guys of Wall Street. Meanwhile, millions of Americans were jobless, some even homeless. The financial crisis had unfolded rapidly, unpredictably, and seemed to hurt those low on the economic totem pole more than anyone at the top.

And in a deeply integrated and hyperglobalized world economy, the pain spread far and wide. A domino effect triggered the European debt crisis, Iceland's banking system collapsed, and unemployment in some nations, like Spain, peaked at 27 percent.

Then there were the problems in the world's second most influential economy. A plunge in demand for Chinese exports was exacerbated by exporters facing payment risks as importers grew short of cash and financing, and rising shipping costs were shuttering factories. The Chinese government feared social unrest driven by massive unemployment as more than 15 percent of some 130 million rural migrant workers returned from cities without jobs, and growth slowed to as low as 5.5 percent in 2008 (roughly half of what it was before the crisis). China blamed the United States for its share of the problems the crisis brought on. The country was heavily exposed to the American economy through its massive positions in U.S. mortgage giants Fannie Mae and Freddie Mac, and also from its investments in American financial institutions. By January 2009, China had lost at least half of its $10.5 billion investment in Blackstone, Morgan Stanley, and TPG Capital.

The global turmoil and China's own domestic woes were a result of America's "blind pursuit of profit" and "a lack of self-discipline," as Chinese Premier Wen Jiabao put it in January 2009, clear violations of the Eight Honors and Eight Shames principles prescribing humility and morality as a way of life that President Hu Jintao had laid out less than three years earlier. Experts and policymakers in the United States had a similar view of the origins of the crisis, with the consensus being that it was the U.S. government's "inaction and mistaken actions" and the "excessive risk-taking" among financial institutions that had led the global financial system to the brink of total collapse. The Made in America crisis reinforced China's skepticism of the West's habit of finger-waving and scolding as it tried to bully Beijing to join the world order—which now looked weak.

With each blow to the economy, governments around the world were pumping more money into the economy. The governor of the People's Bank of China, Zhou Xiaochuan, slashed interest rates five times in three months as he prepared for a worst-case scenario that included a deep global recession and continuing credit freeze as money flowed out of China (investors were looking elsewhere for higher returns). On the fiscal policy front, Chinese leaders unveiled a half-trillion-dollar stimulus package. In the United States, the Federal Reserve had slashed interest rates effectively to zero, so it was up to Congress (the keeper of the nation's purse) to help stimulate the economy. From February 2008 through the end of 2012, the United States' fiscal response to the crisis totaled more than $1.5 trillion, spanning eighteen pieces of legislation.

It was the job of the Treasury department to fill the gaping budget hole that resulted from all the spending bills. They issued Treasuries in open markets, knowing that even amid an American-made crisis, banks and foreign investors would soak up these bonds. The allure and promise of the dollar was strong enough to help dig out of the crisis. But that very element—the Treasuries market—would soon be exposed to shocking volatility that stemmed directly from political grandstanding, threatening to undermine the dollar along with the precious U.S. government bond market.

Deep within the U.S. Treasury department sits a once-secret plan that could bring down the world's reserve currency in one fell swoop. The break-glass plan is so confidential that even now, years after it was made public through transparency rules surrounding Treasury's partner-in-crime, the Federal Reserve, officials who helped create it refuse to talk about it on the record. And in the summer of 2011, Geithner was just one day away from carrying out this unspeakable scheme.

Republicans and Democrats were locked in a battle that was threatening to bring the U.S. economy to a screeching halt, leaving American troops overseas without paychecks, millions of retirees without Social Security checks, and the potential to set off a chain reaction ending with economic destruction. It began because President Obama needed Congress to increase how much debt his Treasury department could issue in financial markets. The level at the time was $14 trillion, but Congress had already made legal a spending package that called for debt issuance to go above that level. Now the federal government needed that added cash to keep the country running.

It's a concept that should be simple: Congress decides how much the federal budget will be, and Treasury finances that spending plan with tax revenue, filling any budget gaps by issuing government bonds for which investors have an insatiable appetite. The limit on U.S. federal debt issuance is a quirk of the system. It was meant to make it easier for Treasury officials to manage public financing during World War I when Congress had to provide approval every time the department issued bonds. To cope with the rapid need for fresh cash amid that global conflict, Congress gave Treasury implicit approval to manage fiscal needs. In order to make sure that authority remained with Congress but could be shared with Treasury, lawmakers imposed a limit on how much debt could be issued.

But after the 2008 financial crisis, the federal deficit had nearly tripled to $1.3 trillion in just three years. So instead of making what was essentially an administrative fix that would allow Treasury to raise the money needed to make good on a budget that was already approved, Republicans (back then the traditionally more fiscally conservative party) were demanding that Democrats outline a plan to eventually bring the country's finances into better order.

Over the course of several months, the standoff between the White House and congressional Republicans approached a tipping point. House Speaker John Boehner stopped taking Obama's calls, so the president summoned him and his colleagues to the White House one Saturday morning to broker a deal.

The entire global financial market was at stake. U.S. federal debt is the gold standard of the world, the most attractive investment on Earth. When investors buy Treasuries, they are buying into a safe system that is free from the risk of default. America pays its debts— that concept is what distinguishes it from almost every other country. Until the 1950s, the debt ceiling was routinely raised on a bipartisan basis without incident, but as Republicans and Democrats became more polarized, they turned to brinkmanship to notch political points. In 2011, with the aftermath of the financial crisis forming a profound political imprint on a still-wounded economy, the parties ended up in deadlock over this seemingly routine fix. Markets faced the most volatile week since the thick of the crisis in 2008, with investors around the world placing bets in markets to hedge against the possibility that the United States wouldn't make good on its loan payments.

To traders, lawmakers looked too angry to realize that disaster was on the horizon.

Breaching the congressionally mandated limit "would shake the basic foundation of the entire global financial system. . . . [The] consequences would last for decades," Geithner told lawmakers. "The consequences would be catastrophic to the United States."

Market analysts were vociferously highlighting those consequences: The immediate ones had to do with missed paychecks and payments to health care providers, the American military, and the like. But beyond that, borrowing costs for U.S. government debt would rapidly increase once the possibility of Treasury leaving its bills unpaid was introduced. Lenders, such as foreign governments, would charge higher interest rates as insurance against trillions of dollars in debt, meaning America's future infrastructure plans, research and development, and military technology would become even more expensive. The uncertainty would crater stock markets, with a plunge in the paper value of retirement funds of millions of Americans—the clearest measure of the economic cataclysm. The U.S. dollar's value—both as a supreme currency and its foreign exchange rate—would erode.

The spillover to the global economy would be just as devastating, since securities everywhere, from the common to the exotic, take their cue from the U.S. bond market. (In subsequent years, as the fight over the debt limit played out repeatedly, JPMorgan Chase's Jamie Dimon would say that a United States default "could cause an immediate, literally cascading catastrophe of unbelievable proportions and damage to America for 100 years.")

The whole scenario forced Geithner and officials at the Federal Reserve to create a contingency plan if the debt ceiling wasn't raised. If lawmakers continued to fight and the legal limit of debt issuance was breached for the first time ever, what exactly would the country's accountants do next? Someone would have to decide which of America's creditors—like China and Japan, which held $1 trillion each—would be paid the interest on those holdings with the remaining funds Treasury had access to, and which would not. The plan needed to remain confidential, because if lawmakers caught even a mere whiff of additional leeway in the drop-dead deadline to raise the debt limit (which in this case was August 2) no one would cave. Plus, the existence of a default plan would damage confidence in American debt.

But America's money managers needed to be ready. To prepare, the Fed started running tabletop exercises—in secret—to check its ability to prioritize debt payments and determine the possible impact on markets. Treasury and the Fed worked through the mechanics of the backup plan: The first to be paid would include those who hold U.S. government debt, and those who received Social Security, veterans benefits, and other similar entitlements. Everyone else (from government contractors and employees to foreign investors) would be at risk of payment delays or partial payments. Put another way, the United States would default on its debt obligations for those in the second category.

The debt prioritization plan revealed two points to investors. First, that the Treasury department was technologically capable of picking and choosing which bondholders to repay. Second, that in 2011 the U.S. was dangerously close to not being able to manage its debt burdens. It was not a scenario Alexander Hamilton envisioned for the country. On his second day as secretary, more than 230 years ago, Hamilton issued a $50,000 loan to the federal government (roughly $1 billion in today's purchasing power) to start building the credit of the young nation that many thought would quickly fail. Hamilton and the rest of America's founding fathers were certain on two points for survival: first, that the United States' best defense against enemies seeking to destroy the new democracy required funding, and second, that the sanctity of the nation's word—that it would pay off its debt in a timely manner—was the key to attaining prosperity.

"A national debt, if it is not excessive, will be to us a national blessing," Hamilton wrote in a letter penned in 1781. "It will be a powerful cement of our Union. . . . There can be no time, no state of things, in which Credit is not essential to a Nation."

In the end, Geithner was saved from having to deal with what would have been a manufactured crisis. On August 1, 2011, lawmakers passed the Budget Control Act, which Obama signed into law the very next day. The bill allowed Geithner's Treasury department to issue another $2.4 trillion in Treasuries, which was enough to cover all debt financing that was due.

But all the fighting over the nation's most sacred asset left its mark. It was that summer that one of the three major credit ratings agencies, which provide a measure of a creditor's ability to repay its debt, downgraded U.S. debt. Standard & Poor's removed the triple-A rating the nation had held for seventy years, saying that the budget deal that lawmakers had hammered out wasn't enough to address the bleak outlook for the country's finances. The credit score that the United States now held, AA+, was a rank below more than a dozen countries. The Treasury department would go on to dispute S&P's controversial move, but the damage was already done. It was self-inflicted: lawmakers had gone a step too far in using the country's finances as a political cudgel.

Then there was the plan itself. Market strategists said that the debt prioritization idea was a terrible one that would damage the U.S. debt market, because investors would begin baking in the possibility of prioritization each time there was a stand-off in Washington over the debt ceiling—which, after this first standoff, seemed to happen every few years.

The 2011 episode was proof that perhaps the biggest threat to the dollar's status lay inside the nation's borders. A weapon as powerful as the dollar, which had emerged from the global financial crisis with barely a chink in its armor, was almost brought down by the nation's leaders. To maintain the power and influence that the United States enjoys through its ownership of the supreme currency, those who govern cannot play chicken with the weapon itself.

12.

NERD WARRIORS
AT WORK

Stuart A. Levey's most exciting moment working at the U.S. Treasury department happened on the day his mom sent tuna salad sandwiches for him to share with his team. They were meant to celebrate his final hours as a government employee after a decade of public service.

It was Friday, February 25, 2011, an overcast and chilly day in the nation's capital. Levey's team had just worked through two days and two nights trying to track down which American banks the Libyan despot Muammar Gaddafi had used to store his government's assets. The stakes were high: The nation of 6.2 million people was in the midst of a rebellion against the dictator, and Gaddafi had told the world he would fight "to the last drop of my blood" and show "no mercy" to the Libyan people in order to retain power. Diplomacy wasn't working, and President Barack Obama was not planning to send American troops in for battle. The next best weapon to force more democratic behavior out of Gaddafi was to turn to the dollar.

Economic sanctions, a novel option when talking failed to solve a problem but kinetic action seemed too extreme, usually take weeks or months to prepare. But if the United States was going to prevent the massacre of millions of innocent people in Libya, not to mention protect the global oil supply chain (Libya was a key cog in energy production), the Treasury department needed to move swiftly in finding Gaddafi's money. It was the best way to pry loose his grip on power— if he couldn't afford to pay his troops, he couldn't afford to resist a rebellion.

Levey got to work. As undersecretary of a unit that ran U.S. sanctions programs (created in the aftermath of 9/11), he marshaled the resources of the Office of Terrorism and Financial Intelligence, and started digging.

Libya had a gross domestic product of $62 billion, its sovereign wealth fund was worth about $40 billion, and the country had another $110 billion in central bank reserves. To establish where Gaddafi kept the Libyan government's money, Treasury's financial detectives and accountants combed through a warren of financial intelligence and data. They reached out to executives at big Wall Street banks for help identifying assets belonging to Gaddafi, his government, his family, or his friends. Levey and his staff figured that with enough determination and some luck, they could locate perhaps $100 million—a sum that would mark a huge moment to demonstrate Treasury's proficiencies and, more importantly, be enormously influential in maximizing the pressure campaign to oust Gaddafi.

At 2:22 p.m. on that final day in government service, just as he polished off his sandwich, Levey opened an email from a lawyer on his team. Sitting in a high-ceilinged fourth-floor office at Treasury with a view of the Washington Monument, Levey's jaw dropped. His snoopers had located $30 billion in just two days. At first, he thought someone had written a "b" where there should have been an "m." At no point did anyone expect to find *billions* of dollars in such a short span of time.

Levey slowly realized just how historic his final day in government would be.

The forty-seven-year-old was concluding an exciting six years in the building. He had consorted with kings and even spent a few hours aboard Gaddafi's private plane, complete with shag carpeting and gold-plated seat belts. Lauded by *The Washington Post* as the "money man in the terror fight," over seven years Levey had turned TFI into a behemoth with the ability to financially carpet-bomb entire nations. He was instrumental in securing the Treasury department a seat at the high-level national security apparatus of the world's most powerful nation, making TFI a permanent part of the foreign policymaking arm of the federal government. He had even served as acting secretary of the Treasury for a short stint during the global financial crisis, covering for a gap between Hank Paulson's departure and Tim Geithner being sworn in. He jokes that he was not important enough to be given a Secret Service detail during that period. (Levey's pals at TFI presented him with a framed chart showing that the stock market had risen 3.9 percent in the six days he was in office.)

But it was his final day, which ended at 8:00 p.m. as Obama signed Executive Order 13566 freezing a substantial portion of the Gaddafi government's wealth, that Levey finds the most memorable. That day, TFI made history: $30 billion was the largest sum of assets the U.S. government had ever seized.

In the decade that followed TFI's creation in 2004, the United States' ability to weaponize the dollar became the cornerstone of numerous international responses to geopolitical strife: Iran's nuclear ambitions, Russia's Obama-era incursion on Ukraine, humanitarian transgressions in Sudan and Libya, to name a few. Economic sanctions were once blunt and often inflexible instruments with mixed or poor results, such as the fifty-year countrywide embargo on Cuba. But TFI turned them into sophisticated efforts driven by financial intelligence prowess and deep cooperation between the public and private sector. Treasury, in conjunction with the State Department, the National Security Council, and the broader intelligence community, sharpened sanctions into a smart, powerful device that could be tailored to situations where diplomacy failed but military force was a step too far.

Take the economic gut punch leveled on Iran starting in 2012 to force it to rein in its nuclear ambitions. The United States first imposed unilateral sanctions on Iranian banks and businesses. When that didn't bring on any change in the nation's nuclear ambitions, American officials traveled the world to encourage the United Nations, the European Union, Canada, Australia, and even nations with traditionally deep ties to Iran such as China, Russia, and India to join their efforts to contain the global threat posed if Iran became a full-blown nuclear power. Slowly, the international pressure on Tehran grew, making financial institutions wary of doing business in the nation.

But the Obama administration needed more weaponry. From this need emerged an even more intricate and severe variation to the sanctions levied so far: secondary sanctions.

It's a low-caliber title for a high-caliber weapon, but the concept behind it is somewhat convoluted. Secondary sanctions essentially widened the net of money flowing to Iran that the United States could immobilize. While primary sanctions blacklisted bad actors of a targeted country from the U.S. financial system, this new breed of sanctions allowed the U.S. government to blacklist entities and individuals outside of that country simply for continuing to do business with the targeted nation. With Iran, primary sanctions blocked members of Iran's authoritarian regime from using the dollar. But secondary sanctions took that pressure one step further by restricting entities in jurisdictions *outside* of Iran.

Treasury's creation of secondary sanctions amounted to a crucial expansion in the dollar's weaponization. Their existence forced America's friends and foes to make a choice between their own economic trade and foreign policy goals, and access to the dollar. For most nations, it isn't worth angering Washington to continue to do business with Iran. Secondary sanctions ramped up America's already enormous power over foreign countries.

But by creating an "us versus them" foreign policy conundrum, the United States also ratcheted up the dollar's ability to fracture the global economic order, which was the opposite of what post–World War II-era economic integration sought to achieve. Countries that were tied to the U.S. dollar for economic purposes now had to consider whether their own democratic ideals aligned with America's, and what their identity was worth. Slowly, the narrative of a central player in the world abusing its power and nudging others to look for ways to live without the dollar was getting stronger. It was a shift that ran against more than a half century of establishing the dollar as unquestioned reserve currency. It would eventually make the world consider the once unthinkable—an alternative to the dollar.

Not everyone agrees that secondary sanctions, or the rise of sanctions use generally, amounts to a weaponization of the dollar. To this day, current and former government officials argue that if the United States' role as owner of the world's fiat currency is to oversee a safe flow of money around the world, it has a duty to disrupt bad behavior in the financial system to maintain its integrity—and sanctions are best used multilaterally.

U.S. economic sanctions devastated Iran. Its economic lifeblood was oil, and without a connection to the dollar (by which virtually all oil prices were settled), it had no way of selling it. The resulting 60 percent drop in Iran's most precious export led to a massive economic contraction, while its currency, the rial, lost 40 percent of its value. The price of basic necessities such as milk, fruit, and vegetables nearly doubled, driving millions of Iranians deeper into poverty.

In 2015, after intense diplomatic efforts, the United States, along with the European Union and half a dozen other nations, signed the Joint Comprehensive Plan of Action (HR JCPOA), a nuclear deal with Iran. For at least a few years (until President Trump overturned it), the Obama administration could boast that its sanctions on Iran made the world a safer place.

By this time, the United States was relying on economic sanctions to help solve more and more geopolitical scuffles. From 2001 to 2015, the Treasury department saw its issuance of new sanctions increase fourfold. These efforts included a multiyear campaign to strike damaging blows to renewable sources of revenue for Al Qaeda,

Hezbollah, the Islamic State, and others. Treasury worked with the rest of the federal government, the private sector, central banks, and foreign finance ministries of allies to develop a surgical approach to curtail terrorists' access to funding, taking a sledgehammer to each group's revenue source (like rogue charities used to launder money, a trust-based system used in Asia and the Middle East called hawala, and other financial conduits).

It was all part of a powerful mission that the Treasury department and its thousands of the dollar's stewards had taken on in absolute secret. A rare look inside the unassuming office where the dollar's blade was sharpened reveals just how rapid its evolution into a weapon of economic warfare has been.

Andrea Gacki was running one of the United States' most powerful agencies. It meant that, for hours at a time, she worked out of a decommissioned bathroom in a dusty old government building across the street from the granite porticoes and neoclassical columns of the main Treasury building. Gacki, a lawyer who is feared by thousands of foreign officials, oligarchs, business tycoons, investors, and terrorists, rarely spoke about her work in public. Even in a private setting she talked with discipline and precision—she knew too many secrets to be too chatty with anyone.

The Michigan native, with her salt-and-pepper hair, black glasses, and a love for comic books, struck an unassuming posture. Confident but always polite, firm in her convictions but not one to boast, one could never guess that the four loops she uses to sign *A. Gacki* on Treasury department stationery had the power to bring down an entire economy or a multibillion-dollar business.

Gacki is among the many custodians of the U.S. dollar who has worked tirelessly and without pomp to fortify a world that runs on dollars. The super-secretive sanctions power center that she runs, the Office of Foreign Assets Control (OFAC pronounced "oh-fack"), is often called the "beating heart of U.S. sanctions," and she and civil servants like her are crucial to its success. As director of that office during the Trump administration and first half of the Biden presidency, Gacki spent much of her day reviewing classified documents from an old toilet in the OFAC director's suite. Disemboweled of its plumbing, commode, and sink to make room for computer equipment and soundproof walls, it has morphed into what is called a sensitive compartmented information facility (SCIF, pronounced "skiff"). While there are SCIFs located across Washington in federal buildings and embassies around the world, inspected regularly and outfitted with countersurveillance measure, Gacki's may be the only one that used to be a loo.

Having spent a majority of her career in public service, she is among the thousands of nonpolitical appointees working across multiple administrations running the government. The power of OFAC is inverse to the size of its actual office. A unit of three hundred lawyers, accountants, intelligence analysts, and investigators, it can freeze assets, block companies and individuals from using the U.S. dollar, and impose fines for running afoul of its sanctions. The historic seventy-two-hour effort to lock away Gaddafi's billions of dollars that Stuart Levey oversaw is proof of how potent OFAC can be.

The office's work is one of a kind. It doesn't need legal rulings to sever anyone's access to the U.S. financial system. While the nation's courts rely on a legal standard of "beyond a reasonable doubt" to dole out punishments, Gacki's crew relied on classified information to provide "a reasonable basis" that sanctions are merited. OFAC works with the entire federal intelligence community, the State, Justice, and Defense departments, along with others, as it manages dozens of U.S. sanctions programs. Final decisions are made by presidents or their appointees, such as the secretary of Treasury or State. But they are carried out and enforced by the lawyers at OFAC. Their work is often confirmed or supported by diplomats, spies, law enforcement officials, and classified intelligence—and no one has ever sued OFAC and won.

OFAC is the keeper of the game-over blacklist of U.S. sanctions: the Specially Designated Nationals and Blocked Persons List (SDN). The addition of a new name on the SDN List posted to Treasury.gov (and scoured by businesses the world over) immediately directs banks and financial institutions to block those listed from accessing the U.S. financial system.

During a rare public speech, Gacki once described the tiny unit's role simply as "protecting the U.S. financial system from abuse." And in a town where real estate is an indication of influence, OFAC is housed in one of Washington's most unremarkable offices. Located opposite main Treasury, the hundred-year-old building is inconspicuous, to say the least. The main door announcing that you are entering the highest perch of sanctions work is a round, beige plaque around the size of a dinner plate. It features a dull green and blue silhouette of half a globe, the full name of the office curving over it. Open that first door and there might still be remnants of the 1970s green, threadbare carpet that embarrassed its workers for decades before it was finally swapped out. If you're lucky enough to secure an after-hours-only guided and guarded tour of the office, you'll find ancient signs taped to dingy cubicle walls stating NO FLOPPY DISKS allowed.

But as unpretentious as the office is by appearance, full access is for a rarefied elite: two entire floors of this building can be accessed only by those with top-secret security clearances, which are bestowed only after background checks about your character, mental stability, and trustworthiness and an extensive review of personal finances and friendships.

It has been part of government operations for decades. The United States started freezing assets as a method of economic aggression more than eighty years ago when President Franklin Roosevelt sought to keep U.S.-held assets of European governments invaded by Germany out of Nazi hands. As terror spread across Europe, Roosevelt signed an executive order in 1940 to keep billions of dollars out of the grasp of Nazis. OFAC as a unit was created a decade later during the Korean War. For the following fifty years, it was a comparatively quiet part of Treasury (some called it an orphan of the agency), mostly for blunt embargo-based actions against Cuba and others. It was out of tragic necessity after 9/11 that the Bush administration expanded sanctions authorities and brought the tiny unit into the center of the battlefield.

The power that OFACers, as some in the private sector call them, wield from this unambiguous office is palpable when they emerge from their dusty government building to meet with Wall Street executives in the sheen and shine of fancy conference rooms in Manhattan high-rises. "One visit from someone in that office can leave us in disarray for hours," shared one New York banking compliance officer. "Running afoul of OFAC is not an option." Penalties for violating sanctions levied by Gacki and her coterie of investigators are costly. BNP Paribas, a French banking behemoth, faced a record fine of $8.9 billion for violating U.S. sanctions against Sudan, Cuba, and Iran. HSBC and JPMorgan Chase have paid tens of millions of dollars in fines in recent years.

Even a tiny cosmetics company wasn't below the scrutiny of Gacki's gang. In 2019 they charged Elf Beauty, Inc., a California-based firm, for importing false eyelash kits that contained materials produced in North Korea. It was a direct violation of U.S. sanctions prohibiting any deal-making with North Korean businesses. The cosmetics company (which voluntarily disclosed the violations and created a detailed plan to avoid future ones) paid a $996,080 fine. It was, as Treasury described in a press release, a "non-egregious" transgression, but the gumshoes at OFAC found out about it nonetheless: Elf imported $4.43 million worth of fake eyelash kits from two suppliers in China, which had sourced materials from North Korea, resulting in 156 sanctions violations.

This level of precision is characteristic of any interaction with Gacki and her brand of apolitical public servant. As head of OFAC, she always knew that it would take a brisk seven-minute walk to get from her office in the Annex to that of her boss, the presidentially appointed undersecretary of Terrorism and Financial Intelligence. That walk involved zigzagging through the underground tunnels that connect the two buildings (which also connect main Treasury to the White House and are rumored to have been used to escort Marilyn Monroe into John F. Kennedy's White House). For those on the inside, Gacki could be spotted easily—sporting her comfortable, heavy-soled black flats, a pistachio green silk scarf ruffling in the air, casually holding some of the nation's most precious secrets.

As the Obama administration coped with more foreign policy problems, cavalier suggestions to solve them with sanctions increased. OFAC's programs, rolled out at a rapid pace during the Bush and

Obama administrations, were drawing demands from both the administration and Congress to turn to economic aggression to combat geopolitical problems. It was an attractive tool in large part because it offered a vast area to explore between diplomacy and war that didn't involve the sacrifice of American troops—military force could not always be the answer when diplomacy failed.

But the prospect of heavier reliance on sanctions was beginning to worry President Obama's second Treasury secretary, Jacob J. Lew. The concerns came down to a core mission of the Treasury department, which was to protect the global financial system and, by extension, the dollar. Each economic sanction that was imposed introduced a new roadblock in the flow of money around the world, making the ability to conduct business complicated. The less predictable the dollar-based system became, the more incentive other countries and businesses had to find alternatives.

And so Lew, a low-profile government technocrat whose illegible loopy signature stamped on the dollar bills drew quips from Obama, issued a stark warning for the U.S. government. "The more we condition use of the dollar and our financial system on adherence to U.S. foreign policy, the more the risk of migration to other currencies and other financial systems in the medium-term grows," he said. He went on to lay out how "overuse" of this tool could undermine the United States' superpower status. "Our central role [in the global economy] must not be taken for granted."

What Lew seemed to be telling the world was that the dollar itself was at a tipping point as a weapon. For more than a century, the U.S. Department of the Treasury worked to smooth the flow of money around the world, eventually achieving the status of ruler of the entire economic system the world relied on. That status was turned into a weapon when the George W. Bush administration used the dollar to protect the nation from a threat on its own soil in 2001. And after two failed wars (Iraq and Afghanistan), the prospect of successful kinetic action was waning. The Obama years saw a preference for fighting with money, not young men and women, so this new tool of financial warfare was given more spikes.

But Jack Lew could not have known just how prescient his warning would become in the years ahead. His words demanding more "strategic and judicious" applications of sanctions were delivered on March 30, 2016, mere weeks after a temperamental candidate was cemented as a surprising front-runner for the Republican Party's nominee for president. In less than a year, the potent weapon that the dollar had become would be in the hands of a strongman leader unafraid of confrontation and who ignored nuance and often aimed to shock.

A new administration would soon be in charge of the mighty dollar.

13.

A TURBULENT
MARRIAGE

Tim Geithner came into the Treasury department as a secretary with a profound understanding of Eastern mores. As a child living in India, he played Holi during the annual Festival of Love, tossing vibrant green, red, and yellow powders onto his family. His high school alma mater is the International School of Bangkok. And over a few summers in Beijing during his college years, he learned enough Mandarin to quote Chinese proverbs.

With that background, Geithner's first interaction with counterparts from the region should have been easy, despite being sworn in as Treasury secretary in the throes of the financial crisis. His predecessor, Hank Paulson, had created the healthiest relationship the two nations had enjoyed in decades. He accomplished that, in part, by neutralizing the protectionist pressure from the U.S. Congress that would have caused damage to China's economy in the midst of a thirty-year cultural and economic transformation. In return, Beijing had allowed the yuan to appreciate 21 percent over the previous two years. As Geithner came into office, the economies of the two nations were deeply intertwined. The trade relationship was worth $28.9 trillion, and China had just become the largest investor in U.S. federal debt (surpassing Japan). China held $628 billion in Treasuries, and another $1.7 trillion in Fannie Mae and Freddie Mac debt, meaning it had significant investments in America's housing sector. That made the United States dependent on the Chinese to keep up its purchases of federal debt to help maintain the credibility of the world's safest asset. American officials needed to handle talks with those in Beijing with great care.

But Geithner goofed up.

Before he could impress his new counterparts with his Mandarin, and even before he'd raised his right hand and pledged to support and defend the U.S. Constitution as secretary of the Treasury (even before that disastrous Cash Room speech), he briefly and accidentally triggered a complete about-face in the United States' stance toward China. It happened in the exhaustion of the first week of the new administration. While Beyoncé was performing at Barack Obama's inauguration ball on January 20, Geithner was preoccupied by the grilling he would get the following day during his confirmation hearing. Completely separate from the topic of China, Geithner first had to deal with something that had cropped up during the financial vetting process of his nomination.

The Senate discovered that Geithner had failed to pay $34,000 in taxes to the Internal Revenue Service due to a mix-up when using TurboTax software a few years back. He wasn't looking forward to having to admit that oversight, and as he feared, it was contentious, a reflection of the economic pain that plagued a nation unable to see what lay ahead. The hearing included a heavy dose of political the-ater, as one senator accused him of "negligence" over his taxes, while repeatedly calling him "Mr. Gitner."

Once the public hazing had concluded, his transition team was handed 289 written questions from members of the Senate Finance Committee. They had just seventeen hours to type up responses as the Senate tried to move Geithner's confirmation vote to the floor quickly, to get him into the Treasury secretary's chair amid the eco-nomic crisis. In a mad early-morning rush, an aide made a mistake that would precipitate the new secretary's first diplomatic gaffe: rather than use what Geithner himself later called a "diplomatic dodge" to get around answering a request from the Democratic senator Chuck Schumer to explain the new administration's stance on China's cur-rency policy, the aide slotted in Obama's fiery campaign rhetoric. "President Obama—backed by the conclusions of a broad range of economists—believes that China is manipulating its currency," read Geithner's reply to the senators (it was later leaked to the press).

With that one sentence, Geithner made an indictment loaded with foreign and economic policy implications. Just as Washington needed to rely on a strong alliance with Beijing to help keep the world econ-omy afloat, Geithner brought the United States to the brink by pub-licly shaming Beijing over its currency policy. While he never intended to make a substantial shift in U.S.-Sino policy in such an indirect man-ner, particularly when Americans were hungry for a shot of strong leadership in the face of the trials ahead, Geithner appeared ready to bulldoze Paulson's policy of diplomacy over confrontation with China.

Investors panicked. As his statement reached markets, a drop in Treasuries sent yields on benchmark 10-year notes to 2.63 percent, the highest level in six weeks. Traders were shedding Treasuries out of fear that a spat between the two powerhouses would undermine their cooperation to counter the global recession. Perhaps it would even drive China to dump some of its own holdings of those bonds, a sell-off that would drive down their value.

The Chinese government reacted quickly and fiercely. "This kind of wrong accusation against China on exchange rate issues will intensify protectionism within the U.S., and will not help resolve the problem," its Commerce Ministry said. A top central bank official said Geithner's allegations were "untrue and misleading."

The episode illustrates the deep-rooted fear among global investors of a fight between the world's two largest economies, with interdependencies and rivalries borne of their contradictory views on governance but shared ambition to expand influence. It was anxiety that crept into how senior U.S. Treasury officials dealt with key economic issues with China for the preceding years, and it continued to serve as the mood music for the next decade.

The risks of a falling-out were huge. In early 2009, America was the single largest buyer of Chinese exports, which helped China grow at a double-digit pace (at least before the financial crisis). In turn, Beijing invested the surplus earnings from selling goods such as toys, clothing, and steel by purchasing Treasury bonds. In 2008 alone it boosted its purchases by 46 percent, making America even more vulnerable to this foreign powerhouse. It was committed to soaking up more American debt so long as the U.S. dollar continued to be the safest bet.

To maintain the unique nature of the relationship, America needed the Chinese to keep buying U.S. Treasuries to fund the drastic stimulus spending necessary to dig itself—and the world—out of recession.

Even a whisper that China might pare back its investments had the potential to sink the value of U.S. government debt, as was evident from the drop in Treasuries when Geithner mistakenly called China a currency manipulator in written testimony. To get through the crisis, investors needed to be 100 percent certain that American credit would remain liquid and practically endless—meaning China had a role to play in protecting the dollar. As Secretary of State Hillary Clinton put it in her first trip to China in 2009, the Chinese needed to carry on with its "very smart decision" to keep buying American bonds. A recovery in the United States would fuel China's growth as well, she said.

With U.S.-China ties integral to the global recovery, in 2009, Geithner needed to strike a tone of equals in his rhetoric both publicly and privately. To that end, he was able to leverage the trust that Paulson had built up with China through the Strategic Economic Dialogue. It led to China's much-needed support for the United States' rescue framework for Fannie Mae and Freddie Mac, since Beijing was a large investor in the two mortgage companies. When the subprime mortgage crisis hit, Fannie and Freddie had $5.4 trillion in securities connected to it, 30 percent of which was held by the Chinese. Officials in Beijing were gravely concerned about the value of their investment, and the U.S. Department of the Treasury had to keep Chinese leadership apprised of their plans and how they were navigating the political theater around it in the U.S. Congress.

The financial crisis only magnified how closely knitted together the two had become. Cooperation would make them both winners. China's economic recovery relied on Americans eating up its exports, and America needed China to keep soaking up its debt as it spent its way through the crisis.

China's currency had become the ultimate trade weapon, supporting its economic ambitions. A highly undervalued renminbi caused a surging current account surplus and a humongous bilateral surplus with America. Even when it belatedly let its currency rise, the central bank continued adding massively to its foreign exchange reserves, slowing the currency's rise. This behavior created huge distortions in the pattern of global trade, hurt many U.S. manufacturing firms and took away U.S. jobs, and generated severe protectionist pressures in America.

China was also becoming more brazen as the world dealt with the American-brewed global financial crisis. The overlords of the U.S. dollar had made huge mistakes, and allies were now paying for them through blowback from the financial meltdown. China's high exposure to dollar-denominated financial assets was damaging to the nation, boosting the case that countries should wean themselves off their dollar addiction. Sick and tired of bullying from America on its currency regime, in 2009 China's central banker called for a "super sovereign reserve currency" to be housed in the International Monetary Fund, to replace the dollar. The concept went nowhere, but it was the introduction to a concept that for decades was considered inconceivable: a world not reliant on the dollar.

For the sake of playing the role of the responsible parent, America declined to designate China a currency manipulator in order to maintain market stability, especially after the havoc of the financial crisis. For years this had been one of the characteristics of how the two nations differed: one was willing to blatantly weaponize its economy and population to achieve global ambitions, the other used a

softer touch and tried to work for the greater good. While U.S. officials set aside the problems for this reason or that (think of Hank
Paulson's explanations of a slow evolution for the Chinese economy,
or Geithner's efforts to barter as he navigated the financial crisis),
China got busy with the business of making real things in their growing number of factories. While Washington's political establishment
chose to disregard insecurities that were breeding just beneath the
surface of a rusting manufacturing sector, the financial elite were
cooking up a crisis and a recession that few could explain and even
fewer could understand. Millions of Americans were in pain. The
topic of China as a currency cheat had become a perennial note to hit
on the domestic campaign trail, because it was one that resonated
with both Democrats and Republicans. And so, from 2000 onward,
China's foreign exchange manipulation became the poster child on
campaign trails across the country for an American currency regime
with no teeth, driving the decline of the nation's manufacturing sector. (Of course, deindustrialization in advanced economies had been
going on for years.)

In the two years since the start of the financial crisis, the yuan had
lost nearly 7 percent of its value against the dollar. Economists started
issuing reports laying out the belief that the yuan's persistent depreciation was faked, leading to it being "undervalued" by anywhere from
12 to 50 percent (a wide range reflecting how difficult it is to determine what its value would be if it was allowed to float freely).

With the U.S. economy in pain (the jobless rate was just shy of 10
percent in early 2010 because of the global financial crisis), a New
York Democrat and a South Carolina Republican doubled down on
joint efforts to try to bully China into better behavior. Chuck Schumer
talked of economists' rulings of undervaluation being the "smoking

gun" that proved Beijing's cheating ways, and Lindsey Graham said he was "fed up." For years, the pair had been trying to correct China's behavior. During Paulson's era, they'd advocated for an enormous tariff on Beijing's exports to the United States, 27.5 percent. Beijing was trying to cushion its economy from the fallout of the economic crisis, and it was unfair to American workers, they said. They rallied more than a dozen of their colleagues to put forth legislation that would slap tariffs on Chinese exports if the nation failed to let its currency rise in value.

Instead of seeing the story of American hardship that was evident between the lines of the lawmakers' proposal, Geithner (just like Paulson before him) put his efforts toward burying that legislation. They were both successful, but the reckoning would come soon enough when the 2016 race for president began.

For the most part, the Obama administration was fearful of the trade war that the measures suggested by Schumer and Graham would almost certainly trigger. The problem was, the economies of the United States and China were so interlinked that inflicting the shame of currency manipulation on one would damage the economic interests of the other, not to mention aggravate a global financial crisis they were only just recovering from.

But there was one person inside of the U.S. Treasury department who felt differently.

The daughter of an American diplomat, Lael Brainard grew up in West Germany before the fall of the Berlin Wall, and then Poland. She followed her father's footsteps and entered public service, and in 2010, she became the custodian of one of the most beautiful offices in

America's capital. Decorated with lush dark blue drapes and matching carpet adorned with neat rows of bright golden-yellow stars, the Treasury department's Andrew Johnson Suite was used by its namesake when he took office after Abraham Lincoln's assassination in 1865. Brainard was Treasury's undersecretary for international affairs, a job once held by economic patriciates like Paul Volcker and John Taylor.

Brainard also became a custodian of the nation's currency policy. As she sat in that office, next to a replica of a Civil War–era Treasury Guard Flag that represented a militia formed to protect Washington from Confederates, it was chock-full of political tensions. While President Obama favored a softer approach to curbing China's interventionist currency regime, he still was aware of the significant problem that it posed. With almost every nation battling their way through the Great Recession, unorthodox monetary policies from central banks in Europe, Japan, and at home (the United States cut rates before most others) began shifting currency values with alarming volatility. Some referred to the interest rate cuts and flood of money into the economy as stimulus, and others called it a currency war.

It was in this context that Brainard was keen to brand China a currency manipulator, a move that the United States had not done since 1994 (even when the charge was clearly warranted). Behind the scenes, she worked to convince her boss, Geithner, and officials on the National Security Council at the White House to use Treasury's semiannual foreign exchange policy report to do just that.

But she was overruled at every turn, even in the face of naked and persistent currency manipulation by China. American policy toward the nation actually went in the opposite direction, with Geithner trying to stave off more congressional demands to find ways to punish China. The reasons for this are complex: Obama's economic team had their hands full and couldn't take on yet another fight. Brainard disagreed, but never allowed her opposition to spill into public view, sticking instead to the administration's official line that the United States had made "measurable gains" in U.S. exports to China without the drama that would come with Treasury's much-feared report on currency policy. Publicly, Geithner did what he could, urging China to unpeg its currency from the dollar (which it did for two years beginning in mid-2008).

During her tenure from 2010 to 2013, Brainard oversaw eight reports reviewing the currency practices of major trading partners, and cleared China of manipulation in each of them. The documents noted China's lack of transparency and said the yuan was "significantly undervalued," and noted that Treasury would "closely monitor" Beijing's activities. Brainard used her public speeches to talk about how incremental progress from China "does not mean we are satisfied," while Geithner seemed to join up with the Federal Reserve chair Ben Bernanke to repeat criticisms and boost the economic soundness of a currency set free. It added up to diplomatic speak to say, *We know what you're up to.* But the U.S. government stopped at words.

As Geithner and Brainard exited the administration in 2013, they handed the perennial China problem to new officials who picked up where they'd left off. Obama-era officials would probably call it strategic patience, but most others thought of it as willful neglect.

Protectionism was once again roaring in Congress, but like the last time, not much would change.

"The single biggest step we could take today to create jobs in American manufacturing is to tackle China's currency manipulation,"

Senator Schumer said in June 2013, just a few months after Jacob J. Lew became the nation's seventy-sixth Treasury chief. Senator Max Baucus, a Democrat from Montana, wanted the United States to go back to the business of "making things" in the "real world," not opaque financial products that had now wreaked havoc in ways most couldn't understand.

Baucus's comments echo precisely what he said to George W. Bush's first Treasury secretary, Paul O'Neill, in January 2001. Not much had changed in two decades, in which politicians and policymakers had been given chances to ease the woes of the American working class but looked away. A decade earlier, O'Neill had been cast as a loner in economic and financial circles for talking about the importance of a world in which real things are made in factories—paper, metal, toys, clothes, etc.—and for chafing against the strong dollar paradigm that undermined that world. As it turned out, he was right about the failings of that policy and the urgent need to address them.

The reckoning for years of strategic patience with China across two presidencies, as Treasury secretaries killed lawmakers' attempts to fight back on behalf of America's disgruntled blue-collar workers, would come as the next presidential cycle kicked off. Beginning with the "escalator ride that changed America," in 2015, America's political landscape would become a stage for bombastic, anti-China slogans from an iconoclastic billionaire who drew thousands to his rallies. American voters would soon hear charges that China was "raping our country." By contrast, the scene unfolding in Washington's upper echelons could not have been more mundane.

The second half of the Obama presidency saw a new Treasury chief take over the China file: Jack Lew. In those final years of the administration, the United States continued to spend its way into a sustained economic recovery, and China's own convalescence was a weak one.

Meanwhile, the initial round of China policy experts that President Obama had hired had left by 2014. Instead of a Treasury chief who had picked up Mandarin in Beijing (as Geithner did), it was budget expert Jack Lew running the agency. The new secretary of state, John Kerry, was focused on peace in the Middle East. Perhaps most alarming of all was the ambassador to China, former Senator Max Baucus, who, as he stepped into his new job, made the jaw-dropping comment that he was "no real expert on China." His long-standing friendship with then Vice President Joe Biden landed him the job, despite the fact that Baucus spoke no Mandarin, unlike most of his predecessors.

With the Hank Paulson–era strategic talks with China now passed down to Lew, the third Treasury secretary to run the dialogue, which had devolved into a somber therapy session between the two nations that ended with a group picture. Once again, China was giving hours-long lectures to Treasury officials about the impact of the Opium Wars in the 1800s on China's centuries-long policy horizon to recover from the shame of Western powers, then led by Britain. One of those group pictures during the final years was taken in the lush surroundings of the eight-hundred-year-old imperial gardens at the historic Diaoyutai State Guesthouse, nestled among gurgling streams, willows, and green pines.

It was a far cry from Smalltown, USA, where empty factories were gathering rust and dust and neighborhoods were falling into disrepair (this deindustrialization was part of a global trend, although such practices made the matter worse). The strategic talks became a lavish celebration of what Lew applauded as "incremental" progress on currency matters and other topics, a notion buried in a 6,589-word statement released to the public. It was an affair that didn't register with the working class, adding to the impression that their fortunes were being decidedly set aside. Meanwhile, the presumptive Democratic candidate for president, Hillary Clinton, was entering the scene with speeches strong on philosophical references to President Franklin Roosevelt from the 1930s, but distinctly lacking reference to globalization's failings. Economists were still closing ranks when talking about the pitfalls of free trade, largely out of fear of giving ammunition to protectionists.

For the down-on-their-luck Americans in the middle, so-called fly-over states, there was just one candidate among nearly two dozen who was willing to point to a villain responsible for their demise. Sure, others who had made it to the White House had shown shades of brazenness as they slammed China while on the campaign trail. But this time, they came from a wilder source, someone who wasn't from the stuffy confines of Washington's inbred establishment.

"We must stand up to China's blackmail and reject corporate America's manipulation of our politicians," said this new politician (if you could call him that—he certainly didn't). He was tall and on the heavy side but dressed in a well-cut suit and a wide, bright red tie. Each rant about China drew wild cheers from jam-packed venues. "We have been too afraid to protect and advance American interests and to challenge China to live up to its obligations."

Donald Trump had a unique method to assess what his supporters wanted from their government. To build a policy platform as he started on the path toward the presidency in 2015 consisted of trial and error during ad-libbed speeches delivered in places like Gary,

Indiana. The level of glee expressed at these rallies became a barometer against which policies were measured. The ecstatic sonic pleasure expressed by the audience was converted directly into border security, abortion, and legal policy. When the Trump campaign said that "the U.S. Treasury's designation of China as a currency manipulator will force China to the negotiating table and open the door to a fair—and far better—trading relationship" and heard the crowd react with jubilation, he knew he was on to something. He listened, very carefully, to his supporters, eschewing the usual focus groups and poll data that costly strategists compiled in their offices. Criticizing China became a staple of his campaign speeches, and talk of 45 percent tariffs on the nation's goods delivered into the United States drew adulation.

Fresh polling provided additional assurance, with one from 2016 showing that almost two-thirds of Americans wanted more restrictions, like tariffs, on imported goods, and 82 percent saying they were willing to pay a bit more for American-made goods if it meant saving American jobs.

Trump saw what others had missed: Economic anxiety had been building for years. In the preceding two decades 5.5 million manufacturing jobs had disappeared, a long-running decline that started in the 1980s and deepened after 2000. While factories had hired workers during the Obama years, it wasn't enough to reverse the protracted losses that hit communities across the Rust Belt and South especially hard, and it was clear that the pain wasn't equally spread around the country. The median income of middle-class households in 2016 was roughly the same as in 2000, while upper-income households had seen an increase. And in that period, the ruling class in Washington and on Wall Street had either ignored that damage or pretended that it was being cured by a redistribution in the labor market. In the meantime, they enjoyed bailouts from Washington when the global financial crisis they caused came to the fore.

For Trump's burgeoning base, where unemployment rates had been higher than the national average during most of the Great Recession, his talk of China as the bogeyman struck a chord.

As establishment politicians and urban voters digested Trump's emergence as the Republican candidate for president, data revealed that roughly half of the counties that supported him in the primaries were still in recession when they cast their vote in 2016, while the rest of the country was experiencing a roughly 2 percent expansion. In fact, new research served to confirm what a lot of ordinary people had been saying all along: free trade, while good overall, harms workers who are exposed to low-wage competition from abroad.

To the millions of voters that favored Trump, it didn't matter that fiscal policy levers available to a president were ill-equipped to reinstate America as a global manufacturing center. They had been lied to by politicians for decades, told by the so-called elites that globalization was in their best interests, only to be decimated by it. Perhaps this new guy, who wasn't really from the swamp of lobbyists that Washington had become, would come through.

During one trip to Nevada in February of 2016, the comments drew roars from the nearly 10,000 people at rallies in Reno and Las Vegas. One such comment: "We're going to take our jobs back from China and all these other countries." His message resonated in a state that, just five years earlier, had the highest unemployment rate in the nation. But while rhetoric blaming China for the decline of the American working class played well on the campaign trail, it belied the reality of their codependent and heavily intertwined economies.

Nevada's economy had grown increasingly hooked to investment from abroad, with Chinese commerce boosting the state's tourism and mining industries, not to mention China's backing of a new $1 billion auto plant, and a new casino. By the time Trump visited, China had become Nevada's second-largest trading partner, with exports of metals, pharmaceuticals, and the like jumping 61 percent. The state went from having one of the highest home foreclosure rates in the country to having the tenth-strongest economic recovery, in large part due to Chinese investment.

But despite all its contradictions, a wave of anti-globalization sentiment heralded a new leader. The stark contrast between Trump and what the ruling political class was doing only invigorated his base, who couldn't connect to what Obama and Clinton were talking about. The sitting administration was trapped in procedural affairs where smiling in a group photograph with foreign leaders and getting twenty signatures on a multigovernment communique appeared to be more important than listening to America's heartland.

The starkness between Obama's erudite and distant views of China policy, delivered in carefully written scripts, and Trump's off-the-cuff pronouncements and astute ability to read the mood music of the electorate persisted throughout 2016.

On July 24, Secretary of the Treasury Jack Lew busied himself with G20 meetings, where the gang of finance ministers and central bankers gathered in Chengdu, China, and pledged to "reject protectionism, promote global trade and investment, [and ensure] broad-based public support for expanded growth in a globalized economy." These were all euphemisms that allowed China to wait out the United States. China, with its authoritarian leadership, had its century-long outlook to nurture, and it wasn't worth shifting those plans because of the demands of an American politician whose job and power was subject to the whims of democracy that changed the constellation of power every two years.

Hours after that G20 agreement was signed, Trump appeared on NBC's *Meet the Press* from New York, making comments that threatened the core principles that world leaders were so afraid to stray from. "We're going to renegotiate [America's trade deals] or we're going to pull out," Trump said, referring to the World Trade Organization. It was a stunning statement. The idea of the United States withdrawing from a group whose roots traced back to the global peace treaties of the post–World War II era was unthinkable. And here was Trump, calling the WTO "a disaster."

Once again, Trump's words acknowledged the tribulations of America's forgotten man, while the Obama administration left the working class as a mere four-word clause tucked amid a banal sentence in a 3,311-word statement from the G20: "But also for workers."

It was only more of an opening for Trump. "The single biggest weapon used against us and to destroy our companies is devaluation of currencies, and the greatest ever at that is China. . . . It is time we make America great again!"

Trump's dark views of a crumbling U.S. economy resonated with roughly 63 million Americans who supported him on November 8, 2016, an Election Day that ended in shock around the world. While his opponent, Hillary Clinton, bragged about the successes of the Obama administration that she was once a part of, Trump tapped into the pent-up frustration of blue-collar workers who had seen stagnant wage growth and trade-related job losses that had reversed an entire generation's climb into the middle class. These workers, squeezed by the rising costs of health care, childcare, and college while having to save more for retirement, felt left behind in Obama's economic revival and ignored by the future Clinton offered. Never mind that the popular vote supported Clinton for president—with a margin of 2.1 percent votes. It was apparent how deeply divided America had become.

Once he became president, Trump immediately showed that he was going to make good on his promises. As a candidate, he had complained that China's negotiation tactics proved that they were "very smart, they are like grand chess masters. And we are like checkers players—but bad ones." And so he tapped longtime China hard-liners as senior advisers and cabinet officers (including one who'd written a book called *Death by China*). With anti-globalists and a volatile president now in the White House, the United States' global role as consensus builder would quickly evaporate.

14.

A TREASURY
HEIRLOOM
SHATTERED

Hollywood producer. A billionaire vulture capitalist with an eye for scooping up companies on the brink of demise. An economist who invented a fake expert to cite in his books. Brought together by a reality TV host, this was the team stepping in as financial and economic masters of the most powerful nation on Earth. And they were running amok.

"You look at what China's doing, you look at what Japan has done over the years. They play the money market, they play the devaluation market. . . . And we sit there like a bunch of dummies," Donald Trump said nine days after he was sworn in as president of the United States, referring to the Asian nations' habit of aggressively forcing down the value of their currencies through purchases in foreign exchange markets.

It was rhetoric that was unheard of from an American president, but it was emblematic of the nationalist America First agenda that carried Trump to power and of his complete disregard for tradition. (Only days earlier, he had tried to institute the infamous "Muslim ban," a failed attempt to block immigrants from certain countries.) The economic and financial literati were appalled at Trump's impromptu policy pronouncements but had little time to recover—he wasn't the only one in his administration who would be talking about currency policy. A day or so after his initial missive, Peter Navarro, the White House's new top trade adviser, went on Fox News to proclaim that the euro was "grossly undervalued." Then his colleague, Wilbur Ross, set off a brief drop in the values of the Mexican peso and the Canadian dollar when he said that as Commerce secretary, he would renegotiate trade deals with America's neighbors.

Even Steven Mnuchin (pronounced "mah-noo-shin," although some lawmakers never got the hang of it and called him "Mr. Munkin"), drove down the greenback when he noted that an "excessively strong" dollar could actually hurt the U.S. economy.

For the first time in almost forty years, the United States had an administration openly pining for a weak dollar.

In Trump's view, the country had tolerated currency manipulations from the ranks of its closest trade partners for too long. It was part of a long-held economic philosophy that he had nurtured, since his days in the real estate business in the 1980s, that pointed to a weaker dollar. But by abandoning decades of verbal discipline, Trump and his staff were eroding America's credibility. They were also putting at risk the stability of the global foreign exchange market that Treasury secretaries through the late 1980s and 1990s had fought hard for, along with the predictable policymaking environment that hundreds of multinational corporations came to expect from the owner of the world's most important currency. Much like its democracy,

America's stewardship of the dollar was based on the nation having dependable economic leaders. And in the same way that Trump's exceedingly wild governing style would raise questions about America's endurance as a world power, his bellicosity would elicit questions of how much longer the buck could reign supreme.

It all started with words. The freewheeling talk around U.S. currency policy was among the first clear symptoms of Trump's desire to redo the world economic order. The problem was that this chatter was only going to undermine Trump's ability to get other nations to stop cheating in the currency game. It threatened to unsettle markets so much that investors feared a return to the rampant currency interventions of the 1980s—or worse, a full-blown currency war.

Bob Rubin's strong dollar paradigm was dead.

"This is my only demand: please don't criticize our currency."

It was a harsh message and it came from a longtime American ally. The unflappable Angela Merkel, Germany's leader, had to quickly adjust to a completely new style of leadership from the United States. She was impelled to publicly reject Trump's accusations that her country was cheating in foreign exchange markets. It was the kind of disagreement between friends that, in the pre-Trump era, would have been resolved behind closed doors. But American diplomacy had changed.

Trump had levied the charge at Germany and others throughout his presidential campaign, and was now making the accusations from his new perch at the White House. Merkel reminded Trump that foreign exchange markets in her country, like in his, worked independently from the political whims of elected leaders. She wasn't the only one having to remind him of this very basic principle of free markets. Fearing a massive policy shift that could lead the new U.S. administration to pursue a weaker greenback and, in turn, damage the Japanese economy heavily reliant on selling goods to American consumers, Finance Minister Tarō Asō sought assurances from the new administration that it would abide by long-held global commitments of nonintervention.

With each rebuke, foreign powers told the United States exactly what it had itself preached for decades.

"The change in Washington puts the European Union in a difficult situation, with the new administration seeming to put into question the last 70 years of American foreign policy," the head of the European Council, Donald Tusk, said within days of Trump taking office. The new president was challenging every pillar of a world standard that could be traced back to the post–World War II era, like America's commitment to the World Trade Organization and other multination pacts that encouraged shared commerce and open trade.

What was lost in Trump's barbs was that his administration's general hostility toward the post–World War II global economic system was related to a desire to help those American workers whom globalization had failed to account for. A lot had happened since the North American Free Trade Agreement was sealed and China entered into the World Trade Organization. While most economists and corporations celebrated the endless supply of cheap labor from China that could trade more easily with the rest of the world, American leaders largely did not acknowledge that the economy could not handle moving a couple million factory workers from one sector to another. The job losses were heavily concentrated in areas that became

Trump's base: small- and medium-sized towns dotted across America's heartland. It was a lesson that was there for all to see and learn, whether through the obliteration of the steel industry that supported the town of Weirton, West Virginia, or the Chinese takeover of an almost historic manufacturing plant in Moraine, Ohio.

Trump was the only presidential candidate in years to directly address the pain of people in Rust Belt states who had been left behind. He was the only one who dared to talk about turning the economic gaze inward, unafraid of turning tradition on its head or of risking chaos in the world economic order. "We've built up these other nations, and now it's time that we rebuild our own country."

The strong dollar mantra, and the globalization that it held up, had decimated American manufacturing, and the new president vowed to change the fortunes of those families.

Geoffrey William Seiji Okamoto had just shipped his black BMW X3 to California when David Malpass called him. An economist who was helping arrange the transition from the Obama Treasury department to the incoming Trump one, Malpass wanted to offer Okamoto a job. The pair had crossed paths when Okamoto was an intern in the Bush White House. Okamoto, an Eagle Scout who grew up on the West Coast, canceled his plans to leave Washington (his SUV made a U-turn) and joined Mnuchin's Treasury as an acting assistant secretary for international finance.

As Okamoto helped navigate the new Treasury team through the early days of a very chaotic administration, Andy Baukol, a civil servant, approached him with a request. Too many people were talking about the U.S. dollar, Baukol said. The Treasury department should be the lead voice—preferably the only voice—for the administration on currency issues, he said. "It's an important principle," he added, "and a sensitive topic for markets." The message the civil service had for the Trump administration was, essentially, to follow the Bob Rubin rule: don't talk about a particular exchange rate for the dollar at any given moment. Like an Olympic torch, it was a message Baukol and his fellow Treasury courtiers had carried forth from one administration to the next.

Okamoto couldn't help but let out a chuckle. The request presumed the capacity for more coordination than the Trump administration would ever have.

Baukol, a former CIA analyst, had worked in the federal government for more than three decades. Since joining Treasury in the 1990s, he had filled in senior posts in government while presidential nominees awaited senate confirmation. In addition, he performed the duties that came with his permanent job as an apolitical staffer, like principal deputy assistant secretary for international monetary policy. Part of the job of such "career professionals," as they often refer to themselves, is to keep the gears turning in times of transition. To that end, Baukol kept a four-inch binder filled with five hundred pages of briefing documents on pertinent macroeconomic and geopolitical issues, through which he supported incoming political officials when an administration changed hands. While there is no section in this binder dedicated specifically to U.S. dollar policy, it does include how to handle the market sensitive topic of foreign exchange rates and the like, laying out the language that has been used by previous secretaries and options for the new secretary.

Baukol and his colleagues participated in more than a hundred meetings during the roughly eight-day transition time between Election Day and Inauguration Day.

"It's the secretary of the Treasury who is the administration's liaison to the Federal Reserve, to finance ministries in other countries, and multilateral organizations like the World Bank and the International Monetary Fund," said John Weeks, who served alongside Baukol as a bureaucrat for seventeen years. "That's why it's the secretary of the Treasury who should be the one—and the only one—to talk about things such as currency matters." It was the job of Treasury's civil service to protect and shepherd the dollar through the turbulence of a new administration getting its bearings, according to Weeks. "And we needed to ensure that the secretary's authority on U.S. currency policy was preserved."

Serving as crucial protectors of America's distinguished currency regime, Baukol and Weeks had given a currency primer to dozens of incoming political officials over the years. In fact, they kept a one-page memo as a mission statement that can be traced back to James Baker's time as secretary during the Reagan administration. During the Obama administration, a half-page iteration of that letter was shared with Tim Geithner and others. Early in the Trump administration, Weeks provided a version of it to Okamoto with the hopes of imbuing some stability in how the new group talked about currencies.

Okamoto gave it a shot. He went directly to Peter Navarro and to Wilbur Ross, gently requesting that they not only refrain from making market sensitive comments themselves, but help persuade the commander in chief to hold back, too.

It didn't work.

A world order arranged around the U.S. dollar was headed into gloomy territory. The Bob Rubin exemplar of discipline and thoughtfulness in public commentary on markets and currencies was set to be obliterated, and leaders from Japan to Europe were trying to figure out how to respond. Somewhat ironically, they quickly rallied around the same demand that the likes of Rubin, Hank Paulson, and Tim Geithner once had of them: don't talk about your exchange rate.

By March 2017, it was China that was defending that regime. Currency complaints and the threat of trade wars from the new American president were making global economic affairs the most toxic they had been in decades.

Mirroring the language that Paulson had used a decade earlier to persuade Beijing to join the global economic world order, Chinese Finance Minister Xiao Jie publicly implored Mnuchin, his American counterpart at Treasury: the world's largest economies should be "adamantly against" protectionism, especially with regards to its currency policy.

Okamoto would go on to serve as a trusted confidant to the Treasury secretary within the Trump administration, at times standing in for Mnuchin at G7 and G20 meetings. (Trump would later place him as the number-two official at the International Monetary Fund.) But he was never able to instill the currency calm that the civil servants at Treasury urged. American-driven unity and multilateralism was not in the cards for the next four years, and on economic policy, Trump's Treasury chief would bear the brunt of the world's confusion and ire over America's new mission.

For Steven Mnuchin's boss, the world was made up of two kinds of people: winners and losers. Donald Trump governed as if he was still the judge on *The Apprentice*, a reality TV show where a loser was kicked off each week. With top White House advisers often learning they'd been sacked on Twitter, the turnover rate was 92 percent at one point. Trump's view of the world was colored by old-fashioned, American business terms: a zero-sum game where there was no victory without being able to stand over the conquered and gloat. It wasn't enough for him to win, his opponent had to actively lose. So when Mnuchin hosted his first formal economic meeting with Chinese counterparts in 2017, his team knew that they had to orchestrate the one-day affair so that it ended with a win for the Trump administration. It was set to be the latest iteration of Hank Paulson's original Strategic Economic Dialogue, but the tone would be very, very different.

Early on July 17, with 90-degree heat already bearing down onto the nation's capital with the swamp-like humidity that chases residents out of town each summer, just over a dozen Chinese officials walked into 1500 Pennsylvania Avenue. Mnuchin's Treasury department was as neutral a turf as China could ask for. Because of Paulson's economic forums, Beijing's diplomats were familiar with the black-and-white-checkered marble that paved the hallways. It helped that Mnuchin was referred to by Trump's aides as a Democrat and "globalist" (albeit pejoratively) simply because he wasn't supportive of their idea of destroying the U.S. relationship with Beijing as a way to rebalance trade. The Chinese were well aware of Mnuchin's mindfulness of disruption in global markets, and found some solace in it.

Mnuchin had already decided what he wanted to achieve from the meeting. In a bid to open up the nation to opportunities for growth for American companies, he planned to push China to lift foreign ownership restrictions in its financial services industry and remove hurdles for information and technology sectors. But before the top officials seated inside Treasury's Cash Room that day even settled back into their chairs after opening remarks, a set of unusually blunt and public words from an American official brought an end to the meeting.

"If this were just the natural product of free-market forces, we could understand it, but it's not," Commerce Secretary Wilbur Ross said in his televised speech as Chinese Vice Premier Wang Yang looked on. "So it's time to rebalance in our trade and investment relationship in a more fair, equitable and reciprocal manner." Ross went on to scold the visiting Chinese officials over their $309 billion trade surplus with the United States, completely offending the visitors from Beijing. Vice Premier Wang was taken aback by being invited into Treasury just to be confronted with an open display of antipathy, and quickly warned that confrontation would "immediately damage" the interests of both global powers. In an unprecedented turn of events, joint statements and the family photo were canceled to limit the embarrassment that China experienced.

Ross's brash criticism of China marked a departure from past versions of the economic dialogue, where the two sides pledged to deepen their relationship as they talked of working through their differences. But whether the meeting was a "win" for the U.S. side depended on who you asked. Mnuchin cast it as a success, saying that the Trump team achieved a "very big step forward" in tackling the trade deficit. Beijing had "heard the direction of the marching orders" that Trump had given them, he said. But officials in Beijing were unaccustomed to "marching orders" from a foreign leader.

The ritual of meeting and talking with the Chinese about economic issues through a carefully nurtured dialogue that Paulson launched a decade ago had shriveled.

For the next eleven months, officials from the two sides barely spoke. Stock markets would gyrate throughout Trump's four years as president as he conducted policy via Twitter, with traders swooning at every whiff of detente or escalation. The president's harsh stance garnered applause even from Chuck Schumer, the Democratic senator who openly loathed everything Trump did and said. There were moments where China got a reprieve, but it all depended on who was "up" and who was "down" in the Oval Office brawls that Trump enjoyed as he decided on policy. His trade adviser, Peter Navarro, fought hard to force the Treasury department to brandish the currency manipulation charge, efforts that Mnuchin staved off, at least for a while. Internal battles over how to punish China for past transgressions broke out into the public as Trump's frustrated team leaked information to reporters.

Volatility in policymaking during the Trump presidency extended to all levels of the government, from currency and foreign policy, to national security and trade. To some, it conjured images of a country coming apart at the seams, with the dollar mixed up in the mania. With American democracy hitting a particularly self-critical moment, the turbulence portended long-lasting consequences to misusing the dollar. A microcosm of this played out with the U.S.-China relationship, as each country levied its economic might to win the rhetorical and actual battles around Trump's bid to rebalance trade relationships.

Steven Terner Mnuchin is known for his meticulousness, his knack for spotting undervalued deals, and his very good luck. He likes forty-mile bike rides and transition lenses for his Ray-Bans (they automatically darken in the sunlight). Strict with his diet and exercise regimen, it wasn't until he met his soon-to-be wife, Louise Linton, that he bought salt for his kitchen. By his fifty-fifth birthday, the New York native had spent nearly two decades at Goldman Sachs, started his own hedge fund, bought and recapitalized a failing California mortgage lender, and become a Hollywood financier. His name appears in the end credits of blockbuster hits such as *Wonder Woman*. And now it was on the front of the American dollar.

Mnuchin bet on Donald Trump for president early on and won the Treasury department as his prize (he became the wealthiest Treasury chief in history). At times, Mnuchin was a solitary force providing constancy to the U.S. economic policy agenda—in large part because of his propensity to hang on to his job. That stability was crucial during the debt limit debates and plans to issue government bonds, among other normal aspects of governing for the Treasury department. Mnuchin persevered through an immense amount of turbulence, including demands from his Yale University classmates who asked that he resign in protest of racist remarks that Trump made in 2017 after a white nationalist rally turned violent in Charlottesville, Virginia.

If you want to understand how he survived four years as Trump's Treasury secretary, you have to know why he sometimes avoided Pebble Beach. The spot on the North Lawn of the White House has nothing to do with the luxurious golf resort in California. Rather, it's where Trump's advisers in the heyday of the notoriously hostile administration would wander over to go live on Fox Business or CNBC with their bitterness over lost policymaking battles. Those were the people who found themselves sacked in a nasty tweet.

But not Mnuchin. He would regularly take a 150-yard jaunt through the west exit of the Treasury department to reach the White House to keep tabs on who was in and out of the Oval Office, and what Trump was up to. He only headed to the live cameras when he was prepared to boost Trump's economic policies—never to offer news anchors evidence of discord inside the West Wing.

When Mnuchin disagreed with the president, he went silent, completely avoiding the reporters who lingered around Pebble Beach. Trump valued absolute fealty above anything else, and more than a decade of friendship meant Mnuchin understood how to stay in the president's good graces. He signed on to Trump's team aware of the mercurial mood swings his boss would likely subject him to, and that the president wasn't a man whose will could easily be bent.

For him, the uphill battle was to win over the Washington insiders and the New York finance elite who, despite his Wall Street pedigree, openly doubted whether the political neophyte would last as long as he did. But for the entire four tumultuous years of Trump's rule, Mnuchin was the voice of prudence, if not reason, amid the turbulence stirred up by his volatile boss.

Not that he ever complained about it.

"Sometimes he'll agree with me and sometimes he won't agree with me," Mnuchin said one afternoon in the summer of 2018, dutifully sticking to his script.

One of the loudest silences Mnuchin ever held was in June of that year. Against his advice, Trump imposed harsh tariffs on Chinese imports into the United States, causing stock markets to drop amid worries of the impact to the domestic economy from a trade tiff. He wanted Trump to take a more measured approach in negotiations with China, but instead the president escalated the dispute by slapping penalties on $50 billion in Chinese goods and then threatening more if the country retaliated for the first round. Trump went live on

CNBC to make the threat: "We are being taken advantage of and I don't like it," he said. The U.S. was "ready to go" with tariffs on $500 billion of Chinese goods.

Investors panicked as they saw signs that the trade war was deepening. The S&P 500 index plunged after Trump's announcement of further tariffs. Shares also dropped across Europe and Asia.

Typically a vocal booster of even Trump's small-bore economic achievements, Mnuchin signaled his displeasure with the trade war by maintaining a deliberate silence in public to show his dissatisfaction. (It was the opposite of what his colleagues did. If Navarro, Trump's top trade adviser, was unhappy, he would call up his favorite reporter to vent. Within a few hours, stories citing "a person familiar with the matter" would emerge, sharing details of shouting matches and slamming doors in the West Wing.)

Mnuchin's absence from the public was noted immediately.

"Would the markets like a positive statement from the secretary of the Treasury? Yes!" said one New York–based money manager as he watched the stock market suffer. But the Treasury chief was nowhere to be seen: not on the Sunday political talk shows, on the usual weekday morning hits on cable news, nor stopping to chat with reporters during his frequent trips to Capitol Hill.

Selective silence was Mnuchin's way of balancing loyalty to the president while preserving his personal credibility with financial markets—he couldn't go out and offer the measured tone that investors wanted to hear because it would be false. But by avoiding an open break with the president's actions, Mnuchin not only maintained influence with him but also created an opportunity to find a way to persuade him to change course.

A month later, another round of belligerent rhetoric by Trump

forced Mnuchin to finally break his silence. That day's Twitter vit-
riol became the Treasury chief's problem as soon as the alert flashed
across his iPhone: in a series of 160-character tweets, the President
of the United States was lashing out at Europe, China, and the Federal Reserve.

"China, the European Union and others have been manipulating their currencies and interest rates lower, while the U.S. is raising
rates while the dollar gets stronger and stronger with each passing
day—taking away our big competitive edge," Trump tweeted on Friday, July 20. "The United States should not be penalized because we
are doing so well."

The barrage of tweets drew the world to the brink of a currency
war just as Mnuchin was facing the very officials Trump had probably irritated the most with his latest tirade. Only hours earlier, he
had landed in Buenos Aires for a gathering of the G20 finance ministers.

That wasn't all. Trump also blasted the Fed for raising rates.

"Tightening now hurts all that we have done. . . . Debt coming due
& we are raising rates—Really?" he tweeted. The comments gave the
appearance of interfering with the central bank's independence, a
notion that was a threat to the entire global financial system because
it was anchored by the U.S. dollar. Protecting the Fed from the impulses of politicians was key to maintaining investor confidence.

Finance ministers gathered in Buenos Aires were questioning
whether Trump's comments marked the beginning of a new era of
greater U.S. intervention in markets, one in which the president and
members of his cabinet were free to weigh in on economic issues that
were traditionally seen as outside the political domain, like monetary policy.

"I can assure you, because I've spoken to the president, that his intention is not in any way to put pressure on the Fed," Mnuchin said, shortly after entering the G20 conference center on Avenida del Libertador in Buenos Aires. He said that there had been no shift in U.S. policy, and investors and finance ministers alike took him at his word. "This is not in any way the president trying to intervene in the currency markets whatsoever," he said.

It was yet another time that the president made Mnuchin's job hard. A Treasury chief is expected to maintain an air of gravitas, which sometimes proved challenging during the Trump years. Sometimes, silence was Mnuchin's only option.

Of course, the scene that unfolded in Davos, Switzerland, in 2018—when Mnuchin inadvertently talked up the benefits of a weak dollar—revealed that it wasn't always Trump who was unsettling markets with loose commentary. One by one, the administration blew up key pillars of dollar governance: to speak about it with care and caution, to project strength, to be stable and predictable with policies, and to refrain from blatantly using it as a cudgel. That final pillar was knocked down in several blows, through economic sanctions levied sloppily but also by Trump's attempt in the summer of 2019 to actively intervene in foreign exchange markets to control the dollar, a bid that Mnuchin ultimately blocked—not through silence but by vociferous lobbying internally and externally.

He didn't always win those battles. On August 5, 2019, just a few weeks after considering manipulating currency markets itself, the United States finally formally designated China with that charge. (The statement came out after Trump insisted that Mnuchin's press release have the words *Currency Manipulator* with a capital "C" and "M.") The move fell flat. The designation didn't cause any major market or diplomatic catastrophe—for the first time, the world saw how hollow that charge really was.

The Trump presidency showed what happens when U.S. leaders are not cautious with power. But the currency channel wasn't the only sphere through which Trump moved the dollar further down the path of weaponization. A round of economic sanctions on a Russian entity that may have proved too big to mess with created even more uncertainty around the United States' ability to manage the dollar.

15.

MNUCHIN, THE OLIGARCH, AND JACK LEW'S NIGHTMARE

The day Steven Mnuchin banned one of Vladimir Putin's best pals from using the dollar, aluminum investors lost so much money that many of them are still unwilling to speak publicly about it.

Early on April 6, 2018, the U.S. Department of the Treasury announced that Oleg Deripaska, and any entity in which he had a majority stake, would be severed from the U.S. financial system. The economic sanctions were intended to be a damaging blow to Moscow for using its oligarchs as conduits to, as Mnuchin said in the sanctions announcement, "engage in a range of malign activity around the globe." Deripaska owned a massive share in the world's second-largest aluminum maker, United Company Rusal, meaning that Mnuchin's sanctions ricocheted across most of the global metals market. Deripaska, a multibillionaire, had a complex business setup, holding a

66 percent stake in a company called En+ Group, which in turn had a 48 percent stake in Rusal. Now that he was on Treasury's blacklist, both companies were facing sanctions.

With Rusal on the brink of becoming a financial pariah, the jobs of thousands of miners and factory workers across Europe's aluminum industry were at risk. Those trading commodities that Friday morning saw the price of aluminum swing wildly throughout the day. Investors didn't know what to do. With Rusal producing 6 percent of the world's aluminum, Treasury had just blown a $10 billion hole in the industry.

"With two paragraphs on an eight-by-eleven piece of paper, the U.S. government fucked up a whole corner of the commodities market, and fucked up the world of a Russian multibillionaire," according to one metals trader based in Canada. Years later, he still refuses to discuss the event on the record and use his name, or even reveal the firm he worked for, because Mnuchin's sanctions surprise had cost traders like him millions of dollars. It was embarrassing.

By the end of the day, commodities markets swung 20 percent, while shares of Rusal closed 18 percent lower. Over the coming weeks, the company's share price would plummet even further, and the ruble would drop an astounding 8 percent as investors braced for the fallout to hit the Russian economy. Metals traders across Wall Street and financial hubs around the world started watching the Treasury department's every move related to the sanctions package, looking for openings to recoup their losses from the April 6 surprise.

The United States went after Deripaska because of his ties to Putin, contrary to the popular theory that Donald Trump only aimed to please the Russian president (sanctions during his presidency indicate otherwise, in large part due to congressional pressure). Once described as Putin's "favorite industrialist," Deripaska was seen as a leading member of a club of billionaires in Russia whose fortunes rise and fall alongside commodity booms and busts. He'd been in Putin's orbit since the pair first met in 2000. To help do Putin's bidding, Deripaska allegedly back-channeled with Trump's campaign adviser, Paul Manafort (contact that was later scrutinized as part of the Mueller investigation into Trump's ties with Russia).

The charge that Mnuchin's Treasury laid against Deripaska was serious. "Worldwide malign activity," the agency called it. With the help of the oligarch, plus half a dozen other business tycoons, twelve companies, and seventeen top Russian government officials named in that day's press release, Putin was able to instigate violence in Ukraine, supply the Syrian dictator Bashar al-Assad with weapons to bomb civilians, and engage in other "malicious" cyber activities to "subvert Western democracies," per Treasury.

"Russian oligarchs and elites who profit from this corrupt system will no longer be insulated from the consequences of their government's destabilizing activities," Mnuchin said in a statement announcing the sanctions. The world had just two months to cut ties with Deripaska and his vast holdings before the Treasury department would levy draconian punishments on anyone found violating the sanctions, such as hefty fines and public naming and shaming.

It was a tall order for the private sector to figure out. The tentacles of Russian oligarchs, and especially Deripaska's stake in Rusal, were notoriously hard to track. A back-of-the-envelope survey of the sector would show that dozens of European metals and auto factories had ties to Deripaska. They would all suffer if they couldn't buy metal from Rusal. If they were forced to close, the impact would be catastrophic. Prices exploded in anticipation of a dearth of supply.

It was new terrain for Treasury, since its actions are usually meant to calm markets. This one led to an eruption of skittishness in a key corner of the commodities sector. It went on to become an embarrassing spectacle—Treasury tried to unwind some of the damage, and with each move managed to trigger more volatility in markets. In one episode just seventeen days after the sanctions were announced, the department issued a statement that laid out a path for Rusal to escape being sanctioned, which included Deripaska relinquishing control of the company. The softening of its position on sanctions sparked a record plunge in aluminum prices, with markets reacting to the expectation of more metals supply in global markets. But those first few weeks of chaos in markets persisted throughout 2018 as Treasury tweaked its program and Deripaska moved closer to shedding his massive stake in Rusal.

This volatility continued. Being the cause of that much instability was the exact behavior that the Treasury department was supposed to refrain from. Prices for aluminum, palladium, nickel, and more were in disarray, but Mnuchin remained steadfast in his defense of the April 6 actions. "We completely understood in sanctioning Deripaska what the impact would be on Rusal, the aluminum market, and on our allies. . . . This was a very well thought through decision."

But behind closed doors, many Treasury officials were shocked at the market reaction.

Multiple accounts from officials who served in the administration in 2018 contradict the secretary's public statements that the sanctions were well thought out. These officials, who spoke on the condition of anonymity to protect their public reputations, say the department did not undertake enough due diligence, such as liaising with private sector executives and allies to assess the full possible impact of banishing the world's second-largest aluminum maker from using the U.S. financial system. The consequences, which became quickly apparent, reached far beyond the borders of the intended target in Moscow.

The looming financial restrictions on Rusal threatened cash flow and factory operations that would require aluminum refineries to be shut down. Take Aughinish Alumina, a metal refinery located in County Limerick in Ireland. The plant was a vital cog in Rusal's ability to supply metal to the global auto and tech industry. After Mnuchin's sanctions were announced, there was speculation that the factory, run by some 450 workers, could become sanctioned and forced to shutter. There were also environmental consequences. Turning off a smelter running at 2,800 degrees Fahrenheit is costly and has to be managed carefully to avoid letting the noxious toxins such as sulfur dioxide pollute air and local water supply. The loss of operating cash from the sanctions would trigger an immediate closure, which had the potential to cause an environmental disaster.

In the end, the plant in Ireland remained open, and the worst of the real-world consequences were avoided after officials in Europe lobbied Mnuchin to tweak the sanctions program. In fact, Rusal escaped sanctions altogether after Deripaska reduced his controlling stake in the company before the sanctions were officially imposed.

Not that the intended prey didn't feel the pressure. Deripaska saw 60 percent of his wealth wiped out. But alongside the business tycoon's pain was a harsh and embarrassing lesson for the United States. The manner in which those sanctions were rolled out was, by some measures, a display of American arrogance. Past administrations had employed tried-and-tested methods of turning to the private sector to investigate the impact of potential sanctions, and took discreet steps to mitigate market turmoil. They also first sought buy-in from key allies around the world, a strategy that maximized impact and curbed mishap.

None of that happened in the case of Mnuchin's attempt to block Deripaska and his companies from to the U.S. financial system. The event instead suggested to the world that perhaps there are some people, like a Russian oligarch with deep ties to the global market, who are too big to be punished, even if they had a hand in trying to interfere with American democracy.

The Treasury department's sanctions on Rusal were born of pressure that had been building across both Republicans and Democrats in Congress over the preceding eighteen months to punish Russia. Lawmakers had been seething since Russia's interference in the 2016 election was disclosed. Capitol Hill was already in tumult over an investigation launched in spring of 2017 by Special Counsel Robert Mueller into whether Trump's presidential campaign colluded with Putin's government, an accusation the president denied.

In the months leading up to the Rusal sanctions, three of Trump's campaign officials and an adviser either had pleaded guilty to charges connected to the investigation or had been indicted (the probe never conclusively tied Russian activity back to Trump). The U.S. intelligence community was issuing jarring warnings that Russia was a continued threat to the United States' democratic process, including the upcoming 2018 midterm elections. "There should be no doubt" that Russia sees the midterms as a target, said Dan Coats, the president's director of national intelligence.

Meanwhile, the U.S. Congress was taking matters into its own hands. All but five lawmakers in the House and Senate passed the Countering America's Adversaries Through Sanctions Act (CAATSA). It was a law that gave the Treasury department parameters and authority to impose crippling sanctions against Russia, Iran, and North Korea, including the ability to name specific economic sectors to target with financial restrictions. But unlike previous sanctions legislation, which enabled the president to remove the financial penalties, CAATSA gave Congress an irrevocable role in the process. If the administration wanted to lift sanctions authorized by the bill, it would need explicit lawmaker approval.

Bit by bit, the scene was being set for Russia to face hefty sanctions. Valued at nearly $10 billion, in just a few months Rusal would be the largest entity that Treasury's Office of Foreign Assets Control had ever blocked. Through CAATSA, Congress directed Mnuchin to create a list of top Russian government officials and billionaires in Putin's orbit, and also to make an assessment of what it would mean for global markets if the U.S. blocked the purchase of some Russian government bonds. Treasury published one of those reports, dubbed by the media the "Russian oligarch list," on January 29, 2018, fifteen minutes before the midnight deadline from Congress. Mnuchin knew it was a deadline not to be pushed. He was due to testify the next day before the Senate Banking Committee in a hearing on financial stability, and appearing after failing to comply would open the floor to snide comments from lawmakers, and risk becoming the kind of public relations disaster he preferred to avoid. Tensions around the U.S. stance toward Russia were at a fever pitch across both political parties.

The Treasury department didn't announce any corresponding sanctions when the list was published, leaving Russia's monied elites surprisingly safe. In a separate classified document, Mnuchin told Congress that the administration had determined it would be too risky to sanction Russia's sovereign debt market, because it could throw global markets into turmoil. It was a clear indicator that the Treasury chief did not want to levy the kinds of sanctions that would trigger too much volatility, laying the groundwork that would prove his folly with the brash Rusal sanctions later. The reports, published without any punitive action, were perceived to be too soft.

One Russia expert called Mnuchin's reports a "disgrace" that proved that the U.S. "isn't serious about sanctions."

That view was quickly fueled, inadvertently, by the report itself.

The unclassified portion of the Russian oligarch list that Treasury submitted to Congress turned out to be identical to a list published in *Forbes* magazine of Russia's wealthiest men, all the way down to the same spelling errors. Instead of a signal for punishments to come, the Trump administration appeared to be indicating that it had no intention of taking Congress's sanctions demands seriously. Global investors with money in Russian businesses, bonds, and the ruble breathed a sigh of relief. "The market has concluded that if restrictions would harm American and European investors, sanctions won't be implemented," one trader said at the time, calling it "good news" for markets. Putin joked that it was "offensive" that he was not included in the oligarch list alongside his friends.

For a moment, it seemed like a tacit acceptance from Treasury that sanctions on Russia weren't worth the trouble they'd cause in markets.

The morning after Treasury released the Russian oligarch list, seated under fluorescent lights in a wood-paneled hearing room on the fifth floor of the Senate Dirksen Building, lawmakers skewered Mnuchin. "This Congress and the American people don't trust the president on Russia, his closeness to Putin," Sherrod Brown, a rumpled and gravelly-voiced Ohio Democrat, told Mnuchin. John Kennedy, a Louisiana Republican with a penchant for delivering flamboyant criticisms in his southern accent, asked why the "thug" who was leading Russia hadn't been punished yet. Feeling the pressure during the ninety-minute hearing, Mnuchin promised lawmakers that his team was "actively working" on financial restrictions on Russian money. "There will be sanctions that come out of this report," he insisted.

Several top Treasury and White House officials were shocked at this revelation. While the Trump administration's policymaking process was chaotic at the best of times, officials who were certain they would be involved if sanctions were coming down the pike hadn't heard of any serious effort to impose them on Russian elites. Such actions needed to move carefully through an interagency process between the intelligence community, State Department, Treasury, and the National Security Council at the White House. But now it appeared that Mnuchin had freelanced policymaking under congressional scrutiny.

The decision would be a fateful one for the Treasury secretary, unleashing chaos in the markets that, in the eyes of many, threatened the sanctity of the department's powers. Mnuchin had used the dollar as a weapon precisely in the truculent way that his immediate predecessor, Jack Lew, had warned against just two years prior (before the notion of a Trump presidency had taken hold in the nation). "Sanctions should not be used lightly," Lew said in his seminal speech on sanctions in 2016. "They can . . . introduce instability into the global economy."

But the Rusal episode was not the realization of what Lew was most fearful of—that still lay ahead.

In a little over a century since Treasury employed its first economic sanctions (just before the War of 1812 with Britain), the agency went from orphan status to having a secretary who boasted about spending half of his time on which enemies to banish from the U.S. financial system and how to do so.

On Mnuchin's first full day in office, he took the stage in the White House briefing room on live television to announce sanctions on the Venezuelan vice president Tareck El Aissami for alleged ties to the narcotics trade. But the real message that day was that the United States was shifting toward a preference for economic aggression over economic diplomacy in more cases than before, a harbinger of how the Trump White House would go on to double the pace of sanctions in the next four years. The president was taking advantage of the weapon he now had full reign over. He turned to it as a tool for his Make America Great Again agenda, using all forms of economic aggression that this weapon bought: import tariffs, export controls, manipulation charges, threats of intervention in the dollar's value, and now sanctions.

Under Trump, the United States imposed roughly 1,000 sanctions per year, double the already amped-up tempo of the Obama administration. The number of individuals and entities cut off from the U.S. financial system (and, by extension, most of the developed world) bloated by more than 900 percent between 2001 and 2020.

The Office of Foreign Assets Control's inviolable Specially Designated Nationals list now included four heads of state (North Korea, Syria, Venezuela, and Zimbabwe). Alleged "malign activities" in half a dozen countries were called out in Mnuchin's press statements in increasingly savage terms: Venezuelan government insiders had turned to "deplorable practices" and created a "corrupt system" in order to "steal from its people," he alleged in one January 2019 press release, slapping sanctions on more than two dozen targets.

Despite the inflammatory language in which the allegations were delivered, Mnuchin insisted that the sanctions "need not be permanent" and were "intended to change behavior." But the notion that sanctions were meant to deter or alter behavior rather than simply punish people, companies, and governments that had run afoul of the United States had become hard to reconcile. Banks, fearful of multimillion-dollar fines and reputational damage from violating Treasury sanctions, asked themselves a simple question: Why would we ever do business with people who the world's most influential nation had at one time deemed deplorable, corrupt thieves?

Back in 2016, Obama's Treasury chief, Jack Lew, had issued an almost clairvoyant warning on the misuse of economic sanctions. He cautioned that unless they were deployed judiciously, "we should not be surprised" if other countries look for ways to avoid the dollar. Just two years later, his prophecy came true: the Treasury department had unleashed a fresh round of sanctions on Iran without the support of any of its allies, and now even its close pals in Europe were arranging plans to circumvent the dollar.

It started with President Trump proclaiming that the Obama administration's Joint Comprehensive Plan of Action, signed by world powers to set limits on Iran's nuclear work, was "the worst deal ever."

In 2018, the administration withdrew from it, saying Iran was dup-
ing everyone and continuing to build on its nuclear capabilities.
Mnuchin reimposed a monstrous number of economic sanctions on
Iran. Eight hundred government officials, Iranian banks, shipping
vessels, and aircraft were blacklisted, dealing a debilitating blow to
Tehran's oil sector.

The United States' withdrawal from the Iran nuclear deal left
China, France, Russia, Germany, the United Kingdom, and the European Union scrambling—they had all signed on to the JCPOA, and
companies in those countries that had signed the agreement had already invested billions of dollars for future projects to help Iran's oil
economy reenter global commerce. Boeing and Airbus alone had ear-
marked $40 billion in aircraft sales to the nation. With the United
States now abandoning the deal, those businesses would have to
choose between the American or the Iranian market.

The Treasury department gave as much as six months to allow
businesses to wind down transactions with Tehran before the sanctions hammer would go down. Companies were immediately prohib-
ited from striking fresh deals in the Iranian oil and energy sector.
After a series of temporary waivers, the Trump administration said
that any nation that continued to buy Iranian oil would be sanctioned.

What happened next was ex–Treasury Secretary Lew's nightmare
come true. The moment had come at last when harsh U.S. sanctions
that lacked global consensus drove foreign governments to rethink
whether they even needed the almighty buck. In 2019, in a bid to salvage the fragile nuclear accord, three European powers came together
with a plan to help companies trade with Iran by working around the
U.S. dollar. The United Kingdom, France, and Germany announced

a Special Purpose Vehicle that, if successful, would almost certainly soften the power of American sanctions and start chipping away at its global dominance—just as Lew had feared. It was a shocking development that was coming from some of America's closest and oldest friends.

"It's a step that makes clear that even when others have a different opinion, we are capable in the EU of going our own way in a united and resolute manner," one German official said.

The proposed trade channel had the potential to prove that the dollar was no longer imperative to trade by insulating companies from U.S. penalties because it would not involve the direct transfer of funds between Iran and Europeans. But the challenge for the Europeans was how to reassure banks that they would be effectively shielded. Being banished from the U.S. financial market is a death blow for most companies.

The Treasury department pushed back hard, using every opportunity to curb Europe's rebellion against the dollar. Sigal Mandelker, the undersecretary for Terrorism and Financial Intelligence, traveled to Paris, Berlin, Rome, and London to tell counterparts and private sector figures that Treasury was "laser focused" on shutting off revenue streams to the Iranian regime. The U.S. administration was prepared to levy financial penalties if the new trade channel was used to deal with Iran.

In the end, the attempt to circumvent the dollar proved ineffective: the Europeans backed off their attempt to circumvent the dollar and work around American sanctions on Iran.

The United States won the battle to save the dollar's supreme status. For now. It came down to America's hold over both the public and private sector. Several major European oil companies had decided to stop purchasing Iranian crude so as not to run afoul of American sanctions, and no European government was willing to sign on as the key owner of a financial conduit whose purpose was to undermine the dollar.

But the mere attempt of close allies trying to bypass the dollar was a troubling sign that put America's precious economic power at risk for the first time since the greenback was crowned king at Bretton Woods seven decades earlier. And this started to worry Mnuchin. He felt that blocking others' access to the U.S. financial system would undermine the dollar's primacy and encourage those like Russia and China to conduct transactions in euros or turn to other financial conduits that helped avoid the greenback.

A gumbo of factors gave Mnuchin's anxieties merit. Sanctions are a valuable tool for American presidents that allow them to take on adversaries without resorting to actual bloodshed. But now it wasn't just European powers seeking to preserve their deals with Iran who wanted to dodge the restriction. Venezuela's economy had been destroyed in part by punitive measures imposed by Trump in hopes of forcing an overthrow of the socialist regime there. And now that government was looking for alternatives to the dollar, too. After some searching, Caracas arrived at a novel solution, announcing it would create a new cryptocurrency called Petro. Backed by its oil reserves, Petro provided a way to keep selling crude to willing buyers in China and Russia.

According to some accounts, this irked Mnuchin, so he turned instead toward efforts to holster what had become one of Trump's favorite weapons in his global economic war to preserve the dollar's pristine status. Those who served in the White House, State Department, and Treasury during the Trump years say they observed firsthand as Mnuchin advised a more judicious approach to economic sanctions starting around 2019. In encounter after encounter, the Treasury chief stood in the way of harsh economic punishment against Venezuela, Russia, China, and others. Mnuchin would later say that during his tenure, Treasury "targeted more rogue regimes, human rights abusers, terrorist organizations and other malign actors than any other administration—and we did so in continual and close coordination with the State Department."

Mnuchin endured four years as Treasury secretary in the wildest era of governing in the nation's history. It was a time that saw one top cabinet officer discover he was sacked as he sat on a toilet with diarrhea on a military flight in Africa. But during his tenure, Mnuchin managed to protect the U.S. dollar from direct assault from Trump— for all the talk of wanting a weak currency and scrutiny of Treasury's ability to intervene in markets, Mnuchin never let it happen.

It was a trying four years. He was often the odd man out at G20 meetings, being ganged up on by all nineteen countries as he coolly held the line on Trump's America First agenda. Hardcore Trump supporters both inside the president's orbit and outside accused Mnuchin of being a closet liberal who supported free trade, and Democrats despised him for sticking with Trump. He was also occasionally punished by the media for not fully understanding the role of a public servant, like when he asked if he could take a $25,000-an-hour military plane to get to his honeymoon destination in Europe (in the end, he did not charter a government jet for his vacation). There's also the time he brought his wife along to check out the first sheets of dollar bills with his signature on them. A photograph of Louise Linton, wearing long leather black gloves and holding up a sheet of uncut bills, inexplicably jounced across Twitter, drawing comparisons to villains from a James Bond movie.

But ask someone who watched Mnuchin's work closely, and that of Trump's other, wackier economic advisers, and regardless of political affiliation you will hear praise. "I give him credit," said Senator Mark Warner, a Virginia Democrat who worked closely with Mnuchin in the spring and summer of 2020 to rescue an economy at risk of being decimated amid the COVID-19 pandemic. "Steve Mnuchin has worked his tail off." It was hard to serve under a volatile, mercurial master, and he did the best he could to protect Trump from some bad decisions, some say. Others are thankful that Mnuchin stayed for the whole term to avoid a vacant seat in the Treasury secretary's office—or worse, a protectionist willing to force down the value of the dollar and try to exert control over the Federal Reserve, at Trump's behest.

However, it is Mnuchin's final moments in office that are the most revealing of the role he played, and the state that the administration left the United States in as power changed hands.

On January 6, 2021, after a short flight from Sudan, Mnuchin landed in Tel Aviv and couldn't believe the headlines flashing across his phone: "Rioters Storm Capitol Hill," "Woman Is Shot to Death During Storming of U.S. Capitol." He scrolled through images of Americans who were carrying Trump flags breaking windows, and a noose allegedly intended for Vice President Mike Pence. Then there were the reports that President Trump was watching the chaos unfold from his West Wing dining room, resisting those who said he should try to calm his supporters. As America's role as a champion of democracy before the world was crumbling, Mnuchin was about to head into a meeting followed by a joint press conference with the Israeli prime minister. Standing alongside Benjamin Netanyahu as he spoke to the media in the early hours of January 7, when most Americans were asleep, Mnuchin delivered carefully measured words.

"The violence that occurred last night at the capitol in Washington, D.C., was completely unacceptable," he began. "Our democratic institutions have been strong for a very long period of time, our democracy will prevail. . . . Now is the time for our nation to come together as one and respect the democratic process in the United States." These would be his final public remarks as U.S. Treasury secretary.

Mnuchin cut his international trip short. Worried that President Trump and his White House were under too much strain to contend with the prospect of foreign adversaries exploiting America's historic political crisis, other top U.S. officials abruptly canceled planned trips abroad. As the world watched the United States in turmoil, Mnuchin was one of only two people in the world with both the personal trust of the president and the constitutional authority (as a cabinet officer) necessary to navigate the ugliness of an insurrection caused by a president who some Americans wanted ousted in the final days of his presidency (the other was Secretary of State Michael Pompeo).

Mnuchin's responsibilities were twofold. As Treasury secretary, it was his job to uphold faith in markets, a concept that is rooted in American rule of law. The U.S. Department of the Treasury has played an increasingly vital role in maintaining the strength of American democracy through its mission to grow the economy and protect the stability of markets. As the most powerful finance minister in the world, Mnuchin was in charge of the dollar. Instability in the American economy or its democracy would damage the preeminent status of the buck.

The second responsibility stemmed from the first: like his fellow cabinet officers (many who resigned in protest a few days before the Trump administration ended), when Mnuchin was sworn in, he took an oath to "support and defend the Constitution of the United States against all enemies, foreign and domestic." And that is where the next responsibility lay—staving off the internal threat.

As the nation and its lawmakers and leaders digested the insurrection and Trump's reaction to it and behavior in the aftermath, there was one aspect of the Constitution that was on everyone's mind: the Twenty-Fifth Amendment, which allowed for the removal of a president from office. Mnuchin and Pompeo briefly discussed removing Trump through this amendment but ultimately rejected the notion. "We both believed that the best outcome was a normal transition of power, which was working, and neither one of us contemplated in any serious format the Twenty-Fifth Amendment," Mnuchin said. He admitted that he had, "out of curiosity," googled the possibility to eject the president from power.

The Trump era brought America into uncharted waters, testing the guardrails of democracy. By 2021, the nation had experienced a president who schemed to overturn democratic elections, applauded dictators, and untethered the nation from economic assumptions of the last generation. Two months after President Trump departed the White House, a member of the old guard of dollar stewards emerged to encourage lawmakers to take urgent action to protect American democracy—and he had an economic case to make.

"For our country to succeed economically, our market-based system must function alongside a strong, effective government," Bob Rubin's op-ed in *The Washington Post* began. "Strong, effective government, in turn, requires a functioning democratic process." Rubin—

the father of the Treasury department's strong dollar mantra that was infused with the strength and power of the United States—was asking Congress to pass twin laws to protect voting integrity and reform campaign finance, and his goal was to secure the nation's "economic future."

It's easy for a Democrat to publicly criticize a Republican president. But Rubin was making a case for protecting both the basic tenets of the nation—democracy—and its market economy that its citizens, and the rest of the world, rely on. In eleven words, Rubin summarized why damage to the nation's electoral process was bad for the U.S. dollar and was in urgent need of repair: "Faith in democracy and faith in markets go hand in hand."

16.

THE SECRET DINNER, AND AN ECONOMIC BLITZKRIEG

One cloudy autumn evening in Washington, a black Chevy Suburban pulled up to an old stone mansion on Sixteenth Street. The iconic white columns of the White House were visible just one block south. A man in a dark suit and an earpiece with a tight coil tube resting on his neck emerged from the front seat and opened the passenger door, placing a small stepping stool on the ground in front of it. A five-foot-three-inch woman with short white hair, the collar of her plum-purple blazer popped up, exited the SUV and swiftly entered the historic Hay-Adams hotel, a Secret Service official in her wake. The 136-year-old building, home to a descendant of one of the nation's Founding Fathers before it became one of Washington, D.C.'s finest luxury hotels, has entertained everyone from members of the literati like Mark Twain to political giants like Henry Kissinger. On the night of October 20, 2021, it was the scene of a secretive gathering of older gentlemen to welcome the first woman to ever become secretary of the Treasury.

Janet Louise Yellen has broken a lot of glass ceilings. The one-time "trailing spouse" of a Nobel-winning husband had become the first woman to serve as chair of the Federal Reserve under President Obama and was now enjoying retirement.

But faced with a pandemic-induced economic slump, President-elect Joe Biden called her back into public service to shatter another ceiling as the first woman secretary of the Treasury. Beyond textbook successes to revive the economy after the global financial crisis, the Brooklyn native was known for her soft-spoken style where she said little but commanded her audience's attention when she did speak. Yellen was known in academic circles as a "small lady with a big IQ." Her retirement from the highest perch in central banking (after being passed over for reappointment by Donald Trump in 2018) brought about emotional protests from self-described Janet Fangirls donning wigs to match her floppy bob to make their point. On her final day at the Fed, #PopYourCollar was trending on Twitter as hundreds of economists and central bankers posted photos with their shirt collars standing straight up in homage to Yellen's signature style.

About ten months into her tenure, as she walked into the foyer of the Hay-Adams hotel and made her way to a private room in the back of the ground-floor restaurant, she was shaking off a day of meetings, including with Republican leadership. That evening's welcome dinner was an event with a storied history in Treasury department lore. The tradition to gather ex-secretaries and Fed chairs to welcome a new Treasury chief to their hallowed club was established in 1953 by the Truman administration alumnus John Snyder, and ever since has marked the investiture of a new member into the informal fraternity of the most elite economic policymakers in the world. The private dinner (no staffers or aides are ever invited) includes all the former Treasury secretaries, as well as the current and former chairmen of the Federal Reserve.

The informal alumni association of past and present secretaries is, in some ways, the celebration of the nonpartisan prestige of the agency that all these luminaries had once led. After all, it's about following money, not political ideology. Each secretary takes an oath to protect the Constitution, after which his or her predecessors gather for a private dinner to toast the newest member to join their ranks. Members of that elite club are uniformly reluctant to discuss their induction dinners, indicative of the political deftness that one needs to survive a job where their every utterance and frown has the power to influence whole economies.

"There's a common bond among Treasury officials because we've all dealt with the same type of issues," said John Snow, who held the post during the George W. Bush administration. "Democrat or Republican, conservative or liberal, the people who have touched Treasury are united by a common set of understandings about the economy, about the premier position of the dollar, the U.S. Treasuries market, and the risks of failing to sustain what makes the American economy so successful, which is critical to our place in the world."

Those who are part of this group are eager to maintain the sanctity of the gatherings and usually shy away from sharing how these evenings unfold. Hank Paulson would only go as far as to say that the dinners "are really fun. We tell war stories and we give each other general advice. They're very friendly." He's attended every single one since his own induction in 2006, and he organized the party in honor of Steven Mnuchin at Washington's posh Metropolitan Club on H Street, one block from the White House, in May 2017. That event, described by one attendee as a stiff and reverent affair, featured red wine paired with rack of spring lamb. Some of the guests had flown in from New York and Chicago for the event. A quick photograph snapped on an iPhone at the end of the evening shows six Treasury secretaries neatly in a row: Paul O'Neill (his final Treasury dinner before his death), standing next to Michael Blumenthal, a Carter administration alum. Next to him stood Tim Geithner, Jack Lew, Mnuchin, and Paulson. Alan Greenspan and Janet Yellen—representing the Federal Reserve—offered polite smiles at the front. The blunt and opinionated Larry Summers hung to the side with a somewhat awkward smile, while Rubin leaned over to have a look at the whole group together.

While in recent years the dinners have been on the simple side, there have been some more elaborate evenings, like the time George Shultz (from the Nixon era) distributed chocolate bars in the shape of dollar bills as souvenirs. It was a recurring motif: after O'Neill's inauguration in 2001, each guest was served an individual chocolate cake topped with reproductions of one-dollar bills, complete with the new secretary's signature.

The group also represents a unique set of American politicians mostly harking from Wall Street or industry, and many have faced questions about their partisan loyalties. Mnuchin was accused of being a Democrat in the Trump administration, Geithner was registered as a Republican before switching parties to join the Clinton administration, and Paulson was challenged over his fealty to Republican ideals by colleagues in the Bush administration.

That's because the Treasury department is not, by design, a particularly partisan agency. It's all about the economy and the dollar.

The only agitator in the room is perhaps Summers, who served in Clinton's Treasury department and then went on to advise Barack Obama. During Mnuchin's tenure, Summers broke an unspoken gentlemen's agreement to refrain from openly criticizing a successor at Treasury. In tweets, blog posts, and op-eds he called Mnuchin a "sycophant" who was "irresponsible," among other things.

In fact, Summers was the only one of the pack that had advice for Yellen that he gave very publicly, before she even stepped into the office: Bring back the strong dollar policy. In an attempt to return U.S. currency policy to predictability and to once again use the dollar to project strength, Summers wanted the Treasury department to restore Rubin's old bumper-sticker phrase, "A strong dollar is in our national interest." But rather than heed that advice, Yellen killed any notion of resuscitating the twenty-six-year-old strong dollar policy in one fell swoop: "The United States does not seek a weaker currency to gain competitive advantage," she said during her confirmation hearing. Markets hardly batted an eye to her pronouncements on U.S. dollar policy, further proof that Treasury's currency regime had entered a new era in which the almighty buck just didn't matter as much.

There were two reasons for that. First, currency markets had grown five-fold since Yellen was last serving in an administration. Treasury's $142 billion Exchange Stabilization Fund (ESF), the account previously tapped to control the dollar, was meager by comparison. The second was that the forces of monetary policy now clearly influenced the dollar's day-to-day value more than anything that the U.S. Treasury secretary could say. With government intervention out of the picture (both actual and verbal), it was the Fed's interest rates, and how they compared to rates in other nations, that influenced foreign exchange markets more than anything else could.

All this talk of the ESF, currency traders, and financial reporters chasing Treasury secretaries around for a comment on the dollar was something that each attendee in the Hay-Adams private dining room celebrating Yellen's new job at Treasury had dealt with in their own time. They had all fought their own version of the battle to protect the U.S. dollar: Rubin created the policy that saved it from political meddling, Paulson and Geithner helped the greenback withstand the pressure of the global financial crisis, Mnuchin staved off a threat from inside the White House. And each had played a role in the buck's evolution into America's most important weapon. But in a matter of months, Yellen would find herself wielding this mighty and potent force in a way that none of her predecessors could have imagined. In fact, it would set off a chain of events that would have America's friends and foes wondering whether U.S. economic dominance, underpinned by the dollar's central role in the world, was worth the trouble.

"This might be the last time you see me alive."

It was the most desperate warning and plea for help the world may have ever heard from a head of state. But Volodymyr Zelenskyy was afraid for his own, and his country's, survival. In the early hours of Thursday, February 24, 2022, the skies of Ukraine (a nation roughly the size of Texas) were filled with hundreds of heavy bomber aircraft and more than one hundred missiles, while Russian troops moved down the Dnieper River and then toward the capital. President

Vladimir Putin appeared to be aiming for full control of Ukraine, with purported plans to remove the government in Kyiv. As the end of that first day approached, it looked like Kyiv would fall before the clock struck midnight. But Zelenskyy, Ukraine's president, had promised Russia, and the world, that they would "see our faces, not our backs." Ukraine was fighting—Kyiv wouldn't fall.

More than five thousand miles away from the bloody scenes of war unfolding in eastern Europe, a financial war was coming together in Washington, D.C. This response to Putin would go on to help Zelenskyy protect Ukraine, and aid in his ability to hold on to the country's freedom despite early predictions that the conflict would end with a win for Russia within a few days.

It was an aspect of the war that the U.S. would not join with field artillery or anti-tank guns. It would turn to a different weapon: the dollar.

President Joe Biden had directed his team as early as September to begin creating a blueprint of economic punishments. First, they were to be wielded as a threat—an ultimatum to discourage Putin from eviscerating the eighty-year global order built around peace and cooperation. Then, if he went through with the invasion, the sanctions were to be unleashed. Adewale "Wally" Adeyemo, the number-two official at the U.S. Department of the Treasury, had canceled his Christmas and New Year's holiday to help draw up this contingency plan. By the time the war broke out, Adeyemo had finished reading *A Gentleman in Moscow*, a fictional account of a poet imprisoned in a Moscow hotel room in the 1920s for penning a revolutionary poem. As it became painfully obvious that U.S.-Russia relations were forever damaged by the events of 2022, Adeyemo would later remark how as he read the book against the backdrop of the war, he realized he would never be able to walk the streets on which the tale unfolded.

Once Putin launched the war, it was time to put into effect all the planning that Adeyemo had done in tandem with Daleep Singh, deputy national security adviser at the White House.

In the first seventy-two hours of Russia's invasion, the Kremlin's forces had moved at breakneck speed, with the army moving by land, air, and sea as Putin attempted to reclaim parts of the old Soviet Union territory. The United States, Canada, and the United Kingdom led the way in response, with a raft of economic measures meant to cripple Putin's economy: they froze the assets of hundreds of Russian oligarchs and government officials, and some $1 trillion in assets belonging to the nation's largest financial institutions.

Adeyemo and Singh had unleashed a full slate of the most painful economic sanctions ever imposed. Some days later, Putin himself would refer to it as an "economic blitzkrieg."

From the outside, it looked as if the measures came rapidly. In the first month of the war, the United States had sanctioned over six hundred targets, including Russian oligarchs, government officials, businesses, and even superyachts belonging to Putin's cronies. For many of these, the White House had the support of thirty allies. But the work to get the G7 nations and the European Union on board had been a herculean effort that involved eighteen-hour days, classified briefings, midnight phone calls, and a lot of Fig Newtons and cappuccinos.

The sticking point of all the negotiating among allies was the unimaginable concept of financially excommunicating the world's eleventh-largest economy. Russia was a member of the Group of

Twenty, meaning it was so deeply woven into world commerce that trying to remove it from supply chains and markets would entail a blowback that would leave families hungry, people jobless, and companies with millions of dollars lost. European nations were especially vulnerable to the pain simply because geographic proximity had led to even deeper economic ties. But once the destruction began on February 24 and photographs of tanks rolling in and blood on the streets were splashed across newspapers and televisions, dozens of countries were ready to unleash the full force of their combined economic might. As the day's events unfolded, France, Italy, the United Kingdom, and finally Germany realized it was time to take once-unthinkable steps that would essentially create an iron curtain between the democratic world and Russia.

The lives of forty-four million Ukrainians were upended as the media circulated scenes of explosions that had killed innocent civilians, and of women and children hiding in underground train tunnels. Rockets pierced the sky for the first time since Nazi Germany attacked Kyiv in 1941, raising fears that it could be quickly seized. Entire cities in Ukraine were on the brink of being pulverized, and President Zelenskyy was posting hurried, passionate videos on social media, vowing to remain with his people despite being hunted by Putin's men.

The first four days of the invasion were crucial in the United States–led economic war. The first signal that the European Union was ready for blistering economic retaliation came on that first day of Russia's invasion. On Thursday, Bjoern Seibert, a top official at the European Commission, sent a WhatsApp message to the White House's Singh at 1:00 a.m. Washington time to say he was very close to securing support across the entire bloc for a hefty economic blow to Putin.

On Friday, Biden himself hit the phones to make the final pitch that it was time for the "nuclear option" in the economic war. The time had come to sanction the Central Bank of Russia, which would immobilize roughly half of Russia's war chest, worth around $640 billion. The funds were stored in different currencies, and gold, around the world.

It was a bold move, but it would take cash out of Putin's hand and hamper his ability to keep financing the invasion. With Western powers plus Japan presenting a united front, freezing Russia's reserves would be like losing the entire GDP of Austria from your bank account overnight. This pot of money was all part of what some analysts referred to as "Fortress Russia," which Putin had been building to sanction-proof the economy. He had dumped more than 60 percent of his dollar reserves, moving Russia's savings into currencies with governments that were friendlier toward Moscow than the United States, like Turkey and China.

The second measure that Biden was proposing was to ban a handful of Russian banks from SWIFT, the global system that financial institutions use to send secure messages about transactions. It had served as a crucial component in cutting off terrorist financing after 9/11, and now the United States was looking toward it to solve another major geopolitical problem. Just as governments, central banks, and financial institutions needed access to the dollar to dabble in global financial markets, they needed SWIFT in order to move money from one account to another.

All of this had to be done in secret, before Russian intelligence got any wind that the country's economy was about to be financially carpet-bombed. If the Kremlin found out about the plans, they might relocate billions of dollars to evade looming sanctions. To avoid asset flight, the announcement to freeze so much Russian money needed to come before Sunday night in Washington, when Asian markets begin their trading day.

By Friday night, Biden had managed to garner the support of more than a dozen world leaders and their economic teams. Even the Federal Reserve was ready for the economic gut-punch: the White House had alerted senior officials at the central bank that the sanctions were imminent (they needed to be aware of any looming risks to financial stability in case the Fed's tools were needed to calm markets). On Saturday morning, they were all moving closer to enacting the largest economic sanctions ever levied. Russia was a massive economy, matching its influence on the world. But it had flouted international rules and values, and the time had come to bar it from the privilege of access to the global financial system. World leaders involved intuited that Russia had no idea what was coming: Putin had never factored in the world's willingness to endure a little pain to punish him.

But one person stood in the way: Janet Yellen. She was worried about what these actions would do to the dollar.

Tuning into a Situation Room meeting through a secure teleconference line early morning on Saturday, she told Biden that the Treasury department would need more time to scrutinize the potential blowback of such massive economic sanctions. If it was referred to as the "nuclear option," it was definitely a massive weaponization of the dollar.

Her main concern was that there was a risk that foreign central banks would start to doubt the United States as a safe place to store assets if that money could be put out of reach through sanctions, which would erode the dollar's standing as the world's bedrock currency. But the president was certain that he'd made the right decision, and that speed was imperative.

Biden ended the National Security Council meeting and directed top White House aides to find a way to button things up with Yellen—he didn't want dissension among his ranks at such a crucial moment.

To smooth things over with the Treasury chief, Singh and his boss, National Security Adviser Jake Sullivan, took the unusual step of arranging for a foreign leader to persuade the U.S. secretary of the Treasury on their behalf. With the help of the European Commission president Ursula von der Leyen, who was also frustrated at the holdup in the United States, by around 1:00 p.m. on Saturday the group was able to get the Italian prime minister Mario Draghi to call Yellen directly in her office at Treasury. The pair had become friends when they worked together during the global financial crisis when she was at the Fed and he was the head of the European Central Bank, and the White House hoped he could use his central bank parlance to persuade Yellen.

Speaking on a secure telephone, Draghi assured her that Europe was joining the measures that Biden's team had crafted, that the unified force of the proclamation of financial war would protect the dollar's status. The trade-off in punishing Putin for short-term pain in the markets was worth it, he said. By 3:00 p.m. in Washington, the G7 statement that had been first drafted four days earlier was ready to launch (Japan would join the action a day later).

That Saturday evening, the European Union and the G7, which together make up half of Russia's international trade, unplugged most of Russia's financial system from the rest of the world, making it the most sanctioned nation on Earth.

By ruling out the notion that American military boots would touch down on the scenes of Putin's war, the United States made the choice to use the dollar as the key weapon. Sanctions as a foreign policy tool had come a long way since 2001, when the terrorist attacks of September 11 forced the U.S. government to reinvent this ancient weapon for the twenty-first century.

With a hot war raging in Europe, and a cold one escalating between countries openly scolding Russia for its crimes, a new age of great power rivalry had dawned.

It is up to America's voters and leaders to ensure that decades from now, quarter past five on the evening of Saturday, February 26, 2022—the precise moment when U.S. sanctions created a tipping point in the buck's weaponization—is a forgotten black mark in the nation's history, rather than the start of a downward spiral. Empires fall imperceptibly over long periods, not overnight.

The events of that day and what they triggered put the dollar at a historic crossroad. The seeds of its weaponization were sown in 1944 as World War II came to an end, began in earnest after September 11, 2001, and may have gone too far in 2022. The timing couldn't be worse: the United States now has the heaviest debt burden of any country, ever. If the currency falls from kingship, then the country won't be the first superpower or empire to collapse because of fiscal mismanagement. While the dollar has changed the world, the world may now change the dollar.

The biggest threat to its dominance doesn't stem from outside its borders but from a rolling series of self-inflicted policy wounds further stoking doubts of whether the United States should remain at the center of the global financial system.

One obvious black eye to the dollar emerges from Capitol Hill.

The U.S. Congress has raised the debt limit seventy-eight times since 1960. Along the way, as the nation has become increasingly polarized, this action has become a political cudgel for lawmakers. By 2023, the stakes of this seemingly routine political jousting became perilously high compared to the last dramatic fight in 2011: Partisanship reached a fever pitch, making investors wonder if Congress might fail to reach an agreement to raise the debt ceiling. The stock of debt that needed refinancing was $17 trillion higher than before, and foreign holdings had more than doubled to $7 trillion. The world's bet on the dollar and Treasuries had grown. The prospect of this manufactured crisis had Wall Street setting up war rooms and some foreign leaders laughing at the nation's potential demise.

The blowback echoed through markets and finally, in the summer, one of three credit ratings agencies downgraded American government debt, a historic act (albeit with nebulous consequences). The most pointed criticism that Fitch, a credit rating agency, gave was about the impact of the January 6, 2021, insurrection in the U.S. Capitol as a key piece of their concern about America's ability to govern the nation, and its massive pile of debt.

Fights over paying debt obligations and questioning election results add to an image of a dwindling nation. This new image doesn't bode well. History has demonstrated the link between a currency and a country's political dominance over hundreds of years. In the eighteenth century, the English pound replaced the Dutch florin as the world's reserve asset. The catalyst was a loss of credibility in economic management by the Dutch, and the acceleration of Britain's economic expansion. The dollar took the crown during the Bretton Woods conference not long after America surpassed Britain as the world's largest economy, and also demonstrably strong economic outlook by comparison.

The consequences of the United States losing its status as the owner of the world's reserve asset are far-reaching. The country would need to live closer within its means and cope with much higher borrowing costs—both of which require smaller fiscal budgets. That, in turn, could hamper the kind of investment and innovation that drives the economy beyond what any other can accomplish. Higher borrowing costs for the government would trickle into the real economy, meaning more expensive homes, cars, and education. The ability to achieve the American dream would get harder. It would also limit Washington's economic statecraft options, weakening a key mechanism to influence geopolitics.

Still, America is likely to continue its reign—which means the dollar will, too.

One key element in the nation's favor is that there is also no obvious alternative to the greenback. China's yuan is hampered by Beijing's reliance on capital controls to guard against sudden exchange rate movements. That requires the kind of government meddling that investors despise (a lesson the United States learned the hard way in the 1980s). On top of that, China is not a democracy underpinned by rule of law that investors can trust, and its markets aren't as open and transparent as the United States'. The other commonly cited alternative, the euro, would struggle to become the world's reserve currency since it doesn't represent a big enough economy. Its debt instruments lack the flexibility and deep liquidity that the U.S. Treasuries market offers. And digital currencies, while talked about often, remain marginal and untested.

A second incumbent advantage for the United States is that for those countries trying to strengthen bilateral trade that sidesteps the dollar, it's proving hard to ditch. Take India and Russia. After Putin's access to the dollar was blunted, India started buying Russian oil with rupees. But Moscow has no use for a stockpile of rupees because they cannot be as easily exchanged as dollars, so India is now paying for Russian oil using the U.S. currency. Even where the dollar isn't wanted, it can't be avoided. Despite all the anti-dollar talk, inertia in the financial system means that roughly 90 percent of all daily transactions (as of 2023) continue to involve the greenback, proof that foreign nations and companies around the world trying to shift away from the buck are addicted to it.

And while the debate rages about the state of America's democracy and global leadership, its economy is not showing any signs of shrinking. With 4 percent of the world's population, it makes up a quarter of global output, and despite erosion in its manufacturing sector and political turmoil, that figure has remained unchanged for four decades. America boasts an economy that is around $7 trillion larger than the world's second biggest, China, largely due to an enviable consumer base that drives global commerce.

Finally, the longer-term outlook for the American economy is growing stronger, raising investor confidence and fortifying the dollar. By 2023, the dramatic decline in the manufacturing sector that defined recent decades has begun to reverse. President Trump's "Buy America" bid became President Biden's. Several policies are driving the shift, including a $52 billion investment from legislation called the CHIPS and Science Act that brought the production of semiconductors (a key component for electronic devices) home. That unlocked hundreds of billions of private sector investment. Where once there was a trend of hollowing out America's heartland, a tsunami of jobs have become available: semiconductor plants in Licking County, Ohio; a production line for socks in Oceanside, California; battery- and dairy-making in Lansing, Michigan. Lego, the famous

Danish toy company, chose Richmond, Virginia, for its first-ever factory in the United States, instead of Mexico. Manufacturing-related construction spending has soared to the highest level on record, and the local economies of each of these towns were boosted with all the added spending and workers: Uber drivers, food trucks, new restaurants. It is America's biggest foray into industrial policy since World War II.

Economic policymakers are finally mitigating some of the painful trade-offs that Bob Rubin's strong dollar policy contributed to. His dollar mantra and the actions behind it helped stabilize foreign exchange markets during a tumultuous era and played a role in the American economic dominance that the world has relied on to provide security. However, there were downsides to the hyperglobalization it supported. By listening carefully to voters in places like Moraine, Ohio, Donald Trump identified that the trade pacts the strong dollar policy bolstered were too big a trade-off for a large chunk of the electorate.

America remains in the midst of this rebalancing.

It is the country's own policies that will ultimately decide its fate. A strong currency needs a strong democracy. Since the United States became independent in 1776, other countries have been waiting for its demise. At first it was the British Empire, hoping to repatriate the jewel it had lost in the American Revolution. During the Civil War, when Secretary of the Treasury Salmon P. Chase found the nation's coffers empty, the world wondered if the newfangled paper currency, seen as an immature and immoral concept, would perhaps even quicken the country's breakup as the North and South fought. But the country pieced together its union and charged forward with the magic trick of illusion and faith that the dollar would slowly come to represent. More recently, desires to usurp American power have come from Russia and China. While a bloc of nations seen making up just under half of the world economy are lining up together to sidestep American dominance, including Brazil and the Gulf states, they are mostly run by autocratic leaders whose demise may trigger the demise of the undemocratic nations they run.

The job of fortifying the buck now belongs to whoever becomes the nation's seventy-ninth and eightieth Treasury secretaries. The men and women who protect the natural resource that the almighty buck is will need to prevail over the future weaponization of it.

Treasury Secretary Henry Morgenthau helped crown the dollar as the reserve asset during the Bretton Woods Conference in 1944. Bob Rubin created a mantra that gave the dollar a mythic quality. Paul O'Neill and John Snow sharpened its teeth. Steven Mnuchin protected it from a volatile president, and Janet Yellen watched as it fought a proxy war. The next secretary will inherit a currency being stretched beyond belief by the biggest public deficit in history and a campaign to use it for war. Past battles to preserve this national treasure will inform how to win the next one: leaders with a unique understanding of how the dollar came to power, panache with markets, and a distinctive combination of trustworthiness and conviction. Their friends at the Federal Reserve, who often join their dinners celebrating a new secretary, may have more power over the dollar's day-to-day value, but it's the public servants at the U.S. Treasury department who are responsible for the industrial, economic, and debt management policies that will decide the currency's long-term fate.

These days, ex–Treasury secretaries and bureaucrats find themselves breathlessly explaining how the buck can survive as long as America remains strong. Mark Sobel, the forty-year veteran of U.S. currency policy, now sums up the problem to those who seek his counsel with a famous line from William Shakespeare's *Julius Caesar*: "The fault, dear Brutus, is not in our stars, / But in ourselves."

ACKNOWLEDGMENTS

It took a village to make this book come true.

My agent, Matt Carlini at Javelin, played a pivotal role helping me fine-tune the concept, lending his support and offering prescient advice every step of the way. My editor, Trish Daly, who I will forever thank for taking a chance on me, helped me find my author voice. I also thank Megan McCormack, Merry Sun, and Penguin's rigorous production team. I am grateful to Mark Sobel for sharing insights from his deep expertise from more than forty years at Treasury, and for reading and commenting on multiple drafts.

I am indebted to many communications professionals who spent both their time and energy to help me secure access to key sources and information. While many were instrumental, I would like to especially thank Joy Fox, Trish Wexler, and Debbie Grubbs. This book benefited from conversations with many current and former Treasury, Federal Reserve, and administration officials, and others who were generous with their time and knowledge. Steven Mnuchin patiently answered my seemingly endless questions over several years as I chased him around the globe. Many others shared invaluable insights: John Snow, Bob Rubin, Hank Paulson, Jack Lew, Tim Geithner, Jay Powell, Lael Brainard, Andy Baukol, Andrea Gacki, Daleep Singh, Jamie Dimon, Rob Nichols, Tim Adams, Geoff Okamoto, Tony Fratto, Brent McIntosh, David Lipton, Jeff Shafer, John Smith, Juan Zarate, Justin Muzinich, Peter Harrell, Michele Davis, John Weeks, Bob Doehner, Stuart Levey, Ted Truman, Danny Glaser, Tony Sayegh, Simon Kennedy, and many, many others, some who prefer not to be named but know who they are.

I am fortunate to have the support of immensely talented friends who suffered through my early drafts. Andrew Mayeda was instrumental in helping crystallize my writing and analysis from the moment I began this project, and Justin Sink was an indefatigable early editor and a morale booster who kept me going. Without these two, I may never have finished this book. I also deeply appreciate my special circle of readers: Dan Flatley, Vina Parel Ayers, Zach Van Hart, Jordan Magill, Chris Anstey, Alex Zerden, Michael Shepard, Jennifer Jacobs, Nick Wadhams, Liz McCormick, and Scott Bessent. Mackenzie Hawkins served as an invaluable data whiz, accomplishing in months what would have taken me years, and Emily Michel was a rigorous fact-checker. The assistance of all of these people was indispensable and made my work more accessible and accurate, although any mistakes or opinions in the book are my own.

I have the incredibly good fortune to work at the greatest financial news organization in the world, Bloomberg News. First-class editors have invested in my career and success, making this venture possible. I am grateful to Reto Gregori for nearly making me fall off my chair when he offered me a job in Oslo in 2013, and to John Micklethwait for setting a new standard in our newsroom by encouraging journalists to become experts and authors. I have great admiration for Michael Shepard, Jennifer Jacobs, Wes Kosova, Marty Schenker, Alex Wayne, Craig Gordon, Jordan Fabian, Josh Wingrove, Nancy Cook, Mario Parker, and Peggy Collins, along with many, many others in Bloomberg's top-notch Washington bureau who have taught me how good journalism works.

I have a wonderful family that offers me encouragement, nurtures my interests, applauds my victories, and helps me learn from mistakes. I dedicate this book to my father, whose interest in all my ventures was never less than my own. He was with me at the start of this journey, but sadly left before I finished writing this book. My mom is, quite simply, the wisest and toughest person in my world. Each and every member of my large and wonderful family are my heroes and my pillars of strength. I deeply appreciate the unconditional support of many friends of whom there are too many to name. My husband was indispensable in tending not only to messy ideas and lost words, but also to the author, offering endless moral support and cooking numerous dinners, and my son provided much-needed respite, lighting up my days with his giggles.

AUTHOR NOTE ON SOURCES

I became Bloomberg News' beat reporter covering the U.S. Department of the Treasury in April 2016. I covered the final months of Jack Lew as secretary, and then the transition as Steven Mnuchin took over the agency. From that point forward, I exhaustively reported on how Mnuchin pivoted economic policy to President Donald Trump's America First vision, how he explained it to global counterparts, and how he navigated the deep policy divisions within the administration. My work as a Treasury reporter encompassed Trump's trade war, economic sanctions, parts of the Federal Reserve and Capitol Hill, and the government's response to the worst public health crisis in nearly a century. I covered the transition into Janet Yellen's tenure as secretary, including her first trip abroad to sell President Joe Biden's Buy America agenda to global allies, her views on rising inflation that threatened to weigh down a tenuous economic recovery, and the U.S. response to Russia's invasion of Ukraine. This book is primarily based on the hundreds of interviews I conducted as a reporter with the government officials who directed those policies, and the articles for Bloomberg News and *Businessweek* that resulted from that work. Many of those stories were reported and written in partnership with extraordinary colleagues, including Jennifer Jacobs, Nick Wadhams, and Liz McCormick, and under the guidance of trusted editors including Alex Wayne, Michael Shepard, Craig Gordon, Wes Kosova, and Cristina Lindblad.

Reporting specifically for this book was done between January 2021 and January 2023. I spoke to more than a hundred current and former Treasury, Federal Reserve, White House, International Monetary Fund, World Bank, and private sector officials, along with current and former foreign diplomats. A majority of the interviews I undertook were done on "background," meaning I could use the information and insights these experts provided but without attribution. Those are cited as "author interviews" in the endnotes that follow.

I relied on the Bloomberg Terminal for a bulk of the economic data and research provided, and have cited the cases that came from another source. I also scoured the work of other journalists, as well as economists, former government officials, and historians who have done extensive research on the historical events covered in this book. I am deeply grateful to these experts. Juan Zarate's *Treasury's War* and John Taylor's *Global Financial Warriors* are exhaustive accounts of the authors' time in government. Eswar Prasad's *The Dollar Trap* is a scholarly resource. Neil Irwin's *The Alchemist*, *The Man Who Ran Washington* by Peter Baker and Susan Glasser, *Keeping at It* by Paul Volcker and Christine Harper, and *Glass House* by Brian Alexander served as important resources. Memoirs by three Treasury secretaries of the period I cover in this book are important pieces of historical record, along with Ron Suskind's *The Price of Loyalty*. My research also benefited from the illuminating oral histories recorded by the University of Virginia's Miller Center.

NOTES

Introduction

xv **vowed to isolate Russia:** "Joint Statement on Further Restrictive Economic Measures," The White House, February 26, 2022.

xv **"act in support":** "Transcript: US Treasury Secretary Janet Yellen on the Next Steps for Russia Sanctions and 'Friend-Shoring' Supply Chains," Atlantic Council, April 13, 2022.

xvi **"Every night I ask myself":** Joe Leahy and Hudson Lockett, "Brazil's Lula Calls for End to Dollar Trade Dominance," *Financial Times*, April 13, 2023.

xvii **biggest pulp producer:** Dayanne Sousa, "World's Biggest Pulp Producer Considers Trading with China in Yuan," Bloomberg News, May 8, 2023.

xvii **brewing mistrust in America:** Serkan Arslanalp, Barry Eichengreen, and Chima Simpson-Bell, "Dollar Dominance and the Rise of Nontraditional Reserve Currencies," *IMFBlog*, June 1, 2022.

xvii **Inside economic circles:** Saleha Mohsin and Enda Curran, "The True Cost of an Extended US Debt-Ceiling Standoff," Bloomberg News, May 18, 2023.

xvii **A low-profile hearing:** *Dollar Dominance: Preserving the U.S. Dollar's Status as the Global Reserve Currency, on H.R. 556 and H.R. 804, Hearing Before the*

Subcommittee on National Security, Illicit Finance, and International Financial Institutions, 118th Cong. (2023).

xvii **little-known research office:** Daniel Fried, "The U.S. Dollar as an International Currency and Its Economic Effects: Working Paper 2023–04," Working Papers 58764, Congressional Budget Office, April 17, 2023.

xix **The dollar won:** Fried, "The U.S. Dollar as an International Currency and Its Economic Effects."

xx **"Faith in democracy":** Robert E. Rubin, "Opinion: H.R. 1 and H.R. 4 Would Reform Our Democracy. They'd Also Help Our Economy," *Washington Post,* March 17, 2021.

Chapter 1. Surviving Donald Trump

1 **"A weaker dollar":** Enda Curran, Matthew Campbell, and Alessandro Speciale, "Mnuchin Pushes to Calm Currency Jitters," Bloomberg News, January 25, 2018.

3 **Mnuchin's words represented "poison":** Patrick Donahue and Tony Czuczka, "Merkel Warns of 'Poison' of Populism in Call for European Stance," Bloomberg News, January 24, 2018.

3 **an example of "buffoonery":** Author interview.

5 **During a campaign rally in Indiana:** Jeremy Diamond, "Trump: 'We Can't Continue to Allow China to Rape Our Country,'" CNN, May 2, 2016.

7 **"a shift in my position":** Curran, Campbell, and Speciale, "Mnuchin Pushes to Calm Currency Jitters."

8 **"love each other":** Laurenz Gehrke and Stephen Brown, "Trump on China's Xi: 'We Love Each Other,'" *Politico,* January 21, 2020.

10 **"Mario Draghi just announced":** Brendan Murray, "Trump Blasts Draghi, China for Weak Currencies to Gain Edge," Bloomberg News, June 18, 2019.

10 **former Fed chair Alan Greenspan:** Author interview.

11 **"responsible for exchange rate policy":** Saleha Mohsin and Katherine Greifeld, "Trump Wants Fed to Weaken Dollar. Powell Says That's Not His Job," Bloomberg News, June 29, 2019.

11 **"China and Europe playing":** Donald J. Trump (@realDonaldTrump), "China and Europe playing big currency manipulation game," X (formerly Twitter)

July 3, 2019, 10:21 a.m., https://twitter.com/realdonaldtrump/status/1146423819906748416.

11 **Trump asked Mnuchin:** Author interview.

12 **Trump called him "my Peter":** Ashley Parker, "From 'My Generals' to 'My Kevin,' Trump's Preferred Possessive Can Be a Sign of Affection or Control," *Washington Post*, September 17, 2019.

12 **dubbed him a "Rasputin-like":** Alan Rappeport, "Peter Navarro Invented an Expert for His Books, Based on Himself," *New York Times*, October 16, 2019.

12 **The threat they brandished:** Peter T. Kilborn, "Policy Shift on the Dollar," *New York Times*, May 22, 1989.

13 **"Who would want to work with us?":** Author interview.

14 **"Could frustration with the Fed":** Katherine Greifeld, "Wall Street Weighs Wild-Card Risk of U.S. Move to Weaken Dollar," Bloomberg News, July 9, 2019.

15 **"Price-level stability":** Saleha Mohsin and Jennifer Jacobs, "Trump Concern over Dollar's Strength Spills into Fed Selection," Bloomberg News, July 10, 2019.

16 **talked out of an intervention:** Saleha Mohsin, "Mnuchin Says No Change to U.S. Dollar Policy 'As of Now, '" Bloomberg News, July 18, 2019.

Chapter 2. The Birth of a Hegemon

17 **It was out of desperation:** Roger Lowenstein, *Ways and Means: Lincoln and His Cabinet and the Financing of the Civil War* (New York: Penguin Press, 2022), 92.

17 **The economic creed:** Lowenstein, *Ways and Means*, 90.

17 **"Immediate action":** Lowenstein, *Ways and Means*, 94.

18 **"carnival of rogues":** Lowenstein, *Ways and Means*, 92.

18 **penetration of Lincoln's currency:** Lowenstein, *Ways and Means*, 104.

22 **doubling of military spending:** Martin Calhoun, "Center for Defense Information: U.S. Military Spending, 1945–1996," July 9, 1996.

22 **But turbulence in the 1970s:** Michael B. Greenwald and Michael A. Margolis, "Why a Digital Dollar Is Good for the World," Belfer Center for Science and International Affairs, Harvard Kennedy School, June 4, 2021.

23　**leading up to 1985:** Jeffrey Frankel, "The Plaza Accord, 30 Years Later," Working Paper 21813, National Bureau of Economic Research, December 2015.

24　**administration's "benign neglect":** Yōichi Funabashi, *Managing the Dollar: From the Plaza to the Louvre* (Washington, D.C.: Institute for International Economics, 988), 9.

24　**was "a blessing":** Funabashi, *Managing the Dollar*, 44.

24　**Amid this turmoil:** Peter Baker and Susan Glasser, *The Man Who Ran Washington: The Life and Times of James A. Baker III* (New York: Anchor Books, 2021), 250.

24　**once failed an economics exam:** Baker and Glasser, *The Man Who Ran Washington*, 247.

24　**In 1984, while serving as:** Paul A. Volcker with Christine Harper, *Keeping At It: The Quest for Sound Money and Good Government* (New York: Public Affairs, 2018), 118.

25　**The so-called Plaza Accord:** Funabashi, *Managing the Dollar*, 177.

Chapter 3. Control Freaks and Vigilantes

28　**"You can't keep a good":** Jonathan Fuerbringer, "Currency Markets: Intervention Fails to Halt Dollar Rise," *New York Times*, January 14, 1989.

29　**Japanese officials verbally intervened:** Jonathan Fuerbringer, "Remarks by Bush and Others Help Dollar to Climb," *New York Times*, November 15, 1988.

29　**"Be calm, be cautious":** Fuerbringer, "Remarks by Bush and Others Help Dollar to Climb."

32　**told to show up:** Michael Lewis, *Liar's Poker* (New York: W. W. Norton, 1989), 22–77.

36　**"I used to think":** Liz Capo McCormick and Daniel Kruger, "Bond Vigilantes Confront Obama as Housing Falters," Bloomberg News, May 29, 2009.

Chapter 4. Bob Rubin's Bumper Sticker

42　**the winning slogan:** Author interview with Tim Geithner.

42　**"It was designed":** Author interview with Geithner.

43 **"We have participated":** Bill Clinton, "The President's News Conference in Naples," available online through the American Presidency Project, UC Santa Barbara, July 8, 1994.

44 **In a routine congressional hearing:** Alan Greenspan, "Testimony by Alan Greenspan Chairman Board of Governors of the Federal Reserve System Before the Committee on Banking, Housing, and Urban Affairs United States Senate," St. Louis Federal Reserve, July 20, 2004.

44 **"The administration believes":** C. Fred Bergsten, *C. Fred Bergsten and the World Economy* (Washington, D.C.: Peterson Institute for International Economics, 2006), 201.

45 **He kept a book:** Clay Chandler, "Rubin Stepping into Spotlight at Treasury," *Washington Post*, December 7, 1994.

46 **revealed to the public:** *Nomination of Robert E. Rubin: Hearing Before the Committee on Finance, United States Senate*, 104th Cong. (January 10, 1995).

46 **"A strong dollar":** *Nomination of Robert E. Rubin*, 104th Cong.

49 **Perhaps for that reason:** Author interview.

49 **"The dollar moved quite high":** Author interviews.

51 **The amount of money:** William P. Osterberg and James B. Thomson, "The Exchange Stabilization Fund: How It Works," Economic Commentary (December 1999), Federal Reserve Bank of Cleveland.

53 **His immediate successor:** "Snow Says China Is 'Intent' on Changing Currency Peg," Bloomberg News, October 7, 2004.

53 **"Journalists would like":** Author interview.

54 **"like a retiring sports star":** "Treasury's Rubin Leaves the World Stage to Sound of Applause," Bloomberg News, May 12, 1999.

Chapter 5. The Bad Dollar

57 **The workforce of the local mill:** "Unemployment Rate in Weirton-Steubenville, WV-OH (MSA)," FRED, Federal Reserve Bank of St. Louis.

58 **From 1997 to 1998:** "Certain Hot-Rolled Flat-Rolled Carbon-Quality Steel Products from Brazil, Japan, and Russia," Publication 3767, U.S. International Trade Commission, 2005.

59 **President Bill Clinton's rescue:** Martin Crutsinger, "Clinton Plan for Steel Panned," Associated Press, January 8, 1999.

60 **By 2016, Donald Trump won:** "Historical Presidential Election Information by State," www.270towin.com.

61 **Rubin and the rest:** "Treasury Secretary Nomination Hearing," C-SPAN, January 17, 2001.

61 **Labor unions and manufacturers:** "Labor Unions, Trade Groups Ask Bush for Weaker Dollar," Bloomberg News, March 21, 2002.

62 **Baucus had already warned:** "Treasury Secretary Nomination Hearing," C-SPAN.

63 **A Midwesterner of humble:** "O'Neill, Byrd Trade Heated Words," *Orlando Sentinel*, February 8, 2002.

63 **In 1987, the year he became CEO:** "O'Neill Says He'll Ensure Sound Financial System," Bloomberg News, January 17, 2001.

64 **By the time he was sixty-five:** Ron Suskind, *The Price of Loyalty: George W. Bush, the White House, and the Education of Paul O'Neill* (New York: Simon & Schuster, 2004), 68.

64 **There seemed to be appreciation:** "Treasury Secretary Nomination Hearing," C-SPAN.

65 **"As an exporter":** Leslie Wayne, "Designee Takes a Deft Touch and a Firm Will to Treasury," *New York Times*, January 16, 2001.

65 **Investors immediately threw a tantrum:** "Dollar Falls vs Yen on Concern O'Neill May Seek Weaker Currency," Bloomberg News, January 16, 2001.

65 **"market-based" secretaries:** "Alcoa's O'Neill Would Bring Washington Experience to Treasury," Bloomberg News, December 18, 2000.

66 **"As long as he keeps":** "Bush Says He's Nominating Alcoa's O'Neill as Treasury Secretary," Bloomberg News, December 20, 2000.

66 **O'Neill and his aides concocted:** Author interview with Chris Smith.

67 **"I've noted in the last few weeks":** "Treasury Secretary Nomination Hearing," C-SPAN.

67 **"Dollar Rises to Near":** "Dollar Rises to Near 1 1/2-Year High vs Yen on O'Neill Remarks," Bloomberg News, January 17, 2001.

68 **By March 2001:** "US Business Cycle Expansions and Contractions," National Bureau of Economic Research.

68 **predicted to cut:** William G. Gale and Samara R. Potter, "An Economic Evaluation of the Economic Growth and Tax Relief Reconciliation Act of 2001," *National Tax Journal* 55, no. 1: 133–86.

69 **"Have you hired Yankee Stadium yet?":** Author interview with Simon Kennedy.

69 **"devoid of intellect":** Author interview.

Chapter 6. A War Office for Treasury

70 **"oasis of luxury":** Ron Suskind, *The Price of Loyalty: George W. Bush, the White House, and the Education of Paul O'Neill* (New York: Simon & Schuster, 2004), 176.

72 **But in the days after 9/11:** "U.S. Markets' Shutdown Will Extend Through Tomorrow," Bloomberg News, September 11, 2001.

72 **"Its traditional safe-haven role":** "Dollar May Fall; Investors May Shun U.S. After Terrorist Attack," Bloomberg News, September 12, 2001.

72 **"In the face of today's tragedy":** "U.S. Treasury's O'Neill Confident Markets Will Function Well," Bloomberg News, September 1, 2001.

72 **Visions of a city ablaze:** John B. Taylor, *Global Financial Warriors: The Untold Story of International Finance in the Post-9/11 World* (New York: W. W. Norton & Company, 2008), 2–3.

73 **The assault on American soil:** Suskind, *Price of Loyalty*, 178.

73 **landed at Joint Base Andrews:** Author interview with Michele Davis.

74 **O'Neill and Secretary of State:** "News Archive—September 2001," The White House, George W. Bush Archives, September 2001.

74 **"We will punish you":** "News Archive—September 2001," The White House.

75 **Protecting the ability:** Taylor, *Global Financial Warriors*, 79.

75 **Hundreds of thousands:** Jeff Ingber, *Resurrecting the Street: How U.S. Markets Prevailed After 9/11* (Charleston, SC: Createspace, 2012), 2.

77 **"money is safe":** Ingber, *Resurrecting the Street*, 123.

77 **"If you own a piece":** "Buffett, Welch Won't Sell Stock When Trading Starts," Bloomberg News, September 16, 2001.

78 **"We're going to show the world":** "Treasury's O'Neill Sees No Recession; Fed Cuts Rates," Bloomberg News, September 17, 2001.

79 **Roughly $300,000 flowed:** John Roth, Douglas Greenburg, and Serena Wille, "National Commission on Terrorist Attacks Upon the United States: Monograph on Terrorist Financing," August 21, 2004.

79 **They used their real names:** David Bruce Bulloch, "Tracking Terrorist Finances: The SWIFT Program and the American Anti-Terrorist Finance Regime," *Amsterdam Law Forum* 3, no. 4 (November 2011): 74–101.

79 **SunTrust in Florida:** "FBI: 9/11 Hijackers Opened Bank Accounts with Fake Data," CNN, July 10, 2002.

79 **around the mere $400,000:** *Terrorist Financing Since 9/11: Assessing an Evolving Al-Qaeda and State Sponsors of Terrorism, Before the Subcommittee on Counterterrorism and Intelligence of the Committee on Homeland Security of the House of Representatives*, 112th Cong. 2 (May 18, 2012).

Chapter 7. The Crystal Ball of Terror

84 **the smell of "unsettled souls":** N. R Kleinfeld, "A Nation Challenged: The Scent; 20 Days Later, an Invisible Reminder Lingers," *New York Times*, October 1, 2001.

84 **$6 trillion in payments:** Author interview with Leonard Schrank.

84 **"If you want to stop":** Author interview with Leonard Schrank.

85 **"rather than threats of sanctions":** David Bruce Bulloch, "Tracking Terrorist Finances: The SWIFT Program and the American Anti-Terrorist Finance Regime," *Amsterdam Law Forum* 3, no. 4 (November 2011): 74–101.

85 **"looking for the clean money:** Author interview with David Aufhauser.

86 **"gentlemen shouldn't read":** Author interview with David Aufhauser.

86 **he flew to Brussels:** Juan Carlos Zarate, *Treasury's War: The Unleashing of a New Era of Financial Warfare* (New York: PublicAffairs, 2013), 56.

87 **"not one bite more":** Author interview with Leonard Schrank.

88 **more than 1,500 other:** Bulloch, "Tracking Terrorist Finances."

88 **"follow the money":** Scott Shane, "Bush Erupts Over the Disclosure of a Secret Everyone Knew—Americas—International Herald Tribune," *New York Times*, June 29, 2006.

89 **"guerillas in gray suits":** Zarate, *Treasury's War*, 17.

Chapter 8. A Secretary's Downfall, In Two Acts

92 **"bunch of crap"**: Author interview.

92 **"regret previous false claims"**: Lawrence Summers, "Why Treasury Secretaries Should Stick with the Strong Dollar Mantra," *Financial Times*, January 25, 2018.

93 **"flickering green screens"**: Will Dunham, "Former U.S. Treasury Secretary and Iraq War Critic Paul O'Neill Dies at 84: WSJ," Reuters, April 18, 2020.

93 **as "show business"**: Dunham, "Former U.S. Treasury Secretary."

95 **worst since Bush Sr.**: "Bush's Popularity Doesn't Stretch to Stock Investors," Bloomberg News, December 31, 2002.

96 **Bush invited the chairman**: Author interview with John Snow.

96 **"People who know me well"**: Ron Suskind, *The Price of Loyalty: George W. Bush, the White House, and the Education of Paul O'Neill* (New York: Simon & Schuster, 2004), 391.

97 **"general with training"**: Author interview.

97 **percent on major indices**: Alexandra Twin, "Bears Tear Through Street— Dec. 9, 2002," CNN, December 9, 2002.

98 **"John, you're going to get asked"**: Author interview.

100 **makeshift briefing room**: "Treasury's Snow, Nichols Comment on Dollar Policy," Bloomberg News, May 17, 2003.

100 **Bloomberg's headline over Kennedy's story**: "Snow's Redefined 'Strong Dollar' May Extend Currency's Slide," Bloomberg News, May 19, 2003.

100 **"the eight-year-old U.S. strategy"**: Michael M. Phillips, "Newly Defined 'Strong Dollar' Signals Change in U.S. Policy," *Wall Street Journal*, May 19, 2003.

102 **"In the past"**: "Bush Soothes Markets After Snow Comments," *Wall Street Journal*, December 15, 2003.

102 **Snow went to Missouri, Ohio**: "Media Advisory: Secretary John Snow to Discuss U.S. Economy in St. Louis, Missouri on Friday," U.S. Department of the Treasury, December 4, 2003.

103 **"Bush's economic agenda"**: "Treasury Secretary John Snow Travels to Ohio to Promote President Bush's Economic Agenda," U.S. Department of the Treasury, March 12, 2003.

103 **put a positive spin:** "The Honorable John W. Snow Prepared Remarks: Nevada Hotel and Lodging Association, Las Vegas, NV, June 18, 2004," U.S. Department of the Treasury, June 18, 2004.

103 **Snow turned and glared:** Author interview with Simon Kennedy.

103 **"there's a strong presumption":** "U.S. Treasury's Snow, Once Set to Be Dumped, Perseveres," Bloomberg News, June 17, 2005.

104 **fighting headline after headline:** "Treasury's Snow, Embraced by Bush, Still Faces Doubts," Bloomberg News, December 9, 2004.

104 **"How could Snow negotiate":** Author interview with Tony Fratto.

Chapter 9. "Just Call Me Hank"

107 **Paulson's annual income:** Henry M. Paulson, *On the Brink: Inside the Race to Stop the Collapse of the Global Financial System* (New York: Business Plus, 2010), 37.

108 **behind Goldman's transformation:** Adrian Cox and Christine Harper, "Goldman's Blankfein Is Frontrunner to Succeed Paulson," Bloomberg News, May 30, 2006.

109 **He had a crow and raccoon:** Paulson, *On the Brink*, 22–30.

109 **parable of billionaire investor:** "The Timeless Parable of Mr. Market," Farnam Street, November 3, 2013.

110 **A Gallup poll showed:** "Presidential Approval Ratings—George W. Bush," Gallup, June 11, 2013.

111 **It left Bolten pondering:** Author interview with Josh Bolten.

111 **His advice for success:** Author interview with Josh Bolten.

112 **They were all fervent liberals:** Paulson, *On the Brink*, 20.

113 **Part of an elite guest:** "History of China State Visits to the White House," White House Historical Association.

113 **"Do you really want to be seventy-five":** Paulson, *On the Brink*, 39.

114 **be the "principal spokesman":** "President Bush Participates in Swearing-in Ceremony for Secretary of the Treasury Henry Paulson," The White House, George W. Bush Archives.

115 **restore the credibility:** Paulson, *On the Brink*, 50.

115 **"Treasury would no longer":** Paulson, *On the Brink*, 47.

115 **first big economic speech:** "Paulson Lauds Global Economy, Backs Strong Dollar," Bloomberg News, August 1, 2006.

117 **"There was no one":** Mark Sobel, "In Conversation with Hank Paulson," OMFIF, June 29, 2020.

118 **bit of a "curmudgeon":** Author interviews.

119 **According to Sobel:** Author interview with Mark Sobel.

119 **had not intervened:** Reuters, "In Mideast, Paulson Offers Reassurances on Dollar," *New York Times*, June 3, 2008.

120 **called a "rhetorical lifeline":** Glenn Somerville, "Paulson's Dollar Policy Tweak May Only Slow Slide," Reuters, November 18, 2007.

121 **cited the nation's giant economy:** Reuters, "In Mideast, Paulson Offers Reassurances on Dollar."

121 **"In collaboration with our colleagues":** "Bernanke Puts the Dollar on Fed's Radar," Bloomberg News, June 3, 2008.

123 **"Speaking together on a podcast":** "Joshua Bolten," Straight Talk with Hank Paulson, Paulson Institute, January 2021.

124 **"this sucker could go down":** David M. Herszenhorn, Carl Hulse, and Sheryl Gay Stolberg, "Talks Implode during a Day of Chaos; Fate of Bailout Plan Remains Unresolved," *New York Times*, September 26, 2008.

124 **"I've clearly lost control":** Paulson, *On the Brink*, 299.

Chapter 10. Chicken Feet in Ohio and China's 1,000-Year Horizon

129 **manufacturing sector was decimated:** "All Employees, Manufacturing/All Employees, Total Nonfarm," FRED, Federal Reserve Bank of St. Louis.

129 **while in China:** Nicholas R. Lardy, "Manufacturing Employment in China," Peterson Institute for International Economics, December 21, 2015.

130 **created a "seismic shock":** David Autor, "Economic and Political Consequences of China's Rise for the United States: Lessons from the China Shock," IFS Annual Lecture, Institute for Fiscal Studies, June 22, 2017, https://ifs.org.uk/sites/default/files/output_url_files/Autor-China-Shock-IFS-Final-vo.pdf.

135 **"frank and energetic":** "Introductory Remarks by Secretary Henry M. Paulson at the U.S.-China Strategic Economic Dialogue," U.S. Department of the Treasury, December 13, 2006.

136 **"a remarkable education"**: Author interview.

137 **"The more fundamental your disagreements"**: Author interview.

140 **"symbol of unfair competition"**: "Paulson Seeks Flexible Yuan, Attacks Protectionism," Bloomberg News, September 13, 2006.

140 **Beijing's Great Hall**: "Yuan Has Highest Close Since 2005 as Paulson Urges Flexibility," Bloomberg News, December 14, 2006.

141 **"worst kept secret"**: "Paulson Is Attacked for Softer Stance on Yuan Policy," Bloomberg News, December 20, 2006.

142 **"trust me, it doesn't work"**: "Paulson Urges Congress to Pass Trade Deals 'Quickly,'" Bloomberg News, January 1, 2007.

Chapter 11. Tim's Cash Room Crash

144 **"There was no thrill"**: Author interview with Tim Geithner.

146 **"no magic bullet"**: "Emerging-Market Bond Spreads Widen on Bank-Rescue Plan Concern," Bloomberg News, February 10, 2009.

146 **Everybody was disappointed**: "Stocks Decline, Treasuries Gain on Skepticism Over Bank Rescue," Bloomberg News, February 10, 2009.

148 **no-win situation for him**: "Former Treasury Secretary Timothy Geithner Sets the Record Straight," CBS News, May 11, 2014.

148 **expected Geithner to be a savior**: "Obama's Troika May Push for Deeper Role in Economy," Bloomberg News, November 24, 2008.

149 **"measure of credibility"**: Robert Edward Rubin and Jacob Weisberg, *In an Uncertain World: Tough Choices from Wall Street to Washington* (New York: Random House Trade Paperbacks, 2004), 192.

149 **terse 150-word statement**: "Statement by Treasury Secretary Robert E. Rubin," U.S. Department of the Treasury, August 17, 1998.

150 **comedian Will Forte**: "Watch Saturday Night Live Highlight: Geithner Cold Open," NBC, March 8, 2009.

151 **projected to shrink**: "World Economy to Shrink for First Time in 50 Years," Bloomberg News, December 18, 2008.

151 **feared social unrest**: Tania Branigan, "Downturn in China Leaves 26 Million Out of Work," *Guardian*, February 2, 2009.

151 **China had lost:** "Clinton Urges China to Keep Buying U.S. Treasury Securities," Bloomberg News, February 22, 2009.

152 **"blind pursuit of profit":** "Analysis: Obama Calls Chinese Leader Amid Strains," Bloomberg News, January 30, 2009.

152 **"excessive risk-taking" among:** "Remarks by Secretary Henry M. Paulson, Jr., at the Ronald Reagan Presidential Library," U.S. Department of the Treasury, November 20, 2008.

152 **fiscal policy front:** "China Central Bank Says Extra Crisis Tools Are Needed," Bloomberg News, December 31, 2008.

152 **eighteen pieces of legislation:** Ben S. Bernanke, Timothy F. Geithner, and Henry M. Paulson, Jr., *First Responders: Inside the U.S. Strategy for Fighting the 2007–2009 Global Financial Crisis* (New Haven: Yale University Press, 2020), 451.

154 **the federal deficit had:** "What Is the National Deficit?," Fiscal Data, updated October 2023.

156 **JPMorgan Chase's Jamie Dimon:** Matt Egan, "'Financial Armageddon.' What's at Stake If the Debt Limit Isn't Raised," CNN, September 8, 2021.

157 **Alexander Hamilton envisioned:** Ron Chernow, *Alexander Hamilton* (London: Apollo, 2020), 288.

Chapter 12. Nerd Warriors at Work

159 **tuna salad sandwiches:** Robert O'Harrow Jr., James V. Grimaldi, and Brady Dennis, "Sanctions in 72 Hours: How the U.S. Pulled off a Major Freeze of Libyan Assets," *Washington Post*, March 23, 2011.

159 **show "no mercy":** Paul Harris, "Barack Obama Defends US Military Intervention in Libya," *Guardian*, March 29, 2011.

161 **the "money man":** Dafna Linzer, "The Money Man in the Terror Fight," *Washington Post*, July 5, 2006.

164 **From 2001 to 2015:** Richard Manfredi, "2022 Year-End Sanctions and Export Controls Update," Gibson Dunn, February 7, 2023.

167 **tiny unit's role:** "Economic Sanctions Outlook," C-SPAN, March 9, 2018.

168 **following fifty years:** "Basic Information on OFAC and Sanctions," U.S. Department of the Treasury, Office of Foreign Assets Control, accessed February 20, 2023.

170 **"condition use of the dollar":** "U.S. Treasury Secretary Jacob J. Lew on the Evolution of Sanctions and Lessons for the Future," Carnegie Endowment for International Peace, March 30, 2016.

Chapter 13. A Turbulent Marriage

172 **learned enough Mandarin:** David J. Lynch, "Obama Faulted for Having Fewer Experts Guiding China Policy," Bloomberg News, November 9, 2014.

174 **called a "diplomatic dodge":** Timothy F. Geithner, *Stress Test: Reflections on Financial Crises* (London: Random House Business, 2014), 274.

174 **"manipulating its currency":** *Treasury Department's Report on International Economic and Exchange Rate Policies, Hearing Before the Committee on Banking, Housing, and Urban Affairs*, 111th Cong. 5 (September 16, 2010).

175 **"untrue and misleading":** "China Rebuts Geithner, Denies Currency Manipulation," Bloomberg News, January 24, 2009.

176 **"very smart decision":** Indira A. R. Lakshmanan, "Clinton Urges China to Keep Buying U.S. Treasury Securities," Bloomberg News, February 22, 2009.

178 **leading to it being "undervalued":** Wayne M. Morrison and Marc Labonte, "China's Currency Policy: An Analysis of the Economic Issues," Congressional Research Services, updated July 22, 2013.

178–179 **being the "smoking gun":** Thomas Ferraro, "U.S. Political Odd Couple Takes on China," Reuters, March 18, 2010.

179 **custodian of one of:** Susan Baer, "Inside Seven Unbelievable Washington Offices," *Washingtonian*, November 1, 2011.

180 **she worked to convince her boss:** Saleha Mohsin, "Lael Brainard Faces China Questions If Biden Picks Her for Treasury," Bloomberg News, November 9, 2020.

181 **incremental progress from China:** Ian Katz, "U.S. Not 'Satisfied' with China's Yuan, Brainard Says," Bloomberg News, February 10, 2011.

181 **"the single biggest step":** Doug Palmer, "Senators Renew Push Against China Currency 'Manipulation' Despite Yuan's Rise," Reuters, June 5, 2013.

182 **"escalator ride that changed America":** Michael Kruse, "The Escalator Ride That Changed America," *Politico*, June 14, 2019.

183 **made the jaw-dropping comment:** Al Kamen, "Presumptive Ambassador to China Baucus: 'I'm No Real Expert on China,'" *Washington Post*, January 13, 2014.

183 **became a lavish celebration:** "Remarks by Treasury Secretary Lew at the 2016 U.S.-China Strategic and Economic Dialogue CEO Roundtable," Press Release, U.S. Department of the Treasury, January 23, 2023.

184 **"We must stand up to China's":** Doug Palmer and Ben Schreckinger, "Trump Vows to Declare China a Currency Manipulator on Day One," *Politico*, November 10, 2015.

185 **two-thirds of Americans:** Enda Curran and Saleha Mohsin, "World's Silence on Weaker Yuan to Be Tested at G-20 Meeting," Bloomberg News, July 21, 2016.

185 **middle-class households:** Rakesh Kochhar, "The American Middle Class Is Stable in Size, but Losing Ground Financially to Upper-Income Families," Pew Research Center, September 6, 2018.

186 **"We're going to take our jobs back":** James Nash, "Nevadans Cheer Trump's China-Bashing Even as Nation Buoys State," Bloomberg News, February 23, 2016.

187 **pledged to "reject protectionism":** "With Globalization in Danger, G-20 Double Down on Defense," Bloomberg News, July 24, 2016.

188 **"The single biggest weapon":** Veronica Stracqualursi, "10 Times Trump Attacked China and Its Trade Relations with the US," ABC News, November 9, 2017.

189 **"like checkers players":** Stracqualursi, "10 Times Trump Attacked China and Its Trade Relations with the US."

Chapter 14. A Treasury Heirloom Shattered

190 **"You look at what China's doing":** Maiko Takahashi and Connor Cislo, "Japan Hits Back at Trump Charge That It Is Devaluing the Yen," Bloomberg News, February 1, 2017.

191 **"excessively strong" dollar:** Saleha Mohsin, "Inside the Mind of Mnuchin: Too-Strong Dollar May Hurt Economy," Bloomberg News, January 23, 2017.

192 **"This is my only demand":** Patrick Donahue and Arne Delfs, "Trans-Atlantic Mood Worsens as Merkel Stands Up to Trump on Euro," Bloomberg News, January 31, 2017.

193 **Fearing a massive policy shift:** Saleha Mohsin, "Mnuchin Warned by Japan, Germany as G-20 Fears Policy Shift," Bloomberg News, February 17, 2017.

193 **"The change in Washington":** Takahashi and Cislo, "Japan Hits Back at Trump Charge That It Is Devaluing the Yen."

196 **"who is the administration's liaison":** Author interview with John Weeks.

198 **With top White House advisers:** Kathryn Dunn Tenpas, "Tracking Turnover in the Trump Administration," Brookings Institution, December 20, 2018.

198 **Ross went on to scold:** Andrew Mayeda and Saleha Mohsin, "Trump's Honeymoon with China Comes to an End," Bloomberg News, July 19, 2017.

199 **"very big step forward":** Ting Shi and Enda Curran, "China Focuses on Avoiding Trade War as Xi-Trump Honeymoon Ends," Bloomberg News, July 20, 2017.

204 **"China, the European Union and others":** Kate Gibson, "Trump Says China, EU 'Manipulating Their Currencies'—and U.S. Dollar Hit," CBS News, July 20, 2018.

Chapter 15. Mnuchin, the Oligarch, and Jack Lew's Nightmare

209 **Putin's "favorite industrialist":** Tim Marcin, "Meet the Man Paul Manafort Worked with to Help Putin," *Newsweek*, March 22, 2017.

209 **"their government's destabilizing activities":** "Treasury Designates Russian Oligarchs, Officials, and Entities in Response to Worldwide Malign Activity," U.S. Department of the Treasury.

210 **seventeen days after:** Jack Farchy, Yuliya Fedorinova, and Saleha Mohsin, "U.S. Softens Stance on Rusal Sanctions; Aluminum Plunges," Bloomberg News, April 23, 2018.

210 **"We completely understood":** "Mnuchin: Rusal U.S. Sanctions Targeted Deripaska, Not Companies," Bloomberg News, October 11, 2018.

212 **"There should be no doubt":** Jeremy Herb, "US Intel Chiefs Unanimous That Russia Is Targeting 2018 Elections," CNN, February 13, 2018.

214 **called Mnuchin's reports a "disgrace":** Leonid Bershidsky, "The U.S. List of Russian Oligarchs Is a Disgrace," Bloomberg News, January 30, 2018.

215 **"There will be sanctions":** Saleha Mohsin, "Mnuchin Says Russia Sanctions Coming After Oligarch Report," Bloomberg News, January 30, 2018.

215 **an interagency process:** Author interviews.

215 **"Sanctions should not be used lightly"**: William J. Lew, Jacob J. Burns, and William J. Burns, "U.S. Treasury Secretary Jacob J. Lew on the Evolution of Sanctions and Lessons for the Future," Carnegie Endowment for International Peace, March 30, 2016.

216 **1,000 sanctions per year**: J. P. Laub, "2019 Year-End Sanctions Update," Gibson Dunn, January 24, 2020.

216 **The number of individuals**: "The Treasury 2021 Sanctions Review," U.S. Department of the Treasury, October 2021.

217 **turned to "deplorable practices"**: "Treasury Targets Venezuela Currency Exchange Network Scheme Generating Billions of Dollars for Corrupt Regime Insiders," U.S. Department of the Treasury, January 28, 2019.

217 **an almost clairvoyant warning**: Jacob J. Lew, "U.S. Treasury Secretary Jacob J. Lew on the Evolution of Sanctions and Lessons for the Future," Carnegie Endowment for International Peace, March 30, 2016.

219 **"It's a step that makes clear"**: Ladane Nasseri, Irina Vilcu, and Patrick Donahue, "EU Unveils Iran Trade Vehicle as It Vows to Salvage Nuclear Deal," Bloomberg News, January 31, 2019.

219 **Treasury was "laser focused"**: Saleha Mohsin, "Treasury Official Doubts EU Can Sidestep U.S. Sanctions on Iran," Bloomberg News, November 12, 2018.

220 **But the mere attempt**: Jacob J. Lew, "Trump's Policies Overuse America's Economic Weapons. U.S. Economic Power Is at Risk," *Barron's*, February 19, 2020.

220 **He felt that blocking others' access**: Saleha Mohsin, Nick Wadhams, and Jennifer Jacobs, "Mnuchin Feared Sanctions Would Undercut U.S. Dollar, Bolton Says," Bloomberg News, June 18, 2020.

221 **observed firsthand as Mnuchin**: Author interviews.

221 **Mnuchin would later say**: Author interview with Steven Mnuchin.

222 **"worked his tail off"**: Saleha Mohsin, "Mnuchin Faces Tougher Tests After Praise for Opening Cash Spigot," Bloomberg News, April 24, 2020.

224 **"We both believed"**: Steven T. Dennis, "Mnuchin Briefly Discussed 25th Amendment to Remove Trump, Jan. 6 Transcript Shows," Bloomberg News, December 27, 2022.

224 **"For our country to succeed"**: Robert E. Rubin, "Opinion: H.R. 1 and H.R. 4 Would Reform Our Democracy. They'd Also Help Our Economy," *Washington Post*, March 17, 2021.

Chapter 16. The Secret Dinner, and an Economic Blitzkrieg

227 **About ten months:** "Calendars and Travel of the Secretary," U.S. Department of the Treasury."

228 **"There's a common bond":** Author interview with John Snow.

228 **"are really fun":** Author interview with Hank Paulson.

229 **a recurring motif:** "O'Neill, Former Treasury Chiefs Form Fraternity," Bloomberg News, December 20, 2001.

230 **"sycophant" who was "irresponsible":** Lawrence H. Summers (@LHSummers), "Why is the Secretary of the Treasury commenting on NFL players," X (formerly Twitter), September 24, 2017, 7:46 p.m., https://twitter.com/lhsummers/status /912040597615185920.

230 **"The United States does not seek":** Saleha Mohsin, "Yellen Says She Won't Seek Weaker Dollar, Wants Market-Set Rates," Bloomberg News, January 19, 2021.

230 **grown five-fold:** "Triennial Central Bank Survey of Foreign Exchange and Over-The-Counter (OTC) Derivatives Markets in 2019," Bank for International Settlements, December 8, 2019.

231 **"last time you see me alive":** Barak Ravid, "Zelensky to EU Leaders: 'This Might Be the Last Time You See Me Alive,'" Axios, February 25, 2022.

231 **the skies of Ukraine:** Natalia Drozdiak and Marc Champion, "Western Allies See Kyiv Falling to Russian Forces Within Hours," Bloomberg News, February 24, 2022.

232 **"see our faces":** Dave Lawler and Zachary Basu, "Ukrainian President Zelensky Delivers Impassioned Address, Telling Russia: 'You Will See Our Faces, Not Our Backs,'" Axios, February 24, 2022.

232 **became painfully obvious:** Author interview with Wally Adeyemo.

233 **six hundred targets:** "Fact Sheet: United States and Allies and Partners Impose Additional Costs on Russia," The White House, March 24, 2022.

236 **But one person stood:** Saleha Mohsin, "Janet Yellen Is Struggling at the Treasury Job She Never Wanted," Bloomberg News, June 15, 2022.

237 **button things up:** Author interviews.

237 **half of Russia's international trade:** "Transcript: US Treasury Secretary Janet Yellen on the Next Steps for Russia Sanctions and 'Friend-Shoring' Supply Chains," Atlantic Council, April 13, 2022.

239 **raised the debt limit:** "Debt Limit," U.S. Department of the Treasury.

239 **$17 trillion higher:** Council of Economic Advisers (U.S.), "Gross Federal Debt," FRED, Federal Reserve Bank of St. Louis, June 30, 1939.

239 **doubled to $7 trillion:** "Table 5: Major Foreign Holders of Treasury Securities," Treasury.gov, 2023.

239 **setting up war rooms:** "JPMorgan's Jamie Dimon Says U.S. 'Probably' Won't Default on Its Debt," Bloomberg News, May 17, 2023.

239 **most pointed criticism:** "Fitch Says U.S. Fiscal Metrics and Governance Spurred Credit-Rating Cut," Bloomberg News, August 2, 2023.

239 **in the eighteenth century:** Daniel Fried, "The U.S. Dollar as an International Currency and Its Economic Effects: Working Paper 2023–04," Working Papers 58764, Congressional Budget Office, April 17, 2023.

241 **India started buying:** "Global Insight: Think Ditching Dollar Is Easy? Ask Putin, Modi," Bloomberg News, May 11, 2023.

241 **America boasts an economy:** Saleha Mohsin and Enda Curran, "The True Cost of an Extended US Debt-Ceiling Standoff," Bloomberg News, May 18, 2023.

242 **America's biggest foray:** Sean Donnan, "$52 Billion Plan to Make Chips in the US Faces a Labor Shortage," Bloomberg News, March 9, 2023.

INDEX